M000198005

Transnational Nomads

STUDIES IN FORCED MIGRATION
General Editors: Stephen Castles and Dawn Chatty

Transnational Nomads

HOW SOMALIS COPE WITH REFUGEE LIFE IN THE DADAAB CAMPS OF KENYA

Cindy Horst

Berghahn Books
New York • Oxford

First published in 2006 by

Berghahn Books
www.berghahnbooks.com

© 2006, 2008 Cindy Horst
First paperback edition published in 2008

All rights reserved.
Except for the quotation of short passages
for the purposes of criticism and review, no part of this book
may be reproduced in any form or by any means, electronic or
mechanical, including photocopying, recording, or any information
storage and retrieval system now known or to be invented,
without written permission of the publisher.

Library of Congress Cataloging-in-Publication Data

Horst, Cindy, 1973-

Transnational nomads : how Somalis cope with refugee life in the Dadaab
camps of Kenya / Cindy Horst.

p. cm. -- (Studies in forced migration ; v. 19)

Includes bibliographical references and index.

ISBN 1-84545-129-5 (alk. paper)

1. Refugees--Somalia. 2. Refugees--Kenya. 3. Refugee camps--Kenya. 4.
Somalis--Kenya. I. Title. II. Series.

HV640.5.S8H67 2006

305.89′35--dc22

2006042835

British Library Cataloguing in Publication Data

A catalogue record for this book is available
from the British Library

Printed in the United States on acid-free paper

ISBN 978-1-84545-129-5 hardback, 978-1-84545-509-5 paperback

Contents

List of Figures

List of Maps

List of Tables

Acknowledgements

Throughout this project, I have received invaluable support and advice from many people. Joke Schrijvers and Ton Dietz at the University of

Amsterdam formed a wonderful and complementary team of critical, challenging but supportive and confident supervisors. When I approached Joke Schrijvers with some vague idea in mind of the research I wanted to do in Dadaab, she responded with great enthusiasm. I received enthusiastic responses from Joke throughout the research, and this has greatly strengthened my confidence. She encouraged me to think critically and always take one extra step, and her personal engagement allowed me to balance my time and thus stay sane. Ton Dietz gave his support to the project at a time when it might have been cancelled due to funding problems. My gratitude in particular goes to the University of Amsterdam for financing the research. Ton's wide knowledge on a variety of topics encouraged me to broaden my scope. Despite our disciplinary differences, he was very supportive of my approach to research and writing and provided me with professional and dedicated supervision.

The time I spent in Dadaab and Nairobi for fieldwork has been incredibly valuable and enjoyable thanks to a great number of people and organisations. UNHCR has allowed my long-term and recurring presence in the camps, and CARE International has facilitated it. CARE and other NGO staff have been extremely helpful in providing me with information as well as sharing their deep knowledge and understanding of the situation in the camps. I am indebted to them, and my special thanks go to Zeinab Ahmed, Steve Gachuhi and Njogu Marangu for their particular contributions and feedback. Then, I was greatly assisted in my research by those who live in Dadaab as refugees. During meetings and casual encounters, Community Development Workers (CDWs) as well as community leaders put up with my constant questioning and were always willing to teach me something about their lives or voice their opinions about the topics I raised. During training sessions and workshops I organised, the active participation of people made the process a learning, as much as a teaching, experience. In Dagahaley, a group of very dedicated young men took the initiative to pass what they learned on to others, which I greatly appreciated. In Ifo, they kept coming back for more and our additional discussions, and the data the participants collected for me, proved very valuable. In Hagadera, the additional reports collected were extremely interesting research material, as various chapters show.

Particular thanks go to the people who have assisted me so much in the research through translations (linguistically and culturally), by organising my thoughts when there was too much for me to absorb, by taking action when I felt lost in a new situation and simply by being friends: Jamaac, Sadio, Hassan K., Abdulahi Q., Shamsa, Moxamed N. and Farah in Eastleigh, amongst many others whom I regret not being able to name. In the blocks and in Eastleigh, there were many people who gave me an immense amount of information, stories and thoughts about their lives in the past and present. I am really grateful for their willingness to share, despite the emotional challenge this at times presented. Halima M., Dhofa and Hassan, Sulub A., Sulub C. and Jawaab: *Mahadsanid*! All those I have mentioned so far have not only made it possible for me to collect the information on which this book is based, but both NGO staff and the refugee community have also contributed to making my stay in the camps a wonderful time, and transformed Dadaab into home (which almost feels inappropriate to say of a place that can never be home for those who live there). Finally, I experienced a far more difficult period doing research in Eastleigh, which was made bearable by the Wabobwa family, who welcomed me into their lives unconditionally. *Asanteni*.

The process of turning my experiences in Kenya and the knowledge I gained there into this book has been particularly challenging. On a number of occasions, I doubted whether I had the capacity to deal with such a large amount of information and it took a long time before I had a sense of direction. This was a gradual process that was mainly established in discussions and e-mail exchanges with a number of people. I want to thank Jeff Crisp for introducing my work to almost anyone dealing with Somalis, refugee livelihoods, protracted refugee situations, transnationalism and refugees in East Africa. He has been the prime source of my success in 'the art of networking' and his confidence in the project has been really encouraging. The current research started off as part of a larger project on refugees in Kenya and Uganda, coordinated by Barbara Harrell-Bond. She always had a radical response available and her work and personal comments have certainly contributed to the shape of this book. Guglielmo Verdirame's research on the human rights of refugees in Kenya (see Verdirame 1999) has been very useful and our various discussions on the situation in Dadaab have inspired me. In a research seminar entitled 'Beyond Home and Exile: Making Sense of Lives on the Move' organised in Arresodal, December 2001, I gained new insights and particularly appreciated Nick Van Hear's comments. In a transnationalism working group at the University of Amsterdam, heated debates challenged me to develop my thoughts on refugees and transnationalism more precisely. I want to thank Valentina Mazzucato for organising these sessions and providing me with useful comments on my preliminary ideas.

Once the book took shape, numerous people helped me refine it through their comments. I was able to reach the Somali diaspora with the generous help of Somalinet and Hiiraan Online and want to thank Axmed Gure and Abdiraxman Ceynte for their role in introducing my work to the wider Somali community. I was deeply impressed with the time and effort that many people invested in not only reading earlier versions of chapters but also providing me with detailed and accurate comments. My gratitude in particular goes to Abdibashi, Bana, Hajir, Ladan, Mulkki, Cawo, Sadiq, Moxamed G., Nasir and Ali Hassan, as well as Ali Abdi, Shukri and the CCF from Hagadera. Marguerite Garling, who has great knowledge of the

Maps

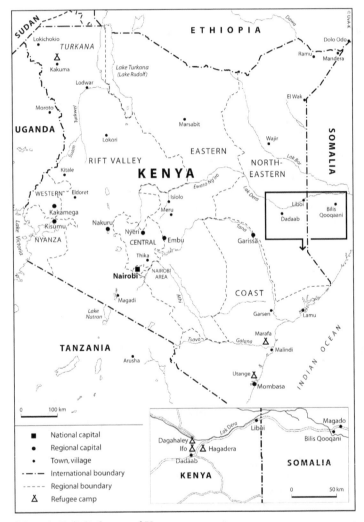

Map 1: *Political map of Kenya.*
UvA Kaartenmakers 2005, Amsterdam.

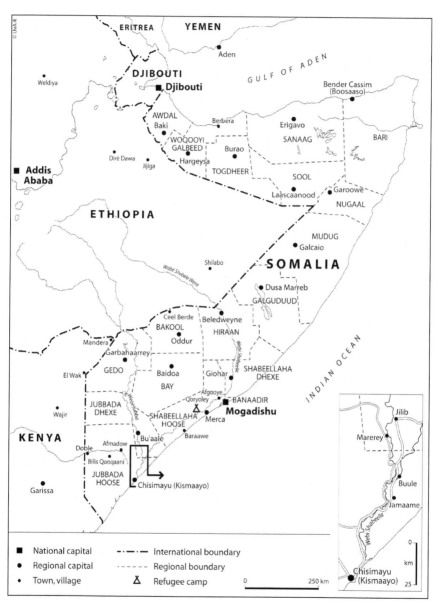

Map 2: *Political map of Somalia.*
UvAKaartenmakers 2005, Amsterdam.

situation of refugees in Kenya and of Somali society, provided me with very useful feedback on earlier chapters as well. My particular thanks go to Dr Tania Kaiser and Prof. I.M. Lewis, who provided me with excellent suggestions on how to improve an earlier manuscript in their reviews for the publisher. Special thanks also go to Dawn Chatty and Marion Berghahn, as well as other staff at Berghahn Books who, through their support and hard work, enabled this book to appear in its current shape.

Finally, my ideas, emotions and the way I was able to translate them into words were formed by who I am to friends and family. I would not have been able to complete this without their continued encouragement and patience while I was struggling to find my way: Mom and dad, for supporting me in all the choices I make; Duncan, spending time and effort on the maps in this book - thanks for simply being a brother; Loes, for enabling me to discuss my work and the difficulties involved by being enthusiastic and understanding what it takes to write this book; Marre, for friendship - you always know what to ask, what to challenge and how to guard my sanity; Ndirangu - Dadaab has become even more precious to me and Kenya is now home because of you. I dedicate this book to all of you.

We are refugees. We are like the sufriye that people make use of to cook on the fire. When you use it the first time, it gets burned badly. But later, it develops a thick layer of charcoal and cooks only slowly. Our hearts are like that. We have experienced so many things that we are now very strong. We have hardened with life.

Hassan Jamaac, Nairobi, Eastleigh, 18 January 2001

1

At a Distance?
An Introduction

On 23 November 1999, I met Axmed[1] in Dagahaley camp during a second interview with his uncle, Roble Abdiraxman.[2] I had been in Dadaab for almost four months by then, and Dagahaley was the second camp in which I stayed. Early in November, I had gone to each section of the camp to introduce myself and explain the purpose of my presence in the area. When I reached block C6, Roble was amongst the people I met. He was very outspoken and wanted to know where I was from, telling me that he would soon go for resettlement to the U.S.A., where his daughter lived. I asked him whether I could come back to ask some questions about that, and he agreed. We had a first interview and I made sure that Roble received a copy of my written report of that interview. A couple of days later, while I was walking through the camp with my translator, Roble stopped us and invited me to visit his house any time in order to discuss the report I had given him and answer my additional questions. When we did, he welcomed us with juice and later with tea and cake, proudly telling me that the cake was made using eggs from his own chicken. While initially the atmosphere was a bit formal, this changed when I was introduced to Axmed, a young boy of maybe thirteen years. Axmed had just come from Mogadishu ten days earlier, travelling alone. He had wanted to go to another uncle in Afmadow, but once there, he learned that his uncle had moved to Nairobi. Thus, he continued on to Dadaab, where he knew his uncle Roble lived.

When Axmed found out that I was from the Netherlands, he enthusiastically started to mention some of the Dutch soccer players he admired and we talked about soccer for a while. Then, the boy related his experiences with the sport in Mogadishu. He told me about a man who was coaching a rival soccer team in the city and had tried to encourage peace through sports activities for young people. Axmed was sad when he recounted: 'He was Hawiye[3], but he was a very good man. He brought us over fifty balls so that we could play football together, and he also paid for the tickets of those who wanted to watch football games in the stadium in Mogadishu. He tried to promote peace through sports but one day the warlords just killed him'. Roble then prompted Axmed to tell me why he had left Somalia and I learned that after a soccer match, he had been threatened with a knife and a gun by one of the players. Roble told me that although the assailant was from a related clan and the fight was only about a soccer match, Axmed's relatives in Somalia had considered it best for the boy to leave Mogadishu and stay with his uncle instead. Listening to Axmed's experiences, I was silenced by the deafening clash between the universality of young boys enthusiastic about their soccer idols and the unique absurdness of this particular boy's memories of the game. At that moment, all I could do was talk about Ruud Gullit and Edgar Davids, as if he was just a boy like my brother once was, crazy about soccer.

Throughout my encounters with refugees, whether during work and research in Europe or in Kenya, what I have always found most striking is the duality of humanness and inhumanity in refugee lives. How the most shocking events become part of ordinary human lives is something I am constantly trying to grapple with. I find it difficult to deal with the contrast of, on the one hand, recognising the human aspect of refugees' experiences, while on the other, never being able to understand the dreadful cruelty of parts of their lives. As such, my research project developed from a wish to provide an alternative to common depictions of refugees, both in the media and in academic literature. As I will argue later in this chapter, refugees are often labelled either as 'vulnerable victims' or as 'cunning crooks', a process that strips them of all humanity. Yet the individuals I got to know, during my work for the Dutch Refugee Council and through various research projects, were human beings trying to deal with the 'inhuman' aspects of their past and present experiences. In an attempt to show this continuity and the agency of refugees, I decided to analyse the social security strategies of a particular refugee community and the links between these strategies and the ones utilised in their (pre-flight) past.

Because of earlier research experience, I chose to conduct research amongst Somalis in the Kenyan refugee camps of Dadaab. My main interest concerned the effects of life in Dadaab on the social security arrangements of Somali refugees, and the level of security or insecurity that NGO and government arrangements provided. Before their flight, the Somali were very familiar with insecurities, which they dealt with through what I will call a 'nomadic heritage'. I define this heritage as consisting of three elements: a mentality of looking for greener pastures; a strong social network that entails the obligation to assist each other in surviving; and risk-reduction through strategically dispersing investments in family members and activities. My main interest was to find out whether refugee life in the Dadaab camps affected such strategies. Between July

1999 and August 2001, I spent various periods of fieldwork amongst the Somali refugees who live in the refugee camps near Dadaab in northeast Kenya, adding up to over one year. During my stay in the camps, I learned that while the three 'nomadic' characteristics had developed from the local circumstances of life in Somalia, they had now acquired a transnational character and were still supporting the Somali refugees in Dadaab in their daily survival.

This book is structured along the historical and transnational lines of my interest in the social security strategies of Somali refugees in Dadaab. Chapters 2 and 3 present the historical background to the ways that Somalis can deal with insecurities in the camps, looking both at the situation in Somalia before and during the war as well as at the history of the refugee regime mandated to provide security to refugees. Then, chapters 4 and 5 analyse the transnational aspects of the refugees' strategies, presenting the ways in which Somalis assist each other across borders as well as the consequent dreams and opportunities of migration from Dadaab. This first chapter will provide insight into the process that led to this historical and transnational focus, presenting the case of Khaliif as an introduction to some of the main points in this book. I describe common refugee labelling processes and suggest an alternative approach that acknowledges both refugee agency and vulnerabilities. Subsequently, I introduce the research setting in Dadaab and the position of Somali refugees in Kenya. In conclusion, the methodological and theoretical basis of research and book will be discussed.

Khaliif: Migration and Choice

During my stay in Dagahaley my Somali teacher Yunis Axmed, who was not only an excellent language teacher but also a great help to the research, introduced me to Khaliif[4] Ibrahim. Yunis had taken it upon himself to introduce me to some of the respected elders and leaders in the camp, and Khaliif was one of them. We paid a visit to his block at the far end of Dagahaley on a Friday, but discovered he was out rounding up his cattle from the bushes next to the camp (Fig. 1.1). One of his sons rushed to tell his father about our visit and we waited for Khaliif to come home. Although we were served tea and welcomed warmly, Khaliif insisted that he had not been expecting us that day and we needed to come back so that his wife could prepare something for us. We agreed to come for lunch on Sunday, and arranged to have an interview afterwards. Although the story that Khaliif told us on that Sunday, 21 November 1999, is not typical in many ways, it serves as a clear introduction of what this book is about. Khaliif has far more opportunities than most refugees in Dadaab due to his socio-economic position, but the way he weighs his options and

Figure 1.1 *Rainy season in Dagahaley.*

makes his choices is exemplary for the decision-making processes related to migration. Besides, Khaliif's situation illustrates the many advantages that 'transnational nomadism' has brought for Somalis in Dadaab. He functions within an extensive transnational network of relatives, which has enabled him to live in Dagahaley in relative prosperity, while also allowing him to migrate from the camps.

When I asked Khaliif to tell me more about his personal background, he started his story by talking about his childhood. He was born in a rural area in Galgaduud near the Ethiopian border where he was brought up in a family of wealthy pastoralists who owned goats, cattle and camels. Khaliif belongs to the *reer* (family, lineage)[5] of former president Siyaad Barre. His grandfather was a respected elder and peacekeeper in the area and when he died, Khaliif's father fulfilled that role. Again, when his father died, his *adeer* (father's brother) took over. Khaliif went to *dugsi* (Koran school) in Galgaduud and, at the age of seventeen, he moved to Mogadishu and joined the armed forces there. At that time, he learned Italian and some English. He was promoted to the rank of colonel and was sent to the USSR and Italy for further military training. Khaliif believes that due to this experience abroad, he is able to evaluate the situation of his family in the camp and compare it to life in resettlement countries in the West; something we discussed extensively that afternoon.

Khaliif is the father of thirteen children, of whom one has died. Ten of his children live with him and his wife, Canab,[6] in Dagahaley, while one of his sons goes to secondary school in Nairobi and another boy lives in the U.S.A. with his mother, whom Khaliif divorced. When I asked about the two boys who do not live in the camps, I realised that Khaliif was not really pleased with the fact that they were out of his reach. He told me,

> Both boys have not stayed with me since 1996, but every now and then I travel to Nairobi to visit my son there. He has really changed a lot since he moved from the camps; in terms of how he speaks, the way he dresses and even his hairstyle. He has become like a Black American now, copied from other boys in Nairobi. When I tried to say something about it, the boy told me: 'Hey dad, I'm free'. His behaviour has made me fear very much for the other children and that is why I cannot take them to the U.S.A. The religion tells us always to go straight, but in the U.S.A. children will learn to make detours.

I asked Khaliif whether he had agreed with the fact that his other son went to the U.S.A. to stay with his mother and he answered that he had not wanted him to go. Yet, the boy's mother insisted because he was her only son and she needed his assistance there. When she went so far as to send her relatives to Dagahaley in order to discuss the issue with Khaliif, he had to let his son go.

Then, Khaliif told me that he was called to Nairobi and offered a sponsorship[7] only four months earlier but that he did not want to opt for resettlement:

> My brothers and sisters pleaded with me to come to the U.S.A. and said that they would provide a sponsorship for my whole family. They told me that there is no reason for me to get killed in these refugee camps, arguing that the children would have nothing if I were to die because I am the only breadwinner in the family. However, it is better to die than to lose my children, my culture and my religion. The camps provide free food, education and medical treatment, clean drinking water, ninety-nine percent security and a piece of land on which we can build our houses without paying rent. There is plenty of grazing land available for the animals I own, so my condition is okay. There are people who take their children back to Somalia although there is still no education and no security and no let-up in the fighting. They are really crazy: what are they looking for? I have a piece of land near Mogadishu close to the river, which I could reclaim when I go back, since I have a letter of ownership for it. But at the moment, there is nothing for us to go back to unless peace is restored. My oldest children are now pupils in standard seven and eight, and for the next two or three years they will be going to Dagahaley secondary school. After that, peace should be restored in Somalia and they can finish their education there and find jobs in foreign embassies.

According to Khaliif, the prospect of opting for resettlement would interfere with these plans.

My children are my most important possession. If I went to the U.S.A., it would be like saying: 'take my children and make them into whatever you want'. The conditions in Dagahaley are good, so why should I risk my future just because of a few years of suffering? If I were to go to the U.S.A., I would have nothing and be nobody, nor would I be able to return to my country. My children would refuse to go back to Somalia and I would be like an old camel, leaving behind all its products. If I returned to Somalia on my own, people would ask me where my children were and why I had left them in the U.S.A. And then they would want to know why I had taken them to the U.S.A. in the first place.

When I asked Khaliif whether other people would agree with his point of view, he told me: 'People are not the same. Some people come from towns, some from rural areas. Some have lived off agriculture and others have moved with their cattle'. My question referred to the widespread existence of *buufis* in the camps, the dream to go for resettlement. Thus, my next question to Khaliif was whether he could explain why some refugees wanted to go to the West, unlike him. Khaliif answered:

First of all, the refugees want to escape the insecurity and the economic problems that they are facing in the camps. Secondly, they assume that they will achieve economic prosperity in the West. There is a clear lack of knowledge about the reality of life there, as the Somali do not realise that people in Western countries work hard for their money. But once people have resettled, they cannot go back because they do not have the money to return and besides, their children would not come with them. As a consequence they are stranded.

Despite his negative attitude towards life in the West, many of Khaliif's relatives live in Western countries and a number of them even enable him to live a comfortable live in Dagahaley. Khaliif has one brother and one sister who live in the U.S.A. and another brother in Denmark. He has received remittances from them on a number of occasions, but only in response to his requests. Khaliif does not like to call his siblings for financial help, since he knows that they have many relatives in Somalia who ask for their assistance. Besides, his siblings have their own family responsibilities, with small children to raise. When I asked him whether he received remittances from others, Khaliif said: 'My son in the U.S.A. is only eighteen and works part-time besides going to school, so it is not possible for him to send any money. At times, my ex-wife sends me some money when she is able. In addition to these occasional remittances, I get a monthly allowance from a group of fifteen of my relatives in Ohio who are in a position to assist me. They are *ilmo* (children) *adeer*, who are usually even more dedicated to assisting than one's own brothers and sisters'. Khaliif supports his large family through these regular remittances from outside the camps, but also has his own sources of income and assets. He owns three camels, six cows and fifteen goats as well as thirty chickens that he keeps for their eggs and for special guests to eat. This enables him to show me in practical terms what Somali traditions of hospitality entail and I am impressed by the wonderful meal of soor (a grain dish) and chicken that his wife has cooked for us. As always, I eat it with the mixed emotions of not wanting to be a burden on the refugees' often tight subsistence, but realizing how important it is for Somalis to still be able to provide hospitality. This is a source of dignity and pride that I would hate to insult by declining the offer.

This brief description of my conversation with Khaliif and his deliberate choice to stay in Dagahaley addresses the main issues relevant to this book. Firstly, it is important to take into account Khaliif's position within the Somali community. He stems from a family of leaders and belongs to the clan of Siyad Barre, the former president of Somalia. He does not go into detail, but Khaliif seems to have occupied an important position in the government before his flight. Currently, although he lives in the semi-desert surroundings of a refugee camp, he can still be considered a wealthy and respected man. His socio-economic position obviously influences the choices that Khaliif is able to make in his life, and it is clear that most refugees do not have the same level of choice. Yet, as I realised from the feedback I acquired on a preliminary version of this chapter, the situation may be rather complex as Khaliif's socio-economic position simultaneously expands as well as restricts his options. Madimba Muse, a Somali who now lives in the U.K. and who sent me valuable comments on all preliminary chapters I sent him, was of the opinion that Khaliif would have been willing to live in Western countries just like he did before, as long as the circumstances were the same.[9] He was unwilling to go purely because he had lost his status of government officer and had to replace it with that of refugee. Indeed, various studies, for example those dealing with the gender aspects of refugee issues, have pointed out how the experience of becoming a refugee at times is more difficult for those who had a higher socio-economic position in their country of origin (see e.g. McSpadden and Moussa 1993; Schrijvers 1997). Besides, Khaliif's current position is complicated by his links with the former government, as a number of Somali readers pointed out.

Listening to other Somalis explain how they were surviving in Dadaab, I realised that the level of power and choice of individual refugees may vary widely and thus needs to be studied and not assumed. A second point of relevance to this book is that Khaliif's story is punctuated with elements of travel and migration. In Somalia, travel is considered to be a learning process and a source of wisdom. 'A man who has travelled, a *wayo' arag*, is one who knows a great deal, has seen things, has lived' (Rousseau et al. 1998: 386). Khaliif came from a family of nomads and left for Mogadishu at the age of seventeen. From there, he ended up in the USSR and Italy. In addition, his family members currently live on a number of continents. These patterns of transnational distribution of family members and a very high mobility rate are widespread amongst the Somali. I became interested in the link between these current patterns and the nomadic lifestyle that for centuries was very common in Somali society. As Aden Yusuf, who now lives in the U.S.A. with his family, remarked in a comment on the concept of 'transnational nomads', 'Somalis treat the U.S.-Canadian border the same as they would treat the Ethiopian-Somali border: "If it rains better today, we move there". They are always on the move and changing their residency and they often do not like to be constrained by rules and regulations. When you define the term transnational nomads for the reader, you might want to include the secondary migration by Somali "nomads" in Europe, U.S.A. or Canada'.

A remarkable feature of the case selected is that Khaliif made the deliberate choice not to go to any of these Western countries. I was more often confronted with those who wished to go, and was particularly fascinated by the extremes of that wish as manifested in *buufis*. While working for a refugee organisation in the Netherlands, I had had to deal with the many problems that refugees face when living in the West. In the camps, I found an idealised image of life abroad, or at least a strong hope to go there. I tried to express my own picture of refugee life in the West but my cautions seemed to have no sounding board at all. This does not mean, however, that I cannot understand why people wish to exchange their lives in the Horn of Africa for a life in the West or assist others in doing so. Through various means of communication, the inequalities in life standards are now well known worldwide. Besides, the fact that Somalis have moved from the camps and send remittances from their new localities of course benefits many refugees in Dadaab. Khaliif was able to live a comfortable life because of monthly remittances and other refugees were able to survive due to an occasional money transfer, while a third group benefited indirectly from the dollars that flow into the camps. Migration has been a good investment for many, and it has improved life in the camps substantially.

A final issue of relevance in Khaliif's story is the fact that he is part of a wider network of relatives. This network is important in the decision-making opportunities of the individual in a number of ways. Although Khaliif's siblings and siblings' children tried to influence and enable his decision to move, he was the one who made the final choice. At the same time, his relatives gave him the luxury of that choice. With their monthly allowance he could have decided to move to Garissa or Nairobi, as quite a number of refugees from the Dadaab camps have done. His relatives offered him the opportunity to go abroad with his family but never forced him to do so. They could have done so by cutting his monthly allowance, as happened to others who did not abide by the wishes of their family members. It was only due to the continued assistance of his relatives abroad, that Khaliif was able to live a comfortable life in Dagahaley. He decided to stay. From his point of view, Khaliif also treated the relationship in a considerate way. He was aware of the family responsibilities of a number of his family members and did not like bothering them. Instead, he preferred to wait for the initiatives of those who could afford to assist. Still, his wide network of relatives overseas was of great help to him for daily survival and in times of special need. To summarise, the book shows the importance for Somali refugees of social (assistance) networks in relation to survival in the camps and migration elsewhere, in particular to the West, without losing sight of the considerable variation between the level of power and choice that individual refugees have.

At a Distance?

The title of this chapter refers to and problematises 'distance' in a number of ways. In the first place, the social networks of Somali refugees often cover a great distance, as relatives live far away from each other. It is very common to find Somalis in the camps who have relatives living in Somalia, Garissa, Nairobi, South Africa, the Middle East, Canada, the U.S.A., Australia or Europe. But at the same time, this physical distance does not necessarily affect the closeness of relationships between them. Somalis travel a lot, and visit their relatives on numerous occasions. If face-to-face contact is not possible, they keep in touch through various means of communication. Many refugees in the camps contact their relatives inside and outside Kenya using the *taar* (radio communication transmitters) or phone, or they send messages and goods via those travelling to a place where relatives live. Another common way for relatives to stay in touch over long distances is through the *xawilaad* (an informal value-transfer system), which enables both communication and remittance sending. Through these means, social ties are kept strong and relatives play an important role in each other's lives and livelihoods, even over large distances.

Secondly, 'distance' refers to the detachment that supposedly exists between researchers and the people they study. In anthropology, there is ambivalence towards that detachment. On the one hand, the discipline's main method of data collection, participant observation, relies on a position of closeness in order to gain knowledge. At the same time, anthropologists realise that total immersion in the research context cannot be attained and they will always remain (partial) outsiders. Even those who do research within their own communities, and who thus share a similar sociocultural background, are at a distance simply because they have come to study others. On the other hand, the shared humanness between the researcher and the researched does bring about very valuable insights, as it is the basis for mutual understanding. There will always be experiences or aspects of life that are recognisable for both sides. In my own research, the crossing of national and cultural boundaries was an experience and position I shared with the Somali, despite the fact that our reasons for crossing were completely different. If the world is seen as a place where moving and dwelling are in constant interplay, sites are not experienced merely by being present in them, but also by leaving them behind (Fog Olwig and Hastrup 1997). The anthropologist may be in a good position to understand what it means to be a transnational nomad, even though her or his level of power and choice is often far greater than that of refugees.

A third meaning of 'distance' relates to the assumption that, after data collection, the researcher needs physical as well as mental distance to analyse his or her fieldwork material 'objectively' and to write about it. It is commonly thought that, in order to be able to see patterns in the data collected and find explanations for these patterns, the researcher must leave the area she or he worked in. Yet, this involves a kind of appropriation of information that in recent years many social scientists have questioned. Various attempts have been made to deal with the ethical questions raised and more participatory ways of analysis and publication have developed in the process (see e.g. Jackson 1995). Furthermore, global developments in transport and communication have shortened the actual distance in time and space between the researcher and the people concerned, facilitating their participation in the analysis and writing-down of results. Personally, after my fieldwork was completed, I frequently visited Kenya, made many phone calls and exchanged information with a number of people in Dadaab. Besides, I have been able to disseminate my preliminary work through the Internet, e-mail and the postal system to Somali refugees, NGO employees and academics for comments. In the course of this book, I will elaborate further on this particular form of 'shared anthropology'.

Lastly, the title of this chapter refers to the attempt by many authors not to appear in their own academic work, keeping the Self safely, but dishonestly, 'at a distance'. The practice of rendering the researcher-author invisible largely stems from the common belief in an objective (exclusive, mastering) academic truth. Yet, knowledge is not simply 'out there'; instead, it is created in a dialectical and dialogical communication process (Schrijvers 1991) in which all those involved exert power. As such, the idea of social science attempting to arrive at an objective truth may need to be replaced with a vision of constructed, partial, fluctuating and conflicting truths. I agree with Haraway (1991: 190) that social scientists cannot arrive at anything but partiality in their attempts to describe and understand the world they are part of. According to her, this is not something they should try to transcend. Rather, the highly specific, wonderfully detailed and different pictures of the world should be investigated. The only way for a researcher to find a larger vision is by being somewhere in particular, by locating one's partial and critically situated knowledge (Haraway 1991: 190). I have tried throughout this text to allow the reader to establish my positionality as researcher and author, although of course this is a limited exercise as I have ultimately been the one deciding which constructed, partial, fluctuating and conflicting truths to select for this book.

Theorizing Refugee Agency and Vulnerability

When starting from a perspective of social sciences as situated knowledge, researchers should be aware of the ethics and politics behind their own and other people's attempts at categorisation and representation. It is important to question categories and analyses of an essentialist nature continuously (Scott 1988), in order to leave room for alternative representations. In the media and academic literature, refugees, in my view, are often depicted as vulnerable victims or cunning crooks. These images do no justice to the multifaceted and fluid humanness that characterise individual refugees, or to the agency that I found so striking in their attempts to deal with life. Agency has been defined as concerning 'events of which an individual is the perpetrator, in the sense that the individual could, at any phase in a given sequence of conduct, have acted differently. Whatever happened would not have happened if that individual had not intervened' (Giddens 1984: 9). Thus, agency firstly implies a level of choice, although the conditions under which a certain choice is made may vary. A range of specifiable circumstances may confine the options, but nevertheless a choice has been made (Giddens 1984: 15).

A second aspect of agency involves power: the power of doing things or leaving them, thus making a difference. According to Giddens, this transformative capacity is of importance irrespective of whether the outcome of someone's actions was intended or not. As such, his structuration theory avoids the common dualism between actor or agent and structure or system that is created by the assumption that an individual's or group's level of choice and power is constrained by larger institutional structures and social systems. In his view, the structural properties of social systems are both the medium and outcome of the practices they recursively organise: 'Structure is not to be equated with constraint but is always both constraining and enabling. This, of course, does not prevent the structured properties of social systems from stretching away, in time and space, beyond the control of any individual actors' (Giddens 1984: 25). Thus, the agency of actors is both enabled through and constrained by the structural properties of social systems, while simultaneously leading to their reproduction. Conversely structure, while seemingly operating independently and decisive, only exists through the actions of individual agents. I will illustrate that current conceptualisations of refugees do not generally acknowledge such agency, and suggest an alternative approach.

Media Images of Refugees

When people are categorised as refugees, they are assigned certain characteristics as a group. This has a function for the different parties involved, such as governments, the UNHCR (United Nations High Commissioner for Refugees) and NGOs, academics, 'the general public' and the refugees themselves. Concepts, both in the sense of conceptions and constructs, are of great importance to people as they assist in classifying and giving meaning to the world, and in justifying actions. However, despite the utility of concepts, they must be used critically. As feminists and other critical researchers have stressed, it is important that academics continuously examine essentialist categories and forms of analysis critically, within both science and the larger society (Mouffe 1992). The issue is what concepts might allow people to think and how they allow them to think. This is particularly urgent, considering the fact that (theoretical) constructs are not only influenced by social reality, but also have an impact on the general discourse within that reality and thus on actions (Wolf 1994). The ideas that exist about refugees, in the end, have a clear effect on the reality of their daily lives. First, the labelling of refugees concerns the images created of them in the media, affecting public opinion. Secondly, it concerns a classification process for policy purposes, through institutional labels. In both cases, what is at stake is people's identity and entitlements: what (or who) is a refugee; and what rights does that give him or her?

In the media, quite standardised discursive and representational forms are used that create a certain image of refugees. First of all, there is a picture of horror and powerlessness. Refugees stop being specific persons, but are reduced to pure victims of the worst in humanity. They are stripped of the particular characteristics of their person, place and history; left only with a humanness of the most basic sense. Common representations of refugees as masses of people or as vulnerable women and children display their raw, bare humanity (Malkki 1996). It is assumed that the confrontation with the most horrific realities in life reduces them to vulnerables in need of protection and someone to represent them, so helplessness and dependency are stressed. Secondly, the representation of refugees amounts to a feeling of shame and unease because they do not fit the national order of things. In a world of 'imagined communities' (Anderson 1983), refugees form a threat and an embarrassment to the nation-state. They are described as people in a liminal position, as being in between: for they have lost their nation, culture, identity and many other certainties in their lives.[10] Thirdly, refugees are always related to problems, and not so much those that caused them to be refugees but rather the problems they themselves are causing simply by existing (Malkki 1996). The crisis is not located in the external factors that have lead to the creation of refugees, but in the existence of refugees in itself. This also leads to common representations of refugees as people who present bogus asylum claims (Kaye 1998). As such, an ambiguous picture is created of, on the one hand, 'masses' of refugees who have no agency at all, mostly remaining in the developing world and, on the other, individual 'crooks' who misuse their agency to come to the West and profit from various resources from which they have no right to benefit.

The public image of refugees as victims, liminal people and the cause of many problems is, in my view, a way of Othering them: of clearly distinguishing Self from Other. The experiences of refugees cannot be grasped by others, because that would entail a most dramatic confrontation with the arbitrariness of fate and the fleeting nature of life. Being in a refugee situation means an annihilation of the substance of a world, a culture, a history and a livelihood (Habib 1996). Those who are not refugees do not want to identify with the situation refugees are in as if it were a human condition: something that could happen to anyone. The image others have of refugees can be understood through the fear of them, as symbol of ultimate disorder and liminality. Visual representations of refugees often depict their bare humanity and extreme vulnerability. Looking at these pictures it becomes difficult to trace any connection between 'us' and 'them', except that bare humanity which is in all of us (Malkki 1996). This enables people who never had to flee to safeguard a sense of security by placing the experiences of refugees outside the Self and by denying any form of responsibility for them or their fate.

Now of course, there are many reasons why the described labelling and related processes of Othering refugees are problematic. First of all, the images presented are simply not true. Extensive empirical evidence shows that refugees conceive an identity very different from that ascribed to them (Zetter 1991). Still, they are constantly confronted with existing images, and they may become Other to themselves. A Kurd from Iran describes the discrepancy between reality and the image of vulnerability very accurately: 'the problem is the gap between the refugee's identity and the perception of the refugee by the host community. Kurdish refugees are survivors; they are strong and can contribute to the host society. Yet, they are still treated as newborn babies, left in an uncertain and unstable situation' (Horst 1997: 22). A Somali in Kenya describes another aspect of the problem, noting that they left Somalia as Somalis and arrived as refugees, as UNHCR statistics (Farah 2000: 16). Another one of Farah's respondents, a Somali man who now resides in Sweden, told him that whereas in Somalia, they were defined by their family and clan responsibilities, in Sweden this was no longer the case. 'Here, we are refugees first, black Africans second and Somalis last' (Farah 2000: 190). What is problematic is that the complex identities of a single person are taken and replaced by one: that of a refugee. In the process, refugees are stripped of the specific features of their society, their place of origin and history.

A related issue is that this de-politicises fundamental inequalities and injustices on national and international levels, erasing the specific, historical, local politics of particular refugees. The practices of representation are very damaging because they actively hide the politico-economic connections that link television viewers' own history with that of 'those poor people over there' (Malkki 1996). The problem is that public images, whether accurate or not, both influence and are part of the politics and policies that determine the lives of refugees. These images, as they are represented in and formed through mass media, are both 'agenda-setting and news framing': they determine which issues are seen as priorities for policy development and political action, while at the same time, 'news' is a frame through which reality is socially constructed, influenced by, for example, the interests of politicians (Kaye 1998).

Institutional Labelling

The refugee regime and governments simultaneously label refugees institutionally, in order to determine their entitlements in terms of aid and protection. But even the various parties involved have great difficulty agreeing on who is a refugee and who is not and thus on who is entitled to aid or protection and who is not. Zetter (1991) describes labelling as a process by which people, conceived as objects of policy, are defined in convenient images. According to him, labelling involves defining a client group in stereotypical, clear-cut ways and then prescribing its assumed set of needs. Malkki (1996) gives a clear example of this process in her study amongst Hutu refugees in Tanzania. According to the Tanzanian aid workers she spoke to, refugees are poor and vulnerable and should look that way. In fact, they are at their 'purest' when they have just arrived, in their most desolate state (Malkki 1996: 385). After this first period of helplessness, refugees cannot be trusted. They are dishonest and make up stories for their own benefit. Such an attitude is rather common amongst government officials, NGO and UNHCR employees dealing with refugees anywhere in the world, including Dadaab.

Being categorised by others, refugees themselves also have an interest in the label they are given. They have an ambivalent attitude towards labelling and its implications because it categorises them in often negative and incorrect ways with which they cannot identify. At the same time, being labelled a refugee entails the entitlement to certain rights. These rights can be claimed by stating that 'indeed we are vulnerable and thus entitled to assistance', a variant that I found very common in the Dadaab camps and will describe extensively. Other groups of refugees claim instead that 'indeed we are politically oppressed and thus need protection as well as recognition from the international community'. Malkki describes such views amongst the Hutu in Tanzania (Malkki 1995a) and I personally found this attitude to be common amongst Kurdish refugees in the U.K. The words of a young Kurd describe this political claim clearly: 'Refugeeness is implicit in the creation and construction of exile politics. It is a concept that turned politics into the cornerstone of our continuous identification process' (Horst 1997: 21). In both instances, inclusion requires conformity; the original story needs to be adapted to the bureaucratic dictates that come with the specific label (Zetter 1991). Thus, the system requires refugees to do what it accuses them of, to make up stories, as chapter 3 will clearly illustrate.

The bureaucratic needs of the international refugee regime and governments make it necessary to label the people that are entitled to assistance. To prevent a blurring of tasks, it is argued, refugee assistance projects should not deal with internally displaced, economic migrants, or locals. The UNHCR and NGOs use clearly earmarked relief money and project managers are accountable for the ways they spend that money. The system requires refugees to be defined and then counted, to prove efficiency (Harrell-Bond et al. 1992). When it comes to the content of the label, the UNHCR and NGOs benefit from the assumption that refugees are passive victims needing charitable dispensation. The assumed identity of refugees creates and imposes an institutional dependency; to become a refugee is to accept the passive role of recipient. This is taken to facilitate the distribution of aid and, moreover, the assumption of helplessness and a need for care is the cornerstone of nearly all appeals for funds. Lastly, labelling refugees has great political advantages because it enables segregation and control. The movement of refugees can only be directed and restrained if they are clearly distinguishable.

There are two main problems related to the kind of labelling occurring within the international refugee regime. In the first place, the idea of refugee dependency is presently seen as an absolute and fixed truth, whereas historically refugees have not always been treated as vulnerable victims in need of assistance. The refugees fleeing from Eastern Europe after the Second World War, for example, were seen as a unique potential for economic growth and also a proof of the failure of communism. These refugees were welcomed to help the underpopulated and 'underdeveloped' democracies of the U.S.A., Canada and Australia build up their economies; their education and skills were gratefully utilised (Harrell-Bond 1996).

But not only is the label incorrect and variable through space and time, it is also damaging. Such labelling serves to confine people's agency by placing constraints on refugees' attempts to utilise their own strengths. Since institutional labels often start from the premise that refugees are vulnerable victims in need of assistance, policies based on such labels do not recognise, let alone stimulate, people's own initiatives and in fact often obstruct them by, for example, regulating or restricting refugee movements and economic activities. According to some, there is a risk that a vicious circle will develop that leads to the so-called 'refugee dependency syndrome' (Buchwald 1991). When policies reflect the idea that refugees are vulnerable, their own resources, capabilities and views are disregarded completely. This may discourage them from taking initiatives while, at the same time, teaching them to conform to the label ascribed to them. A number of researchers (e.g. Harrell-Bond 1986; Buchwald 1991) and refugee assistance workers claim that this leads to a certain state of apathy and dependency. Various studies deny the existence of a dependency syndrome amongst refugees, and rather observe a strategic use of the label and what is expected (Kibreab 1993). But no matter whether the syndrome is factual or pretended, nonparticipatory policies are damaging to the dignity of refugees as well as the efficiency of policies.

An Alternative Approach

The dominant conceptualisation of refugees is highly problematic because it is incorrect and damaging to those conceptualised. On a number of occasions, I discussed this problem with refugees in the camps. Once, on a Wednesday morning, 15 December 1999, I visited Halimo Hassan in her block in Dagahaley for an interview. She answered my questions elaborately, understood what I wanted to learn and taught me a great deal. We talked about the misconceptions that exist concerning refugees and I commented how difficult it is for people to imagine that they could become refugees themselves. Halimo agreed, telling me about her own experiences. She recalled the time when she was living in Berbera (Somaliland). Her father worked as a sailor and she lived with her mother and her three brothers and three sisters.

> In those days, I used to see Somali refugees from Ethiopia, and I never understood them. Who were they, and why were they there? But now, ironically, I have been a refugee myself twice. In 1988, one day before the fighting broke out, I fled with my husband and two children from Berbera to Mogadishu. Many followed us later, when the problems in Somaliland intensified. The inhabitants of Mogadishu regarded the refugees from the north with great suspicion and it was then that I was able to understand the position of the

Ethiopian refugees in Berbera. When the civil war started in 1991, we had to flee together with our hosts and came to Kenya as refugees.

According to Halimo, the Kenyans despised the Somali refugees who had come to their country. She wished she could warn them about the risk of becoming a refugee: 'Please, keep your government because we also had a government once, and look what happened when we threw it away'. She had been living the life of a refugee for over twelve years and had experienced great hardships.

> During our second flight, we were captured by militia on the way to Kismaayo and taken hostage for one year. In 1992, after we were freed, we reached Liboya on the Kenyan side of the border. Two years later, we were transferred from Liboya to the Dadaab camps. Here, I sell *sambuusi* [samosa] at the market to supplement the food rations that are insufficient to sustain my family. I have also travelled to Garissa and Nairobi in order to try to communicate with my siblings and cousins in Europe. I had hoped that they could send me a monthly allowance, a sponsorship or even some money to return to Somaliland. But at the time of the interview, Halimo had not been able to communicate with any of her relatives.

Halimo's story illustrates two points that are of relevance to this book. In the first place, it expresses the self protective inability of human beings to understand the humanness in refugees and their experiences. Halimo could not understand the situation of the Somali refugees from Ethiopia she encountered until she became a refugee herself. This is a very common phenomenon that has been described in a number of studies on refugee situations throughout the world. In the film *We Are All Neighbours* (Christie 1990) about the civil war in former Yugoslavia, it is shocking to see how long it takes before people accept that they are part of the war. Even when the fighting is only some miles away, they do not realise that they themselves are involved in an ethnopolitical conflict. They cannot make the link between what they see happening around them and their own situation since, after all, in their village, people are all neighbours. Habib (1996) expresses the same type of 'ignorance' in relation to the war in Lebanon, when she writes that she only understood the reality of the situation in which she found herself, after family and friends were killed. She assumes that the main reason for not accepting that this was happening to her was probably the impossibility to understand and give meaning to her experiences.

Secondly, Halimo's observations and her attempts to sustain her family in the best way also provide an illustration of the fact that refugees are not simply victims, no matter how tragic the experiences they undergo. People always create their own history and future, even if they do it in conditions that are not of their choosing (Giddens 1984). Forced migrants are active agents who, despite unfavourable conditions, will try to utilise the options open to them in order to be able to cope with life. As Jackson (1987: 22) argues, that is where the truth lies about which anthropologists should write: 'Truth is seen pragmatically: not as an essence but as an aspect of existence; not as some abstraction like Science, Rationality, Beauty, or God, to be respected whatever the circumstances, but as a means of coping with life'. To cope with life means learning not only to accept what one cannot change, but also to fight for those things one is able to change and to distinguish correctly between the two. The actor-oriented approach that I used in my research in a similar way ascribes a central role to human action and consciousness. It assumes that people are capable and knowledgeable when it comes to dealing with life, both in giving direction to it as well as in accepting it (Long and Long 1992). As such, I wanted to find a way to express the strength that I observe in refugees and to convey my understanding of their lives. Throughout this book, I have tried to do this by extensively quoting the refugees I spoke to in Dadaab and those who commented on my earlier work, as I will shortly explain further.

In order to understand the situation of Somali refugees in Dadaab, I also found it essential to place that specific situation in a historical context. In the academic world as well as within relief-providing organisations, crises are largely seen as external events interfering with a certain stable social reality. This viewpoint obscures the fact that insecurity is the normal state of affairs for many, and people have developed socio-economic security mechanisms to deal with it (Davis 1993). De Bruijn and van Dijk (1995) argue the same in their study on nomadic pastoralists in Mali, for whom insecurity paradoxically constitutes life's only certainty. According to these authors and others (e.g. Aronson 1980; Hjort af Ornäs 1990; Braun 1992), nomadic pastoralism is an adaptation to an ecologically insecure environment, so there is a danger of focusing on 'normal' conditions that are not very likely to occur anyway. With mobility being the most suitable strategy to cope with climate fluctuations, instability becomes an inherent characteristic of nomadic life. Similarly, the Somalis who had become refugees in the Dadaab area had faced all kinds of insecurities before the collapse of their state and developed various ways of dealing with those insecurities. As will be described in further detail in the next chapter, these were mainly based on mobility, strong social networks and dispersing investments within those networks. In situations of extreme scarcity or crisis, such as after flight from one's country, alternative means of survival may need to be sought. Yet, adaptation to insecure circumstances is often determined not only by survival functions but also by cultural values and history. The experience of the threat to a way of life may be more real than the experience of the threat of starvation (De Waal 1989). This is a very essential factor to take into account when studying the continuity or change in the social security mechanisms of refugees.

Somali Refugees in Dadaab: National and Regional Policies

At the end of 1991 and in early 1992, three refugee camps were set up close to Dadaab, to host the large influx of Somalis fleeing the collapse of their state. At present, approximately 135,000 refugees are still living in Ifo, Dagahaley and Hagadera. Most of the refugees in Dadaab originated from the regions of Jubbada Hoose and Shabeellaha Hoose, the lowlands of the two main rivers in South Somalia. There are also smaller groups of refugees from Ethiopia and Sudan, and a few individuals from Uganda and Zaire. Although the largest influx of refugees into Kenya took place in the early 1990s, up to this day new arrivals are registered in the camps. Their livelihoods in Dadaab are affected both by developments in Kenya's national refugee policy, as well as by the problematic location of the camps in Northeastern Province.

The Development of Refugee Policies in Kenya

Kenya did not host many refugees until it experienced an increasing influx from the late 1980s onwards, first as a result of the continued conflict in Uganda after 1986 and later from Ethiopia and Somalia. In 1990–1991, the arrival of 400,000 Somalis occurred simultaneously with the arrival of a large group of Sudanese young men, who had walked from Ethiopian camps after their stay there was no longer safe. Before this large influx, the involvement of foreign NGOs had almost been negligible and the government of Kenya was responsible for status determination on a largely individual case basis (Verdirame 1999: 56–57). Under pressure from increasing numbers, however, the government lost its ability to deal with the refugees and sought assistance from the international community. In order to attract funding, it agreed to designate specific areas to house refugees in camps and the UNHCR set up a number of camps throughout the country. The Sudanese were largely settled in Kakuma, a camp in the Turkana region of northern Kenya. The Ethiopians mainly stayed in Mandera, which is on the border between Kenya, Somalia and Ethiopia.

The Somali were initially spread over a number of camps. Those who came by boat from Kismaayo, Brava and other seaports in Somalia, arrived in Mombasa and were settled in Utange, Marafa and similar refugee camps close to Mombasa. These were amongst the better off communities, but also contained minority groups who had been particularly targeted during the war. Then, other well off Somalis came straight to the capital, Nairobi. Many settled in town while others were registered in Thika, a reception centre that had been set up by the government before 1991. The majority of less well off Somali refugees came into the country by road, on foot or packed into any type of vehicle able to make the journey. They were mainly from the south of Somalia and many of them spent time in Liboi and Mandera, before being moved to the Dadaab camps. Those who had relatives in Kenya, such as in Garissa town, were at times able to settle with them. Unlike Thika, the Mombasa and Dadaab camps were administered by the UNHCR. Another difference was that the refugees were required to stay in the camps 'until a durable solution was found' (Verdirame 1999: 57).

The shift in responsibility for the care of the refugees from the government to the international community had the positive effect of attracting external funds. The negative consequence was, however, that the laissez-faire policy before 1991 had provided few obstacles to the local integration of the refugees, except maybe that the overall situation of poverty in the country was a complicating factor. The refugees had a right to employment, education and freedom of movement. When the UNHCR took over, none of these positive aspects were preserved. It was not very efficient for the UNHCR to operate a large number of smaller refugee camps, and the government of Kenya was also not happy with the dispersal of refugees across a large number of campsites throughout the country. In Mombasa and Thika, tensions between the refugees and the local population also began to rise. Although many of the refugees had been forced to live in the camps, these camps were not far from the urban area and soon, a large number of self-settled refugees could be found in Mombasa. Some started businesses and were highly visible in the local market. There was unfair competition due to tax evasion by refugees, which was unacceptable to the local community. As a result, between 1994 and 1997, the government decided to close the majority of the camps in Kenya. The UNHCR's response was to organise a relocation of the refugees to Dadaab and Kakuma, the two camps in Kenya's most remote areas (Verdirame 1999: 68–69).

Despite the longstanding presence of refugees in the country, Kenya has no refugee legislation. Kenya is party both to the main refugee-specific international instruments as well as to general human rights treaties. It has signed the 1951 Convention, which defines a refugee as a person who, 'owing to well-founded fear of being persecuted for reasons of race, religion, nationality, membership of a particular social group or political opinion, is outside the country of his nationality and is unable or, owing to such fear, is unwilling to avail himself of the protection of that country' (UNHCR 1996: 22). It has also accepted the OAU 1969 Convention governing the specific aspects of refugee problems in Africa, which forms the basis for UNHCR activities in Africa. This regional agreement broke new ground by extending protection to all persons compelled to flee across national borders by reason of any manmade disaster, whether or not they can be said to fear persecution (Hathaway 1991: 16). In Kenya, the issue is not lack of applicable refugee law at an international level, but

Figure 1.2 *Compound in Dagahaley.*

rather the deficiency in the implementation of the international treaties at a domestic level (Hyndman and Nylund 1998: 29). A draft Refugee Bill has been in existence for several years, but has never reached parliament. This has led to a situation where the refugees are not granted Convention status or any other legal certainty, but they are rather provided with temporary asylum on the basis of group determination. Their prima facie status offers few, if any, political solutions to the refugees (Hyndman and Nylund 1998: 47), as they are forced to stay in a place like Dadaab.

Refugee Camps in One of Kenya's Most Marginal Areas

It is common for refugee populations to be concentrated in camps that are located in remote, ecologically and politically marginal areas. This has negative consequences for their level of security, as is also the case for the Dadaab camps in the northeast. Kenya's Northeastern Province is a vast stretch of semi-arid land (Fig. 1.2) that has been the object of dispute between Kenya and Somalia since independence. Colonial borders have made the Somali a dispersed people and their fate is depicted in the five angles of the star on the Somali flag. These represent the Somali people in the British Protectorate in the Northwestern Somali region, the Southern Somali region under Italian rule, Djibouti, Ethiopia and Kenya. During and after colonisation, efforts were made to bring the parts together, although only Northwestern Somalia and Southern Somalia formed a union in 1960, soon after both gained independence. This union was put under pressure when in 1991, Northwestern Somalia seceded from Somalia to form what became known as the, internationally not recognised, Republic of Somaliland.

In Kenya, Somali *'sijui'* live in the semi-desert of the Northeastern Province.[11] It represents 20 percent of the country and is mainly inhabited by Somali nomadic pastoralists, who constitute 1–2 percent of the total Kenyan population (Central Bureau of Statistics 1994). The contact between the Kenyan state and the Somali inhabitants of Northeastern Province has been limited. The state had no interest in the infertile land and was only concerned with preventing a revolt. This was not easy, since it inherited a potentially explosive situation from the British. In the colonial period, there was hardly any interference in social structures, although an attempt was made to reduce mobility. This attempt only led to stronger feelings of ethnicity and a call for separation from Kenya (Farah 1993). The British encouraged the desire to unite with the Somali Republic by investigating the wishes of the people through special commissions. In 1962, the Northern Frontier Commission was appointed to 'ascertain and report on public opinion in the Northern Frontier District (comprising the Districts of Isiolo, Garissa, Mandera, Marsabit, Moyale and Wajir), regarding arrangements to be made for the future of the area in the light of the likely course of constitutional development in Kenya' (quoted in Farah 1993: 79). In the same year, the Regional Boundaries Commission was to create new regional boundaries, taking into consideration the existing boundaries and the wishes of the people.

The postcolonial state in Kenya wanted to avert a further aggravation of the conflict situation. It applied its central power, using instrumental strategies such as the penetration of the province through administrative units. The Somali elite was given the chance to take part in state institutions. This made them feel recognised and gave them resources to distribute. The Kenyan government achieved its goal by creating an elite that could identify with the political centre and its values. Besides, political units were based on clan units, weakening ethnical sentiments through the stimulation of clan sentiments. Therefore, after the Somali state failed to take possession of Northeastern Kenya in 1967, resistance was tamed. This does not mean, however, that all friction has gone. Neither side has forgotten the past and present relationships are built on distrust and frustrations. Ali Bashir, a Kenyan Somali working for an NGO in Dadaab, claimed that the problem of banditry by Somalis was actually caused by the Kenyan government: 'Besides underdevelopment, the province faces repression. Innocent men are put into prison and tortured to get information. How can they go back to their families when they have been treated this way? When their pride is injured, when they have been rendered powerless? Their reaction is predictable: they turn to criminal activity, they rebel and become bandits. This was a predetermined plan of the government to put the Somali in a bad light'.

During the British colonial occupation, the Province was run with special powers to bypass the national judicial system, under the guise of preserving state security. The postcolonial Kenyan government maintained emergency rules that to the present day give the national security forces wide-ranging powers. The Dadaab camps have been set up right in the middle of this politically sensitive, environmentally fragile and quite underdeveloped region of Kenya. The consequences are, of course, numerous. First of all, Dadaab is a very isolated area. Refugees travel from and to Nairobi by bus, passing the Garissa bridge checkpoint that makes it almost impossible to move in and out without being noticed. The busses nowadays operate on a daily basis; a great improvement compared to the once-a-week rides in 1995. From Dagahaley, there is also transport to Wajir, but otherwise there are few roads into 'down-Kenya'. Besides, the main roads are not passable in every season. When the rains start, transport by road becomes impossible at a certain point in time. UNHCR staff members mainly travel by plane, except for the local staff from Northeastern Province.

This is not only because of the length and discomfort of travelling by road, but also because the roads from Dadaab are often not safe due to frequent attacks by *shifta* (bandits). These *shifta* operate on the roads and near the camps where they are feared for stealing cattle and raping women who go out of the camps to collect firewood. A lot of attacks even occur inside the camps. Thus, although the refugees left their country to gain safety and security, they still live in fear in the refugee camps. Another clear and important consequence of the location of the camps in Northeastern Province is that refugees and locals are very hard to distinguish between. Both groups use this fact with great skill in order to survive. Destitute Kenyan Somali nomads and others come to the camps if they have lost all ways of making a living or simply need an additional source of income. Here, they receive the rations that the UNHCR distributes. Refugees buy Kenyan IDs from local Somalis in order to be able to move freely through Kenya. Thus, people claim other labels than they are supposed to, simply in order to survive. This has led to a mix of substantial numbers of Somalis in the camps who are locals and large numbers of refugees who live in town despite the fact that they are not allowed to. The reality of Somalis coping with life through the flexible use of their identities forms another reason to acknowledge the inappropriateness of existing labels.

Collecting Information

Between July 1999 and June 2000, I carried out my main fieldwork in the three refugee camps of Dadaab as well as in Garissa town and Eastleigh, an area of Nairobi where most Somali refugees can be found. Additional data collection followed in July and August 2001, both in the refugee camps and amongst the urban refugees in Eastleigh. Doing research in a camp setting in an isolated and marginal area of Kenya brought conditions with it that are not necessarily common to 'mainstream' anthropological research. First of all, the security or insecurity of all those involved in the research, including myself, was an important factor in determining the nature of the fieldwork. Secondly, the rather artificial environment of the camps, being isolated and operating with a very hierarchical structure, shaped to a large extent the relations that I was able to establish with the refugees. It also affected the high level of unexpected and unpredictable fluctuations in day-to-day activities, including my own research activities, as schedules often changed at the last minute. The lack of communication and long-term planning 'from the top down' led to a situation in which I had to be very flexible in order to make use of my time in Dadaab as efficiently as possible. As I had been in the Dadaab region in 1995 for MA research, I at least had an idea of the possible effects of the specific conditions of life in the refugee camps in Northeastern Province on my research.

As I mentioned earlier, the worst problem with processes of refugee labelling is that they lead to policies that do not enable refugees to regain control over their lives. Thus, deconstruction of these common images is important in order to work towards creating a better position for refugees (Horst 2002). In line with Giddens (1984), such an approach would recognise the central role of human action and consciousness in transforming and sustaining the status quo while realising that the structured qualities of social systems, which are both constraining and enabling, are always beyond the control of individual actors. The concept of human agency attributes to the individual actor the capacity to devise ways of coping with life, even under the most extreme forms of coercion. Within specific contexts and limitations, individuals are knowledgeable and capable. Yet, they are not the only deciding and acting entities, as collectivities also have means of formulating decisions and acting. Agency, in terms of choice and power, depends crucially on the emergence of a network of actors who become (partially) involved in the lives of others. It requires the strategic generation or manipulation of a social network. As such, research cannot focus on the individual actor alone, but will have to focus on individuals within the context of a larger network of 'meaningful others'.

Another important aspect of understanding human agency is related to the ways in which people interpret their experiences. Individuals use certain narratives, or discursive means, to reach decisions and justify them. In most cases, there are various types of discourse to choose from, so actors face alternative ways of representing themselves, formulating their objectives and acting. I do not occupy a privileged position as researcher, but necessarily influence the communication process as others do, with intervention occurring both ways. By seeing academic knowledge-creation as a dialogic process, the strong polarisation of 'local' versus 'academic' knowledge is questioned. In my opinion, the separation between the two has little to do with epistemological issues, being far more a matter of power and control. I believe that social scientists need less essentialist ways of thinking and acting; focusing on the interactional, multi-layered, fragmentary and diffuse aspects of knowledge. Academic knowledge creation thus takes place through the 'dialectics of a dialogical ideal' (Schrijvers 1991). Accepting people's agency is not only a theoretical choice or political stance, but is also clearly reflected in research methods and epistemology. If one accepts the fact that refugees have a certain level of power and choice in determining their lives and livelihoods, this surely also includes the power and choice to create knowledge about and give meaning to their own situation. As such, research methods, in my view, need to involve dialogue between refugees, agencies and academics; leading to an exchange and discussion of ideas, concepts and theories.

I have tried actively to involve Somali refugees, policy makers and practitioners in both data collection and analysis, for which in particular various participatory approaches have proven relevant. Participatory research developed in the 1960s from a wish to counter the traditional subject–object approach, which was seen to be hierarchical and 'exploitative'. Rather, these approaches and methods tried to work from a more equal perspective, in which the research and research results should be of use to all those involved, often leading to subsequent action for change. I acknowledge the difficulties and dilemmas related to a fully participatory approach, not in the least because it is the researcher who initiates a certain research. Yet, I do believe that applying participatory techniques and being aware of the power involved in knowledge creation is highly valuable (see also Nelson and Wright 1995). Discussions with refugees in Dadaab on my research questions and methods proved vital for my fieldwork and research assistants have played an active and independent role in collecting data. These assistants were refugees who had participated in a workshop on 'Data collection and report writing' that I organised in each of the camps. During these workshops I used, and taught, visual participatory techniques such as mapping, matrix exercises, flow diagrams and pie charts, as well as group discussions (see e.g. Pretty et al. 1995). These exercises provided not only relevant feedback on my findings, but also opportunities to collect new research data. Besides, throughout the fieldwork I have engaged in multiple dialogues relating to my data and various stages of analysis. This included sharing and discussing interview reports, fieldwork reports and later articles and preliminary chapters with Somalis, policy makers and implementers and academics. It also included organising sessions to discuss my research findings and writings with various groups in the community, including elders, CDWs and teachers.

Even after finishing fieldwork, I was still able to continue this process of receiving feedback and collecting new research data. Through e-mail, I sent preliminary chapters and articles to NGO staff members, who printed the texts and passed them on to the refugees involved in my research. In this way, I received interesting comments on earlier texts, some of which are included in the chapters concerned. Furthermore, I was able to establish contact with a number of refugees who had left Dadaab and were now living in Western countries. One of them, Abukar Rashid, advised me to send an article to a Somali Internet site, and after that, I frequently published my texts on various sites and received comments as well as new information from Somalis throughout the diaspora. Somalinet, for example, published my field reports, and added a 'forum discussion' through which anybody could respond to the writings. Interesting debates followed, to which I personally contributed a number of times in order to respond to various comments. In a few cases, the discussions went on in the less public space of e-mail. Somalinet then published a preliminary version of the first chapter to my thesis, adding my e-mail address and encouraging readers to send their remarks to me. Furthermore, I sent a number of my writings to a UNHCR staff member, who invited me to have it published as a working paper; appearing both on the Internet site as well as in hard copy (Horst 2001). This gave me feedback from policy makers, UN or NGO staff and researchers. I thus built up a list of e-mail addresses of a very specialised group of interested readers, combining Somalis in the diaspora with refugee 'specialists', and decided to utilise that resource.

Starting up a mailing list, I introduced my initiative as follows: 'Some days ago, a Somali student at Melbourne University asked me whether I had ever thought about "setting up a group of Somali people living around the world to give you advice on the methods you use, the areas you need to do more research on, or any other support you may need". At the same moment, I was going through some articles on diasporas, transnationalism and global networks. In many of these articles it was suggested that research in this field should be carried out within a transnational, transdisciplinary network consisting of academics, practitioners, policy makers and the "transnational migrants" themselves. I fully agree. The suggestion was brilliant and perfectly timed'. I would send any of my writings through this mailing list, and had discussions with its individual members on my analyses of the research material and other topics. I have added some of the remarks of these commentators, who were mainly Somali students and professionals with a keen personal interest in my work. The 'transnational dialogues' between us added a fascinating dimension to my research (see also Mazzucato et al. 2004).

My understanding of refugee life in the camps and in town, as described in this book, stems from the combination of various ways of collecting data. These include common anthropological fieldwork methods such as participatory observation and the collection of life histories, as well as more interactive, dialogical and participatory methods. I have selected certain sections from, for example, an individual's life history, not only on the basis of that particular story, but also based on my observations in the camps, my participation in various events, interviews collected by research assistants and essays I received from refugee school children while teaching English composition. I have chosen to make use of direct quotations in order to do justice to the words and thoughts of refugees as much as possible, although it must be noted that these quotations are edited and selected based on their relevance to a certain topic. Much of these quotations stem from taped material as well as texts received from refugees, but I have allowed myself some more freedom in including quotations from group discussions and interviews that were not taped. Furthermore, most of the interviews and discussions did not take place in English. I have a basic knowledge of the Somali language, but felt that this was insufficient to capture the complexity of themes my research was dealing with. As such, the quotes included are based on translations. In what follows, I will never be able to present the immense amount of data collected, but I have made a selection based on the insights gained throughout my fieldwork. Furthermore, I decided not to write an extensive separate methodological account here, but instead, I have integrated information on my methodological approach in the text. This, I believe, does more justice to the idea of dialogical knowledge creation and it also sheds light on the situatedness of the information gathered.

Dilemmas Faced

Doing fieldwork in refugee camps and amongst urban refugees involves many dilemmas, a number of which I will discuss here. First of all, doing research amongst refugees who often live in terrible circumstances feels like highly inappropriate voyeurism when one can do nothing in practical terms to improve people's misery. During my fieldwork, I felt very uncomfortable when I was trying to explain what I was doing there, and how I hoped that the book I was planning to write would in the end contribute to better policies for refugees. It seemed so improbable and so minor, considering the conditions people were surviving in. Furthermore, through asking questions I at times triggered painful memories. I preferred not to ask too much, because I did not want to encourage refugees to talk about traumatic experiences while I was in no position to assist them with the possible consequences of remembering such events. As both Malkki (1995a) and Hyndman (2001) argue, building trust may in the first place be related to the researcher's willingness to leave some stones unturned and to learn not to pry when this is not wanted. I do feel that as a consequence, people did at times narrate traumatic experiences to me and it is a great responsibility to try to convey what they have witnessed.

Another problem I faced was related to the image that people had of me, which determined the kind of information I was given. Having been in the Dadaab camps for nearly a decade, the Somali refugees were used to various types of white visitors. Only a very small number of those white visitors were students on long-term research projects like mine, whereas the majority were donors, evaluators, resettlement officers or journalists. Many of these people had something to offer in the form of financial assistance, projects or resettlement opportunities, and it was in everybody's interest to present the problems that refugees were facing in their daily lives. This, of course, stood in sharp contrast with my own interest to counter the refugee label by showing how Somalis were dealing with insecurity themselves. Whereas I tried to discover how Somali refugees helped themselves and each other, they tried to tell me about the problems they were facing and how they needed external assistance to solve those problems. And not only did this stereotyped image of me initially determine the answers I would get, it also created a picture of how I should think and act. I tried to counteract this picture by not confirming to what was expected of me, for example by going into the blocks on foot instead of by car and by dressing more according to Somali than Western standards. Small things like that, and simply being there for such a long time, gradually reduced the stereotypes.

Related to this is the problem of 'truth', which I will touch upon in most of the chapters. When I initially asked questions on refugee livelihoods and additional sources of income besides the food rations, most refugees would tell me that the ration card was their only source of income. Later, staying in the camps long enough to observe people's daily activities, I learned that most refugees did have additional resources. There was often also a great deal of suspicion towards the questions I asked and hence a reluctance to answer them. The *xawilaad* and *taar* operate with low profiles, because these businesses are mostly illegal in Kenya. Thus, it is not surprising that their owners were reluctant to talk to me and if they did, reluctant to provide me with much information. While I was in Garissa, the police was just carrying out a campaign against the *taar* in town, which made it completely impossible for me to get any valid information. However, not only *xawilaad* and *taar* owners regarded me with suspicion: Somalis in Dadaab were suspicious of my goals, and the research assistants were even suspected of being *shifta* who were out to steal remittances. Urban refugees were reluctant to disclose themselves to me because they often lived in Garissa or Nairobi illegally. During my fieldwork, I tried to deal with these issues by being as explicit as possible about my own position and by checking the information I received through different informants or methods. In the writing of this book, I have tried to include dubious or contradictory cases, in order to give the reader an insight in the dilemmas I faced and the way I dealt with them. Besides, many Somalis in Dadaab and elsewhere have read earlier texts and their critical but positive comments have given me confidence in the analyses presented.

A final dilemma I want to mention here is of an ethical nature. In the current climate of restrictive trends in international migration, combined with post-'9/11' fears for Islamic terrorism, the material I have collected is sensitive and runs the risk of being misused by those having interests different to mine. I discussed the disadvantages of publishing certain information with my research assistants in Ifo. According to them, there are practices in and outside the camps that refugees would not want to be widely known, and some of these activities could be branded 'illegal'. It was suggested that donors might reduce or stop humanitarian aid if they would find out that refugees are assisting each other. Also, the Kenyan government might take action against taar and xawilaad offices. In general, they feared that negative decisions might be taken that would deteriorate the already poor living conditions in the camps. Throughout my research, I have been aware of the fact that collecting information is one thing, but using it in texts that are openly accessible is another. In my view, the only caution one can take to avoid that research information is misused, is to be very specific to oneself and others about the aim of the research and subsequent publications. This at times means leaving out information that could be easily misinterpreted or misused.

Transnational Nomads

Soon after my arrival in Dadaab, I realised the continued importance of the Somali nomadic heritage, including a high degree of mobility, strong social networks and a dispersal of investments, for refugee livelihoods there. Yet, this heritage has also changed, becoming largely transnational in kind. The links that Somalis maintain with relatives outside the camps are essential for their daily survival. These links do not only operate between Somalis in Dadaab and elsewhere in Kenya, Somalia or Ethiopia, but reach relatives throughout the larger diaspora as well. At least 10–15 percent of the refugees receive remittances, enabling a much larger part of the camp population to survive in the camps despite limited regional opportunities and insufficient international aid. These remittances are largely sent through the *xawilaad*, which is an informal system of communication and banking operated by Somalis around the world. On a smaller scale, money can be transferred within Africa by using *taar*. Overall, Somalis make huge investments in such communication and transfer technologies, as staying in touch and assisting each other is of vital importance to them. The funds that are received by Somalis in Dadaab enable them to survive in the camps while simultaneously improving the general economic situation here. As a consequence of these monetary flows and the accompanying images of life in, for example, North America and Europe, many refugees in Dadaab dream of going for resettlement, and migration has become a popular investment. Such themes of interest, which link the lives and livelihoods of people in different places, closely match recent theoretical developments within studies related to transnationalism and diasporas. As these studies still largely ignore refugees, this book hopes to make a contribution in explicitly introducing a transnational approach to the study of refugees.

Transnationalism and Diasporas

During the last century, there has been a technological explosion in the domain of transport and communication that according to Appadurai (1996) has lead to a new condition of neighbourliness amongst people. Information and communication technologies provide ever-widening circulations of material and interaction in real time. Faster and cheaper modes of transport also serve to move and connect people, commodities and ideas in greater numbers than ever (Rogers et al. 2001). This is not to say that there are no historical precedents to current patterns, because these surely exist. It is just that today, these systems of ties, interactions, exchanges and mobility function intensively and in real time while being spread throughout the world (Vertovec 1999). Technological developments have enabled transnational flows over large distances with much greater frequency, speed and regularity than was possible in the past, thus affecting a much wider group of people, including refugees in relatively remote camps such as Dadaab. Developments in transport created the possibilities to sustain transnational networks, while simultaneously the increased spread of information globally created the incentive to do so.

In this respect, Appadurai's discussions on 'media-scapes'[12] and 'collective imagination' are highly relevant. He suggests that the existence of the mass media has made imagination a collective social fact instead of an individual, private experience. His 'media-scapes' constitute the distribution of electronic capabilities to produce and disseminate information and images of the world created by these media. They provide large and complex repertoires of images and narratives to viewers throughout the world. Thus, media-scapes in the end create images of the lives of others and of possible lives to be lived (Appadurai 1996). This does not imply happiness, since it produces images of well-being that cannot be satisfied by local standards of living and consumer capabilities. Instead, the process merely highlights inequalities. However, collective imagination can also stimulate agency, as it allows people to consider migration or design new forms of (transnational) civic association and collaboration (Appadurai 2000). This is exactly what, to me, constitutes the duality of buufis: on the one hand, images cannot be satisfied and only lead to frustrations about global inequality. But on the other hand, *buufis* as a form of collective imagination provides hope in quite a hopeless situation, and also increases people's level of power and choice.

The technological developments described also inspired developments in academic theorising, when the limits of existing theories and methodologies became evident. The concept of transnationalism was first put forward as an alternative to the dominant approach in migration studies during the 1970s and 1980s that limited itself to two possible conceptualisations of the migrant: either as someone who completely adapts to the culture of the receiving country or as a temporary sojourner who eventually returns to the home country (Rouse 1995). Rather than conceiving migration in terms of one or a few discrete moves, transnationalism conceptualises migration as a continuous flow of people, goods, money and ideas that transgresses national boundaries and in so doing connects different physical, social, economic and political spaces (Mazzucato et al. 2004). What sets transnational analyses apart from previous approaches is the focus on migration within a globalising economy and the questioning of the central role of the nation-state in determining migrants' activities and identities.

Whereas debates on transnationalism overlap with globalisation theories, they typically have a more geographically bounded scope. In globalisation theory, global processes are largely analysed as decentred from specific national territories and as taking place in a global space. Transnational processes, on the other hand, are seen to be anchored in and transcending one or more nation-states. Globalisation implies more abstract, impersonal, less institutionalised and less intentional processes occurring without reference to nations (Kearney 1995), whereas transnationalism brings about a sense of social networks and sees the flows within those networks as human accomplishments. The interest in global networks reflects the current movement away from general, macroscopic views of globalisation towards an intense study of networks and networking as the lineaments of the new world (Rogers et al. 2001). Thus, the study of transnationalism and diasporas has become increasingly popular over the last couple of years. Research programmes have been set up, new journals and book series are being published and transnational networks of multidisciplinary teams of social scientists are being established, with inequalities in the international exchange between social scientists being a point of discussion. At the same time, the terms have acquired metaphorical implications and are used more and more by displaced people who feel, maintain, invent or revive a connection with a prior home (Shuval 2000).

In the excited rush, there is, not surprisingly, much conceptual muddling. It is important to review definitions and interpretations of transnationalism and diasporas, two concepts that are closely linked and often used in one breath. Transnationalism is used to indicate that the social relations emerging from contemporary global developments are not easily confined within the borders of nation-states. The term indicates a relation over and beyond, rather than between or in, nation-states, without disregarding the importance of borders. Basch et al. (1994: 7) define transnationalism as 'the processes by which immigrants forge and sustain multi-stranded social relations that link together their societies of origin and settlement. We call these processes transnationalism to emphasise that many immigrants today build fields that cross geographic, cultural and political borders'. Research often focuses on various types of flows within transnational networks, such as the movement of capital, commodities, cultural artefacts and (forced) migrants (Castles 2001). Transnational networks are the frameworks within which the communication, regulation and management of such flows take place, involving individuals, groups or institutions in different nation-states.

Diasporas are closely linked to transnationalism, as they have been defined as the 'exemplary communities of the transnational moment' (Tölölyan 1996: 4). A diaspora is a transnational social organisation or community of a particular kind. In theoretical work about diasporas, concepts of place and space, roots and routes are often linked and the main difference between the conceptualisation of diasporas and transnational communities seems to be the extent to which people's 'roots' are stressed. The word 'diaspora' is derived from the Greek verb *speiro* (to sow) and the preposition *dia* (over) and was used by the Greeks to mean migration and colonisation. For Jews, Africans, Palestinians and Armenians, it meant 'exile' (Van Hear 1998b). In this original meaning, the diaspora experience was related to traumatic occurrences, forceful dispersal and the not feeling at home of diasporic people in their new places of settlement. This may closely match the experiences of many refugees worldwide. Yet, currently, a wider range of experiences is being identified as diasporic. There seems to be a reasonable consensus on the main characteristics of diasporas, though various authors warn that these characteristics should not be interpreted as adding up to an 'ideal type'.[13]

Diasporas are expatriate minority communities that (1) have been dispersed from the homeland to at least two other places. This dispersal is often forced and involves uprooting and loss, but not in all instances; (2)

have a collective memory and myth about their homeland; (3) believe in an eventual return to their (idealised) home; (4) are committed to the maintenance or restoration of their homeland; (5) have a collective identity, group consciousness and solidarity. Whereas Safran (1991) assumes that this group consciousness is defined by the relationship with the homeland, Van Hear (1998b) and Clifford (1994) argue that a collective identity does not necessarily stem from the link with one place, but rather from the identification with co-ethnics in other countries; (6) are not fully accepted by, or have a troubled relationship with the host country and society; and (7) have a rich culture, selectively preserving and recovering their traditions. What occurs to me, as is also remarked on by Van Hear, is that these traits are still closely linked to ideas on ethnicity and the nation-state. Smith (1991) came up with similar lists for the definition of ethnic and national identity and they differ from the above only in not explicitly mentioning elements of migration. Whereas theories of transnationalism and diasporas provide social scientists working on migration and migrants with an interesting new focus and innovative research questions to ask, at the same time we should not overestimate their transformative power, as they are based on old theoretical models of ethnicity and nationalism.

Transnationalism and Refugee Studies

While the analytical perspective I just described has been applied widely to other groups of migrants in recent years, refugee studies largely remained uninformed by the discussions on diasporas and transnationalism. The academic discourse and practical efforts dealing with refugees continue to be informed by the assumption of a rigid separation between the exile's country of origin and country of asylum (Crisp 1999a). First, this reflects longstanding academic divisions between refugee studies and migration studies, where the first discipline supposedly deals with political or forced migration and the second with economic or voluntary migration. Refugee studies is still very much policy-oriented work of a reactive nature, with only a small number of publications making an effort to discuss conceptual or theoretical questions or understand individual migration strategies (Wahlbeck 2002). Secondly, it is tempting to treat refugees as a separate case because they enjoy a specific legal status due to the involuntary nature of their departure. This legal status does not allow them to go back to their country of origin, which obviously complicates the possibility of retaining transnational ties. Yet, in reality, many refugees are not legally recognised and thus do not have a separate status from other migrants.

A third reason for the limited interest within refugee studies for transnational processes is that it does not seem appropriate to understand the role of transnational networks in forced migration, because that would fuel arguments that these refugees are fraudulent. Yet, I fully agree with Crisp (1999a) that it is essential to separate means and motivation clearly: fleeing through the assistance of others does not necessarily mean that migration was voluntary. On top of this, it has become increasingly difficult to make a clear distinction between voluntary and involuntary population movements, with political, ethnic, economic, environmental and human rights factors combining to cause people to move. Besides, refugees live alongside compatriots and co-ethnics who are part of a transnational community but who are not refugees. It is more profitable to focus on such communities as a whole than on those people who have been recognised as refugees (Crisp 1999a), as these different categories of people often make up one and the same family. I believe that the theoretical debates on transnationalism and diasporas can provide refugee studies with more adequate theories and clearly defined concepts, allowing researchers to study refugees in an increasingly interlinked world.

At the same time, I do recognise, and want to be explicit about, the possible drawbacks of a transnational approach for refugees. First of all, many refugees are not in a position to profit from transnational networks. Crossing national borders by means of communication or travel requires resources that not everybody can afford. Secondly, an idealised image of migration or other transnational flows may cause disappointments and a shift in people's attention from the here and now to the 'elsewhere and later'. Refugees may no longer be ready to invest in their present situation, because they imagine leaving that situation behind. Thirdly, even for those who do manage to migrate, life abroad may not bring what they were expecting. In the words of Adoy Moxamed, a young Somali woman in Ifo refugee camp: 'when we fled the war, we prayed only for peace. Then when we arrived here we wanted shelter and food as well. Now if we go abroad again we will have new complaints. Life is a struggle and a human being will never be satisfied with what is there'. These are just some of the cautions that need to be taken into account. Others will become apparent later.

Throughout this book, I will illustrate how a transnational approach to the study of refugees might take shape. A transnational perspective calls into question the common assumption that sedentary life is the 'natural' state of society, and research amongst the Somali refugees in Kenya has provided a particularly stimulating case in this respect. As refugees, the Somalis have lost their homeland and the security of living in a place they can call their own. As 'a nomadic people', mobility, including mobility that crosses borders, is and has always been an essential part of their livelihoods and identities. The Somali are a particularly interesting transnational community because of the challenges they pose to existing concepts of the nation-state and categories of migration. For years, the Somali have not had a proper nation-state and some authors even argue that they never had one (Brons 2001). Somalis can be found in every country in the world, but they largely operate past or above nations. With their diaspora mentality they pose a threat to the nation-state and they cause further confusion because they do not clearly fit into a particular category of migrants.

Transnational networks perform important functions for many refugees, both in enabling their migration as well as in enabling their stay in a certain place. These networks are an important source of information about migration routes and countries of destination. For Somalis in Dadaab, transnational networks also contribute to feelings of *buufis*, of wanting to migrate, in the first place. Besides, these networks often provide the financial resources for migration and create the organisational infrastructure to enable migration through a variety of (illegal) ways. Upon arrival, transnational networks assist the newly arrived with subsistence and teach them how to survive in the new country. But not only do transnational social networks enable migration, they also enable people to stay put in a certain area, as in the case of Khaliif. The *xawilaad* system enables relatives and friends to send each other amounts of money that enable their survival in otherwise marginal areas. The relatively small amounts of money that migrants around the world transfer as remittances to their relatives and co-ethnics, now add up to at least 75 billion dollars a year, worldwide (Vertovec 1999). In the Horn of Africa, the annual total of remittances sent from the Somali diaspora is estimated to be approximately 130 million dollars (Perouse de Montclos 2000).

These considerable amounts of remittances may help people to survive in areas where this would otherwise not be possible, financial assistance from relatives in Western countries can be used for the development of those areas, and it also contributes to peace efforts in various regions (see e.g. Koser 2001b).[14] What the remittances and other transnational flows of goods and ideas do most importantly, in sharp contrast to the established discourse on refugees as passive recipients, is that they give refugees a greater level of power and choice. A Kenyan hotel manager and good friend to Nuruddin Farah, the famous Somali novelist, illustrates this point most vividly. She tells him that in Kenya, generally speaking, 'Somalis are thought to be spendthrifts both of talk and of money, wasteful, loud-mouthed and uncouth. The impression is that they have an uninterrupted supply of money in hard currency, thanks to their families' remittances from their bases in Europe or North America. Implicit in our criticism is this: Do they behave in the way someone applying for refugee status behaves?' (Farah 2000: 32). Her words express the main point of this book perfectly: Somalis, as refugees, are supposed to behave according to the label that others attach to them. But since they are part of a network of transnational nomads, they are able to do otherwise.

Notes

1. Throughout this book, names of people and geographical names are spelled according to Somali official orthography. This script is not fully standardized, and I have chosen to use the Somali-English Dictionary of Zorc and Osman (1993) and McNally's *Atlas of the World* (1993). The letter 'x' in Somali is technically known as a voiceless pharyngeal fricative (Orwin 1995: 5). It is pronounced as a guttural h.

2. All names of those who participated in the research are pseudonyms, so as to respect the privacy of informants. In addition, people who might otherwise be identified easily are not named and neither is their gender revealed.

3. 'Hawiye' is the name of one of the Somali clan lineages. In Somalia, a complex clan system exists that determines social relations and one's position in society. Somalis from the clan lineages of the Darod, Isaq, Hawiye and Dir are by tradition nomadic-pastoralists and speak af-soomaali; whereas those of the Digil and Mirifle clan lineages, known collectively as Rahanweyne, are traditionally agro-pastoralists who speak af-maaymaay (Gardner and El Bushra 2004: 7). See further chapter 2, under 'Somali Identity?'.

4. 'Kh' is the sound generally used for the Scottish pronunciation of the word 'loch'. In Somali, it is only found in loanwords from Arabic (Orwin 1995: 5).

5. A number of words are written in Somali throughout the book. These words are translated in parentheses on their first occurrence, and can also be found in the glossary.

6. The 'c' sound is made in the same part of the throat as the sound 'x' but with vibration of the vocal cords (Orwin 1995: 6). It is the 'ayn of Arabic, somewhat similar to the 'aaaa' sound a doctor may ask for.

7. The term 'sponsorship' refers to arranging the migration of a subsequent (forced) migrant; usually involving considerable amounts of money (Shah and Menon 1999: 362).

8. In Kenya, education officially takes place according to the '8-4-4' system. Pupils from the age of six spend eight years in primary, four years in secondary, and then four years in university.

9. Names of commentators involved during the writing phase are also pseudonyms. An exception is made for those who are interested in the topic academically, because this allows the reader to see their comments in light of their present or future academic work.

10. The concept of liminality stems from Victor Turner (1967) and has been used by a number of academics to describe the situation of refugees (see e.g. Malkki 1995b; Turner 1999).

11. Somali 'sijui' are the Kenyan Somali. *Sijui* means 'I don't know' in Swahili, and various explanations exist as to the origins of the term. Most commonly, people say it is used by Somalis from Somalia to express the lack of knowledge of their original language and culture amongst the Kenyan Somalis.

12. Appadurai uses 'scape' to refer to realities of a fluid, irregular character that are not objectively given but rather depend on constructs.

13. Safran (1991) and Van Hear (1998b) offer a list of the main characteristics of diasporas, which I have combined here.

14. It should not be forgotten, however, that these remittances can also contribute to the continuation of war, for example by supporting warring factions (Koser 2001b; Van Hear 2001: 222). I will discuss this and other negative aspects of remittance sending in subsequent chapters.

2

A Nomadic Heritage:
Past Ways of Coping With
Insecurity Amongst the Somali

Maanta waa aniga, berina waa adiga[1]

In a meeting with a group of CDWs in Dagahaley, I introduced an analysis of the Somali 'nomadic heritage' of mobility, diversification and a strong social network. Afterwards, many points related to my findings were discussed. Yasiin Hussein, an elderly Somali CDW, stepped forward and made a poignant comment. He had heard me explain how the refugees in Dadaab managed to survive through certain sociocultural practices, but he had not heard any account of their suffering in the camps. In kind words, Yasiin told me that this was a great omission, since the refugees were confined to the camps like prisoners and faced a great many problems. Moxamed Faarax added to Yasiin's argument:

> It is true that the Somali assist each other a lot and are highly mobile. You talk about the Somali culture and you do so accurately. But it is obvious that people try to survive and have their own ways of doing so. What you should rather write about is the problems we are facing as refugees: we cannot move freely, there is great insecurity in and around the camps, the rations are insufficient, the health facilities are poor and we hardly have any work or educational opportunities here.

With their remarks, Moxamed and Yasiin were pointing out a dilemma in my approach. When starting out from an actor-oriented perspective that looks at people's ways of coping, I certainly do not want to deny the reality of the many difficulties that Somali refugees are facing in Dadaab. They are facing hardships that to a large extent shape their daily lives as refugees, as I will discuss in chapter 3. My main point, however, is that this experience cannot be seen in a vacuum, as if flight brought about a radical breach with people's past, caused by external events interfering with the equilibrium of their social reality. It is important to look also at the continuation in the experiences of the people who became refugees. In trying to understand Somali history as well as individual life stories, it first of all becomes clear that refugees are people with a past. Or in the words of Ayaan Moxamed, a 51-year-old woman from Hagadera:

> The word 'refugee' is a very bad word. It is as if refugees are not human beings. But like everybody else, anywhere in the world, refugees are individuals. They are all different. They are merely people who have moved from their country, and just like there were different people in that country, the same is true for refugees. They are people of all trades and characters. Someone who becomes a refugee does not all of a sudden change his or her character; he or she will think and act like before.

Through placing the refugee experience in the wider perspective of (life) histories, refugees are no longer depicted as an abstraction but acquire human faces. It enables a move beyond stereotypes of vulnerability and cunningness, towards a picture of people trying to cope with life.

Secondly, the histories show that insecurity has been a constant factor in the lives of the Somali, with which they have tried to cope. It is clear from the literature that Somalis faced many unpredictable fluctuations in their livelihoods before the war. What these insecurities meant in 'real life', however, I learned from Dahabo Axmed. Most remarkable to me was the way she described how the war affected their plans to better her family's future: 'In our minds, we were planning to move to Mogadishu during the week that the war started. But Allah determined that we should not move. The house was almost finished and we had acquired a transfer to Mogadishu, but bad luck resulted in our plans never coming to fruition'. Whereas the translator chooses 'bad luck', the actual Somali word Dahabo uses is *nasiib*, which means 'luck, fate, destiny, fortune or chance' (Zorc and Osman 1993). Going over the different experiences she told me about, I indeed found a great level of chance in the way her life changed from one day to the next. Dahabo faced quite unpredictable fluctuations in her life circumstances, and needed socio-economic strategies that gave her some sense of security and enabled her to rebuild her life from scratch when necessary. After introducing Dahabo's story and its implications for an understanding of the position of Somali refugees in Dadaab, this chapter will outline the insecurities that the Somali faced before and during the war. Then, it will describe the various social security mechanisms that Somalis made use of before their flight to Kenya.

Nasiib: Dealing With a Variable Livelihood

Dahabo Axmed and her husband Nuradin Yusuf were living in Hagadera, close to the market. Sahra Yusuf, the half-sister to Nuradin who worked as my translator in Hagadera and Ifo, introduced me to the family. After our first visit on 23 August 1999, I spent many hours with the family; initially only in the company of Sahra, but later also on my own or with others. Nuradin was well known amongst the agencies and many of the refugees, since he had worked with CARE and the UNHCR for several years. According to Dahabo, he had stopped working because of 'security problems' and his most important work nowadays was to follow up on their resettlement case: they were hoping to go overseas one day. Meanwhile, Nuradin's eighteen-year-old daughter from an earlier marriage, who had moved to the U.S.A. with her mother, was supporting them. She tried to send her father one hundred dollars a month, and this amount was enough to cater for the family's daily needs.

On my visits I would usually find Dahabo and her youngest son Ibrahim in the house, while the older two boys were going to *dugsi*. Nuradin was only in when I specifically announced my visit. He spent much of his time at the market and with the agencies, and visited the other camps frequently. Alhough neither Dahabo nor her husband spoke English and my Somali remained insufficient for extensive conversations, I felt very much at ease in their homestead even without a translator. Dahabo always welcomed me with a strikingly open and cheerful face and I really enjoyed watching her play with her young son and going about her chores. Dahabo told me she had been a cook for the *gaal cadeen* (white non-Muslims) and therefore knew very well what to prepare for me. She always made sure that I was at least served a cup of black tea and she often added a small bite to eat. I had lunch with them on many occasions, sometimes when I had been invited or otherwise when I just popped in to say hi. Thus, when I went back to Dadaab in order to collect a number of personal life histories, Dahabo was one of the first people I approached. She accepted without hesitation, almost as if she found it obvious that I asked her.

On the morning of 18 July 2001, I went to Dahabo's house with Ubax Abdi, who was translating for me during my second fieldwork period. Sahra, my original translator, had moved to Nairobi to try her luck there. I had worked a lot with Ubax before, since she was a CDW coordinator who was always keen to assist and at the same time learn. She often visited me in the CARE compound after working hours and always actively participated in any of the trainings or presentations I organised. Ubax was very open, sharp and pleasant to work with. That morning, equipped with a small tape recorder and sufficient cassettes, we were going to conduct our first life history. In the previous days, we had gone through the questions and I had taped a trial interview with Ubax herself. Therefore, she had a good understanding of what I wanted to achieve with my questions. Of course, neither of us knew how Dahabo, or anybody else, would respond. It was only through the experience of asking and listening that a certain routine developed.

When we were all settled for the interview, I explained to Dahabo why I had come to Dadaab, although this was something she was already largely familiar with. I told her about the discrepancy that I had experienced while I was working for a refugee organisation in the Netherlands; refugees were often depicted in the media in a very different way to how I had experienced them through my work. I wanted to write a book about how the Somali themselves were trying to cope with their lives as refugees, basing the story on an image of human complexity instead of vulnerability or cunningness. What I had found remarkable in the literature about the Somali was their strong kinship networks and the way those networks were used to cope with the harsh conditions in Somalia before the war. I wanted to see whether these practices were still operating after the Somali were forced to flee. During my first fieldwork period, I had indeed found the importance of assistance within dispersed kinship networks, through studying the *xawilaad* system and *buufis*. I had come back to Dadaab because I found I needed to acquire a better understanding of the lives of the people I was writing about. I explained to Dahabo that I wanted to hear various life histories from Somalis in Dadaab in order to place their ability to cope with refugee life in a broader perspective.

After this introduction, I mentioned the different periods in her life that I would like Dahabo to talk about. I was going to ask her questions about the time she was born, the way she had grown up, the time the war started, the way she had to flee from Somalia and the time she came to Kenya. When I asked my first question, Dahabo started her story as follows.

> I was born in a region called Beled Weyne. When I was four years old, my father died. When my father died, my mother raised me and my brothers and sisters by herself. My mother was a farmer and also a firewood seller: she used to go to the bush to collect firewood and sell that firewood from home. Thus, I was brought up in rather poor circumstances. My mother gave birth to nine children, four of whom have since died; one was younger than me, the other three were older. A number of my brothers and sisters died, until we were left with three girls and two boys only.

Dahabo continued her story until she arrived at her present life in Hagadera. I chose not to interrupt her and after she finished, I chronologically returned to the different periods she had talked about, asking her to clarify and elaborate on a number of issues. The story that follows is constructed through a combination of Dahabo's monologue and the answers she later provided to my questions.

Because our father died and mother was alone, we assisted her at home and in the farm. We would also go into the bush to get firewood with her. We were just trying hard for the boys to finish school. My eldest brother became a soldier after standard eight and two of the other boys went to school up to form four. We had a small café in the afternoon shift, where we sold tea and at least earned some income. When I was ten years old, I started baking cakes and bread that I would sell at the market. When we were older and started working our mother no longer needed to work but stayed at home. Myself, one of my sisters and one of my brothers were the only ones working for the family. My eldest brother got married, as did my second sister. During the first few years, our life was very poor but things improved once we started working. My sister used to clean and wash clothes for American doctors who worked in the hospital in Beled Weyne. She would bring her salary to our mother, who was responsible for managing the household. We would give her whatever money we earned and she would then buy us clothes and the like. My eldest brother died shortly after he got married, and the two boys who were in secondary school finished form four. One of them joined the army and died in the first war in Hargeisa. The other one got a job in the sugar factory in Marere and he sent money to our mother at that time. The fact that my brother eventually acquired a good job meant our life was comfortable. He now lives in South Africa.

I used to sell cakes and breads at the market and was always there early in the morning. The market was an open place, just like in Hagadera where you sit on the street in the open. At the end of the day, I would give whatever I had earned to my mother. Then, when I was fourteen or fifteen, CARE employed me as a cleaner. CARE and other agencies were assisting refugees who had come after the 1977 war between Ethiopia and Somalia. Some people from Ethiopia and even Somalia had problems at that time and were taken to that place as a refugee. After I had worked there for one year, one of the cooks left. The CARE people decided that they would give that position to the small girl who was never rude. They just decided amongst themselves that I would be employed as a cook; the selection did not take place on the basis of an interview or whatever. After being a cook for one year, I was again promoted to a more senior post, where I was in charge of all the cleaners and cooks. I worked for CARE between 1981 and 1991 and in 1983 I was promoted to that senior position.

My husband, Nuradin, worked for the UNHCR in Beled Weyne where he was a driver. He had money so he looked rich and I married him. When I was working in Somalia I used to earn 45,000 Somali shillings, which was good money. Nuradin was paid 55,000 Somali shillings; 10,000 more than me. I was very happy because when I received my 45,000 I would just divide it – half for my family and the other half for my mother. I would bring half of the money to my mother and she could use it for whatever she wanted. And I believe my siblings were doing the same. In Somali culture, when women become old they like to be given something so that at least they can manage themselves. They want to be able to support anybody and they want to assist other poor people. Old women always like it like that, so I did not want to manage the money for my mother. Before the war, three children were born and we were comfortable since my husband and I were both working. I had two house girls working for me: one was employed to take care of the children and the other one to cook for the family. Our life was very good before the war began and we were comfortable. We did not even have to pay for the food we ate at home: Nuradin was working for the UNHCR as a driver and drivers used to be given pasta, rice and oil. But I was working for CARE and we were not allowed food. The reason why we were not given it was because we were always dealing with food. The UNHCR thought that CARE officers were constantly stealing food, so they were not prepared to give us any. Only UNHCR staff were given food.

At that time, we were preparing to build a house in Mogadishu, the capital city. We had bought a piece of land and construction had started. It was 1991 and that is when the Somali war broke out and we were faced with a lot of problems in Somalia. Nuradin was in Mogadishu when the war started; he was monitoring the construction of the house. He had been granted some leave from his work and I was at home with my children. So when the war occurred, we were separated, with Nuradin being in Mogadishu while I was in Beled Weyne. We lost track of one another and I tried to look for him, but during those three months that I was travelling to find him, I missed my children too much. I gave up searching and came back to Beled Weyne. It was wonderful when Nuradin came with the military cars and their air force. When they came, he advised us to move from there to Mogadishu and we just fled. During our flight, we met another militia that was against the government and at least for some hours we were caught up in an exchange of fire. I was carrying some water and milk for the children and it started leaking. I thought that one of the children had died because I assumed that it was blood. Those were dreadful hours and I was afraid that nobody would survive. But luckily we had a radio transmitter in the car and the soldiers who were with us were able to communicate to a division nearby. That is how we acquired some assistance and we were able to continue our journey. I have faced a lot of problems in my life, but the time we were heading to Mogadishu was the worst.

By the time we reached Mogadishu, the fighting there had escalated. The first time we fled, it was the districts that were experiencing problems and we were heading to the city. Soon after we reached Mogadishu, we again fled to Kismaayo. Nuradin's family lived near Kismaayo, at a place called Buule. When we arrived in Kismaayo, Nuradin went to Buule to see his father who was sick at that time. He was away for one week when the conflict started in Kismaayo. That is why we were separated again, but this time for six years. Nuradin just decided to move from Kismaayo; he left us with his family and went to Kenya. That is how we separated again. Myself, I remained behind and my husband fled with the other people who were going to Kenya. When the war intensified and it turned into a conflict between the clans, I left Nuradin's family and returned to our home in Mogadishu.[2] I went there to stay with my sister and my mother. I went with my children and I was separated from my husband for six years because he was here in Kenya.

After I had been in Mogadishu for three days, the Hawiye started fighting amongst themselves. They were divided into Abgaal and another sub-clan of Hawiye. I was somehow shocked to see this. After three days of fighting, a number of elders came to negotiate for peace. However, their efforts were in vain since the fighting started again. After another week of fighting, I proposed to my mother that we move from Mogadishu to Beled Weyne. Before we actually went, agencies like CARE and the UNHCR were calling the people who had worked for them. We were given an allowance, a payment. CARE gave me 500,000 shillings. I used some of that money to move my mother and children from Mogadishu to Beled Weyne. With the rest, I opened a small shop. I also gave 100,000 to my brother-in-law, the husband of my sister, who was a butcher. That money enabled him to work and we used to share the income. The 500,000 became two million and I started going to Mogadishu twice a month as a wholesaler. I used to take some goods from Mogadishu to Beled Weyne and people would buy them from me. My standard of living improved greatly, to the level it was at before the war. However, another conflict erupted between the Abgaal and the Hawadleh, who were also a sub-clan of the Hawiye. In Beled Weyne, my clan was very small so we could not defend ourselves. At that time, they looted all my property. I ended up in the same position as before and lost everything. Some of our people were killed, including some of my relatives. Eighteen male relatives were killed there, in the same war, while others ran away. Only the children and women remained in the town. We moved back to Mogadishu again. At that time my brother was working with UNICEF in Mogadishu and he was able to support us.

For those six years that I was separated from my husband, I worked to support my children and we just lived from one day to the next; fleeing from one district to another. I did not think it possible that my husband was alive, but I stayed single and tried to provide for my children using my own strength. I would tell people that my children did not have a father; that their father had been killed. Later I talked about it with my husband and he told me the same: He did not think that I was alive. Nuradin married another woman here in the camp, but that is no problem because our religion allows him to have four wives. But things are different for women. Even if you are apart for six years, women are expected to refrain from remarrying. Men are free because our religion allows for it. The only thing that occupied my mind at that time, was how I would raise my children and what they would wear. I was not thinking about my husband because I was not sure whether he was alive or dead.

But after four years, I received his letter through the ICRC (International Committee of the Red Cross). I received information that Nuradin was alive and that he was staying in Hagadera camp. I moved from Kismaayo to Dadaab in 1996 and from that time on, I have been here. I am okay now that I have found my husband. Luckily, we are all together now: I am here with my husband and my children. I miss my family in Somalia and think about them a lot; but otherwise our life is okay, or at least somehow okay. When I first arrived in Hagadera, I could not adjust. The conditions were very poor; I could not adapt to them. Now, when you look at the children, they look ill. When we arrived, they were well fed and healthy. We faced a lot of problems in Somalia in terms of war and fighting, but as regards health and food we were okay; we did not have any problems. However, the quality of life in Hagadera is poor. My husband does not work and I do not work either. Sometimes, Nuradin's daughter gives us a morale boost by sending us dollars every couple of months. This money enables us to pay the people from whom we buy on credit at the market. However, the only thing that we are certain to get is the food that is distributed by CARE, nothing else. Nobody works for the family. At first, I wanted to go back to Somalia because of the harsh conditions. But then I saw that education is better in the camps and I decided to forget about food and focus on education instead. The children are the future, not food. Now, I have adapted to life in Hagadera; I have got used to it.

Refugee life in the Dadaab camps of Kenya is very insecure in many ways, but Dahabo's story shows that this insecurity is not necessarily new to the Somali. Listening to her story, what was most striking to me was the degree to which her life was determined by unstable and unpredictable factors, and the way in which, despite that, Dahabo tried hard to make a living. Unexpected events led to considerable variations in her livelihood circumstances and those of her family members, while their reciprocal assistance and readiness to migrate mitigated the effects of these fluctuations. While the fact that Dahabo's father died when she was still young had major implications for the family's well-being, they were gradually able to build up a stable life for themselves. Throughout those years, providing assistance was of utmost importance both for those receiving and those assisting, because it gave both parties a certain level of power and choice. Dahabo, for example, was happy that she was in a position to give her mother half of her monthly salary, while this simultaneously gave her mother the opportunity to use the money to assist others. Yet, the results of their joined efforts towards greater stability were shattered when the civil war broke out and they had to leave most of their possessions behind. From one day to the next, Dahabo and Nuradin's main concern was to survive the war. This urge to survive even led the couple to flee in different directions, as migration was largely determined by the origin of one's family and clan members. Like many other Somalis, husband and wife were not from the same tribe and thus were not necessarily safe in the same area.

Whereas having control over one's life may be one of the most basic human needs, Dahabo's life has been determined by events that she did not have the power to alter and that left her with limited choices as to how to (re)act. On a number of occasions in her life, conditions changed unexpectedly and events were beyond her control. Looking at these great fluctuations in Dahabo's life, her use of the word *nasiib* may not be surprising. It is not uncommon for people to ascribe to destiny, changes over which they have no control. The fact that life is seen as inherently risky and governed by fate rather than self-determination is related to a person's image of his or her own powerlessness towards events (Gardner 1995). As Dahabo's story shows, this realisation of one's own lack of power does not mean that an individual will not try to protect himself or herself against risks and just wait passively for things to happen. Rather, views on fate and destiny assist people to rationalise and justify the course of events or the impossibility of changing it (Benda-Beckmann and Benda-Beckmann 1994: 17). *Nasiib* assists Somalis to accept the things they cannot change because it removes their need to explain why. At the same time, most Somalis do try to influence what they can modify and secure themselves against the unexpected. After all, one should always 'pray to God and tie one's camel'.

Somali Identity?

Before describing in detail the insecurities that the Somali were facing prior to and during the war, as well as how they were trying to handle those insecurities, it is important to analyse the concept of 'the Somali' in some more detail. This is vital in order to place the subsequent informa-tion in perspective: which Somalis am I really talking about? I find it dif-ficult to discover a middle way between two forms of describing reality. On the one hand, it is incorrect to write about 'the Somali' as if it is unproblematic to categorise them as a homogeneous group, ascribing all kinds of shared traits to a group, based on the encounters I had with indi-vidual Somalis. On the other hand, I might be stretching things too far when I mention only individuals with their very personal and unique characteristics, as if it is not possible to draw any type of comparison. In the past, many studies have been written that tried to establish what binds the Somali together as an ethnic community. Elements such as eth-nicity, language, religion and livelihood have been focused on to illustrate a homogeneity amongst the Somali (see e.g. Lewis 1961; 1994; Laitin and Samatar 1986).

Many authors mention that the Somali are the only people in Africa who have a country that is ethnically homogeneous. Rather than finding themselves sharing national territory with other people, they have been scattered across different countries due to colonial border drawing. The Somali are commonly represented as one people (the Somali) with one language (*af-soomaali*), one livelihood (nomadic pastoralism) and one reli-gion (Islam). Only the role of the clan is depicted as more ambiguous, having not only uniting but also divisive effects, with the segmentary lin-eage structure presented as a vital organising mechanism. In recent years, however, increasing criticism has been voiced against this vision. According to Besteman (1996: 123), 'cleavages in Somali society not only derive from clan but, more critically, draw upon shifting cultural con-structions of difference such as race, language, and status, and on eco-nomic divisions such as occupation and class'. Brons (2001) illustrates that it was mainly for the purpose of creating a nation-state that ethnic homo-geneity has been idealised as a core characteristic of Somali national identity, at the cost of those who did not fit this identity. Images created within the government and by academics reinforced each other in this respect. Brons (2001) asserts that it was the numerically and politically dominant pastoral groups who projected the image of Somalia as the land of the nomad. This is not only a matter of livelihood, but also of clan and region, since different clans largely engage in different economic activities and are concentrated in different areas.

The Somali clan structure is a complex system, which has been classified in various ways. A widely used categorisation stems from Lewis (see e.g. 1994), who distinguishes six larger clan-families: Darod, Dir, Isaaq[3], Hawiye, Digil and Rahanweyn[4]. Within the first four, nomadic pastoralist clans, there are 'outcast' groups such as the Tumal, Midgan, Eyle, Yahar and Yibr (Gardner and El Bushra 2004). The latter two, agropastoral clans, have shown an enormous flexibility in adopting members, especially those descending from slaves imported from East Africa during the nineteenth century, often referred to as 'Somali Bantu' or Jareer. This has also influenced the common language spoken in many Southern areas, *af-maaymaay*, as well as their relatively 'inferior' position within Somali society. Besides these variations in status within the clan system, there are other groups that exist outside the Somali clan system, including some Jareer but also for example the Barawan and Bajuni coastal communities, who are mainly artisans, traders and fishermen. These groups are often in similar or even worse positions than the agropastoral clans. Clan and livelihood strategy are closely related to region, as, for example, it is only the fertile interriverine areas that allow extensive cultivation. Originally, agricultural clans largely occupied these regions, whereas the pastoral clans occupied the semidesert areas. But due to ecological and other pressures, people have migrated for decades. Although it is possible to identify 'home areas' that reflect the strongholds and traditional locations of the different Somali clans, in actual fact there is a great mix of people from different clans living together in different places.

Similarly, pastoralism and crop cultivation cannot be easily distinguished as unique livelihood strategies, since people often engage in a mix of activities. Large parts of Somalia consist of semi-arid regions with extreme climatic and ecological variations from season to season and place to place. This greatly limits the scope for controlling one's environment, and thus the possibility of securing a livelihood. In those areas, nomadic pastoralism is one of the few viable options, and it indeed may form the backbone of the Somali economy. A large part of the population is dependent on livestock-related earnings and before the war three-quarters of exports were attributable to this sector.[5] On the other hand, the culture of southern Somalia has a strong agricultural component, supported by the regular flooding of the two rivers in the region: the Jubba and the Shabeelle. This region permits extensive rain-fed cultivation during the main rainy season, and flood-recession cultivation during the minor rainy season (Menkhaus 1991).

However, the distinction is not absolute, since pastoralists use cropping as a (temporary) strategy to overcome periods of hardship, just like sedentary cultivators often keep livestock. Mixed strategies are essential to survive the unpredictable ecological conditions in Somalia and it is quite common to shift between cultivation and pastoralism, between a sedentary and mobile life (see e.g. Salzman 1980; Merryman 1982). Many farmers and pastoralists also engage in nonagricultural activities and a number of Somali work in 'white collar' jobs with the government or (I)NGOs, or are engaged in business activities. In fact, many Somalis are traders and businessmen, while others make their living as seamen, fishermen, labour migrants etcetera. In the end, being a pastoralist or a farmer or anything else is not so much a question of activities, but rather one of self-definition, aspirations and values (Bruijn and Dijk 1995). Nunow (2000) observed the same amongst Somalis in the Garissa district of Kenya. Although some of the people he spoke to had lost all their animals and were now trying to survive at the margins of Garissa town, they still identified themselves as pastoralists. My own use of the term 'nomadic heritage' similarly goes far beyond the actual activity of moving around with animals by an individual or even his/her parents. It rather refers to a strategy of coping with life by looking for greener pastures elsewhere, and of minimising risks by investing in different activities and people in different places.

The background of the Somali refugees in Dadaab is that about 80 percent are Darod, mainly of Ogaden subdivisions such as Moxamed Zubeir, Aulihan, Abdalla, Abdwak and Makhabul (CASA Consulting 2001: 87). An important reason for this is that during the war, the significance of clan grew and flight also followed clan patterns. Not only did people flee in the direction of the strongholds and traditional locations of their clans within Somalia, but also across borders. On both sides of the Kenyan-Somali border, the above-mentioned subclans of the Ogaden can be found. The remaining 20 percent of the Dadaab refugees are from a variety of other clans such as the Hawiye and Dir. Besides, there is also a large group of Somali Bantu in the camps. As the majority of refugees are Ogaden, they belong to a nomadic pastoral clan family. But in terms of livelihood, before their flight they engaged in a wider mix of livelihood strategies. As I will describe in further detail, many Ogaden had already shifted place and livelihood a generation earlier. The refugees in Dadaab mainly originated from the interriverine area between the Jubba and the Shabeelle, from where it was geographically most convenient to flee to Kenya. In Somalia, quite a number of them were agropastoralists, others were nomadic pastoralists, farmers and some engaged in business or had formal jobs with the government.

In describing insecurities and social security mechanisms, I will focus on pastoralism and agriculture because these were vital aspects of the livelihoods of many Somali refugees in Dadaab before the war. The main reason for my particular interest in nomadic pastoralism is because the majority of refugees are Darod, and they were therefore familiar with the framework of nomadic ways of coping with insecurity, irrespective of their actual livelihood experiences. This also became obvious from the choices that many refugees made in trying to secure a living in or outside Dadaab. As such, the focus of this book is limited to a section of the population in the camps, even though this section forms the majority. Yet, I do not claim to make observations that can be generalised for all Somali refugees in Dadaab, as there are great differences amongst them; not only based on the mentioned aspects of clan, region and livelihood, but also on gender, age, race, class etcetera. My aim is not to come to absolute generalisations based on the experiences of individuals, without acknowledging the many differences and contradictions within Somali society. Rather, I hope to show how 'ethnographies of the particular' (Abu-Lughod 1991) can contribute to an increased understanding of lives in Dadaab. Abu-Lughod argues that, as anthropologists are representing others through their ethnographic writing, the degree to which the people they study appear 'other' must be partly a function of how anthropologists write about them. The same may be true for the way in which refugees have commonly been represented. According to Abu-Lughod (1993: 149–50), one powerful tool for subverting this process is to write 'ethnographies of the particular' instead of attempting to come to the generalised conclusions so common in the social sciences. These generalisations not only create a gap between the professional and authoritative discourses of social science and the languages of everyday life, but also flatten out differences amongst the people studied.

Pre-war Insecurities

Insecurity to a greater or lesser extent is part of everybody's life. According to Brons (2001: 27), the prevailing and inherently dominant factor in determining people's choices and subsequently identities is the search for relative security. We are all looking for safety, protection, stability, confidence and certainty. As she phrases it: 'A permanent search for security is under way in all the different spheres of societal life, which in the end can at best result in less insecurity' (Brons 2001: 70). More so, insecurity is an intrinsic part of the lives of the Somali, who are facing highly uncertain and unpredictable ecological and political circumstances. In trying to understand the causal factors, it is important to realise that insecurity is not easily separated from security: what to some can represent security might to others mean insecurity. Besides, attempts to create security may actually lead to further insecurity.

A Fragile Ecology

The livelihood strategies people in Somalia and the Northeastern Province of Kenya are able to pursue are constrained by a number of factors. For one, they are highly dependent on ecological features. The temperature is continuously high in the region, although small variations do make a difference (Quaye 1994). The amount, timing and distribution of rainfall are essential, since water is one of the most critical resources. Rainfall patterns in the area are characterised by an erratic spatial distribution and may bring floods as well as droughts. In 1998, for example, a dramatic flood occurred, which was nicknamed 'El Niño' and destroyed many people's livelihoods. A moderate drought, on the other hand, is expected every four to five years, with a major drought expected once per decade. There were serious droughts in 1964–1965, 1970–1975 (Dabadheer, or Long Tail), 1983–1986, 1990–1992 and 1996–1997. Besides these temporary crises, pressures on the land are rising permanently due to increasing desertification in the north (Brons 2001). As a consequence, the herding capacity of the pastoral lands in the north is diminishing and many pastoralists are moving to the south.

In semi-arid environments with extreme climatic and ecological variations from season to season and region to region, the scope for controlling one's environment is very limited (Braun 1992: 112). These conditions require very fragile economic adaptive strategies with low productivity and uncertain yields. Nomads face drought, hunger and death as a regular part of life and are mainly interested in getting through the dry season with as few losses as possible (Unruh 1990). Indeed, a number of the people I interviewed mentioned very harsh conditions when remembering their childhood in rural areas. Nadar Moxamuud, a woman from Ifo of approximately thirty-five years had, like Dahabo, lost her father when she was still young, and most of her siblings had died at an early age. Her mother was cultivating a small piece of land, but Nadar instead was introduced to a nomadic life. When she was sixteen her mother arranged for her to get married to a pastoral nomad.

> I can only remember that we were following our animals and that I suffered great hardship. We were going to places that took us days to walk to and we were always moving from place to place, covering substantial distances. And yet, even when we arrived at our destination there was still the possibility of there not being any resources available. My children were crying for milk because they were so thirsty, but I did not even have water to give them. After staying in those far-off places for a long time, we would come back all the way to the city to buy some maize. It was really a hard life. After I had lived that life

for twelve years we were looted by *shifta* carrying guns. They took my husband's property, all his animals. That was before the big fighting started; at that time, there were small, armed groups who would come to loot people. When my husband's property was taken, he died due to the shock.

From then on, with nothing but her four children, Nadar joined a group of nomadic pastoralists from the same area who had also lost their animals to looters. They were surviving by begging from other people, because according to her, 'I did not have any relatives to go to, and by then the war had started and there was not even a place to go back to'.

In such a fragile ecological environment, overgrazing is common in certain areas and human and stock populations are a heavy burden on the scarce resources that are available: there is constant competition for access to land and water. This is most acute in the dry season but it is a general characteristic of the pastoral life as a whole (Lewis 1994: 28). Since water and pasture are scarce and not constantly available, social networks are very important, but the formation of bigger stable groups has to be prevented. To satisfy both needs, the total clan system functions as a constant framework within which small groups can conclude temporary cooperation contracts; the *xeer*. Obligations can consist of helping to protect and rebuild a herd, taking care of vulnerable people and paying compensational payments (*diya*) in the event of homicide and the like.[6] This system guarantees physical strength and livelihood collaboration within the *diya*-paying groups, and thus security.

However, at the same time, due to its flexibility, this system of 'segmentary opposition' is also highly unstable. Depending on the circumstances, a *diya*-paying group may fight another *diya*-paying group, or cooperate with it to fight another lineage, up to the level of subclan and clan (Lewis 1994). Those who once were enemies may become allies, and vice versa. Thus, cooperation is always fragile except at the most intimate level of kin relationship. Although assistance is guaranteed, the security that this provides only extends to the intragroup level, while at the intergroup level it creates further insecurity: after all, cooperation serves to protect the group members against others. Hostilities can take a number of forms, more or less directly related to the competition for resources. First of all, looting each other's animals is a common practice. Often, the use of the term *shifta* here is a bit misleading, because these activities involve far more than mere banditry and are often related to problems between clans. An additional form a conflict can take is a blood feud, where two groups are engaged in a series of attacks and counter-attacks. This can escalate into outright fighting, from the most local level up to state level.

Indeed, the security situation in both Somalia and northeast Kenya has never been optimal and these states have not been able to protect their citizens. In fact, the government at times actually increased insecurity, as I will illustrate shortly. Conflict situations lead to physical insecurity because people's lives are directly threatened. But far more than that, they also lead to economic insecurity because people's livelihoods are affected. Certain good pastures have always been undergrazed by the Somali for fear of raiders (Baxter 1994) and tsetse flies. Situations of outright war are accompanied by a general state of lawlessness, in which *shifta* are highly active. This curtails the mobility that is so essential to Somali livelihoods, and people also face the risk of losing their productive assets. Farmers see their agricultural activities disrupted in times of hostility and may find that their produce is looted. Thus, conflict situations leave many nomads and farmers pauperised. It should be noted that economic insecurity is not necessarily a side-effect of war, but may well be one of the tactics of war. Constraining enemy livelihoods can be just as effective in winning a war as threatening enemy lives in more direct ways. Besides, there are always beneficiaries when people's survival strategies are under threat (Keen 1994).

The Somali Nation-state

The socio-economic policies of a government can have positive as well as negative effects on people's daily lives, due both to deliberate actions as well as the unforeseen consequences of those actions. The Somali state had a very clear and conventional idea of modernity and development, in which economic growth and solid bureaucratisation were main goals. According to Braun (1992: 114), the aim of these measures – implicitly or explicitly – was state control and sedentarisation of the nomadic population. Most countries with a nomadic population regard the sedentarisation of nomads as a prerequisite for efficient, state-led development and modernisation. Besides, a number of governments try to influence the size of the herds of (nomadic) pastoralists, who are often perceived as having too many animals. Pastoralists are put under pressure to decrease the size of their herds and flocks either directly, by compelling them to sell animals, introducing quotas or confiscating livestock, or indirectly, by refusing them access to veterinary care (Dietz 1996). It is assumed that a nomadic population can only gain access to infrastructural improvements, government social services in the health and education sectors and agropastoral consulting once it has been environmentally stabilised and politically controlled. Only when they are forced to settle, can nomads develop. Despite the large percentage of nomads in the country, the Somali state was no exception to this.

According to Braun (1992), government policies that start from such a premise are doomed to fail. They do not take into account the simple fact that nomads have to be security maximisers because they live in an ecologically fragile environment. Trying to restrict the movements of nomadic pastoralists clearly limits their livelihood opportunities. This is especially problematic because of the scarcity of economic alternatives they have in semi-arid and arid areas, where only few subsistence activities are possible. On top of that, governments are often not ready to invest in such areas for a host of reasons. Kenya for example has largely been neglecting its Northeastern Province in terms of infrastructure, health and education; because its relationship with the Somali population has never been particularly good. Besides, there is also little to be gained by a government investing so much in infertile lands with 'stateless' populations.

Besides neglect, Somali nomads and farmers also faced the negative effects of explicit government policies. In the 1970s, attempts were made by the Somali government to incorporate marginal areas into the market economy, with a focus on large-scale mechanised agricultural projects. The land of subsistence producers was appropriated and all investments went into export production, disregarding the importance of subsistence crops for people's livelihoods. Commercialisation policies did not take into account the proper way of controlling the terms of trade, nor did they try to protect agropastoral production (Ahmed 1994). These policies had the effect of marginalising all subsistence producers; both farmers and pastoralists. At the same time, in 1974–1975, the worst drought in recent Somali history occurred (Lewis 1994). It coincided with a large and highly ambitious Rural Development Campaign that the Somali government organised. The programme was adapted to the crisis situation and camps were established where drought-stricken nomads were temporary settled. There, they formed a 'captive audience' for the awareness and educational campaigns the government had originally planned. Afterwards, the nomads were resettled in crash farming schemes and fishing communities. It was both through state and international (mainly USSR) intervention that drought-stricken nomads from the north were relocated in settlements in the south. This pattern of pastoral population moving into agricultural areas continued and intensified due to prolonged droughts and forced migration after the Somali–Ethiopian war of 1978.

The Somali state has in many ways been a state in constant conflict; both with its own citizens as well as with surrounding countries. According to Bastlund (1994), the basic internal factor of the civil war in Somalia is the contradiction that has always existed between the clan system and the state. As I mentioned earlier, the Somali function within a segmentary lineage system that requires a flexible loyalty, mainly on the level of the *diya*-paying group. There is no such loyalty to the idea of a nation-state, and both systems function according to separate principles of economic, political, military and sociocultural organisation. There have certainly been attempts to create a true nation-state, built on the concept of the Somali as one people. According to some, however, these attempts were never really successful (e.g. Brons 2001). When president Siyad Barre came to power in 1969, his policies provided a concrete plan of action to develop Somalia economically, which was quite popular after the first years of independence had been characterised by nepotism and corruption. Moreover, his nationalist pan-Somali aspirations to unite the Somalis living in five countries in the Horn of Africa were warmly welcomed within the country. At the same time, president Barre found that he needed to do away with the dividing forces within Somalia, and he declared clannism taboo.

No matter how strictly the clan system was banned, the president himself needed it and used it to consolidate his own position. He pitted one clan against the other in a divide-and-rule strategy, directing attention away from ever worsening socio-economic conditions (Makinda 1993). Especially his own clan, the Marehan, and that of his mother, the Ogaden (both are subclans of the Darod), were favoured. The economy was negatively affected within this system through growing corruption and the uneven distribution of national resources. Access to state power became imperative for human welfare and such access was not equally available. As a result, the state became the object of conflict, as well as the means by which the conflict was waged (Doornbos et al. 1992: 4). Opposition grew and was increasingly repressed. Outside the country, president Barre was making few friends. His nationalist claims did not find any support in Africa or elsewhere, because they did not respect the principle of territorial sovereignty. If other OAU states were to recognise these claims, the basis for their own borders would be threatened as well. Thus, Somalia had no supporters when it invaded Ethiopia's Ogaden region in 1977. Although progress was made initially, the war ended in a complete humiliation because the Soviet Union decided to abandon its former ally and assist Ethiopia instead. After his defeat, having suffered heavy losses, president Barre no longer had any grassroots support. His rule turned into a dictatorship; the strong government characteristic of most weak states (Buzan 1988).

The defeat of Somalia in the Ogaden war in 1978 generated a vast refugee influx of hundreds of thousands of Ogaden (ethnic Somalis who were Ethiopian nationals). It led to further overstocking in the north and later (temporary) settlement in the south, where the Somali government opened refugee camps. The first camps were opened in 1979, including the Qorioley camps in the Lower Shabeelle region and eight camps in Beled Weyne. The Qorioley camps had a population of 68,000 and the total number of refugees was estimated to be 1.5 million. Through drought-related pastoral migration from the north and war-related migration away from the Ogaden, pastoralists who were predominantly from the Darod clan settled in the south and north-west (Brons 2001: 106). The dominant perception among the local population was that they received unequal treatment in comparison to the refugees. This was explained by the fact that the refugees were Ogaden like the president's mother, whereas many of the local people were marginalised Rahanweyn and Digil. Unrest grew, particularly when parcels of land began to be distributed to refugees for cultivation.

In Nairobi, I talked to Shukri Hassan, who came from Ethiopia to Somalia in 1978 and was now again a refugee in Kenya. Shukri left Ethiopia when she was sixteen years old with a soldier from Somalia whom she had just married. They had met during the war and got married in a cave in the mountains where the family had fled to. Her father did not agree with the marriage since the man could not offer him anything for his daughter, but she followed her husband to Somalia all the same. After some time, the husband left the army and became a driver and Shukri stayed in the refugee camps at Qorioley. She told me that they had relatives around Qorioley and that she also had a farm. 'At that time, the farm was too big so I always had to call the neighbours. We would call all the adolescent boys and girls together. I would prepare lunch for them and they would go to the farm directly, to plough the land and plant for me. When it was time for harvesting I would call all of them again'. I asked Shukri how she acquired the farm and who had given it to her. She told me the government gave her the farm. I was amazed and asked whether she had been given land because she was a refugee. Shukri told me that all the refugees had been given land and they also received rations. 'We were just like them, the people who were settled there. It is only now that we have become refugees. There, our life was quite okay'.

So in fact, the Somali had been quite familiar with refugees for decades. Talking with refugees in Dadaab about life in Somalia, I learned that many people had met refugees, some had worked in the refugee camps and others had actually been refugees before. Thus, they had already known the insecurity of refugee life, though they had not necessarily related it to their own vulnerability. The problem with flight within the Horn of Africa is that the whole region is quite fragile ecologically and politically. Similar semi-arid conditions can be found in large parts of Somalia, the Ethiopian Ogaden region, northeastern Kenya and Djibouti. Moreover, their governments are not amongst the most stable and those of Ethiopia and Kenya are not necessarily on good terms with Somalia or their own ethnic Somali citizens. Thus, those who flee within the region, a group that constitutes the majority of refugees, are likely to continue to face great insecurities even after their flight from Somalia. On top of that, the influx of displaced people into these already fragile areas may also have negative effects for the regions concerned (Keen 1993). I only learned just how much this was true in the case of the Ogaden refugees when I received comments on Shukri's story from Somalis in the diaspora.

Sulub Abdi wrote that I was wrong to imply that the government took land from the local farmers to give it to the refugees. According to him, the refugees were just as poor as the locals and they were assisted by the UNHCR and not by the government. Madimba Muse, on the other hand, noted that the fact that Shukri and other refugees received some of the most fertile and irrigated lands in the country was a typical example of the injustice that ultimately ruined the country. Such (contradictory) disagreements with the text did not occur often and were mostly related to the reader's opinion on whether a certain clan or individual mentioned in my work was disadvantaged or privileged during president Siyad Barre's reign. Such diverging viewpoints are most commonly caused by someone's clan position. This makes it hard to judge the 'truth' in the matter, but it does clearly illustrate the complexity of solving the current crisis in Somalia, as these diverging views do form an individual's 'truth' and thus the basis of his or her actions. The judgement on whether the aid provided to the Ogaden refugees was just and fair has to come from a certain positionedness, and that is why, in Madimba's words: 'to date, the arrival of relief aid in Somalia sparks tribal or factional fighting'.

The development policies and political stance taken by the Somali government cannot be seen in isolation. Outside interference in Somalia's economy and politics throughout the years also did the country no good. Its colonial history has contributed to the creation of an uneven development both between Somalia and the colonisers, and within the country itself. Intensive agricultural development projects had already been set up in the colonial era. Both the colonial and postcolonial projects were exclusively devoted to large-scale irrigated agriculture (Menkhaus 1991). The Italian colonial administration, for example, set up an export-oriented plantation system in the south of Somalia, in order to supply the home market with agricultural products like bananas. Because of the unequal terms of trade for primary products compared to manufactured products on the world market, this system contributed to the peripheral and dependent position of Somalia (Bastlund 1994).

The refugee flows that followed the Ogaden war in Ethiopia caused the government to launch an international appeal for assistance in 1979. Soon after, Somalia had become a major focus of the international aid regime (Kibreab 1993). The government had a strong economic interest in institutionalising the refugee problem, since the amount of aid it received constituted a considerable proportion of Somalia's GNP. President Barre's forces, like the rest of the state, depended heavily on supplies of food aid that were officially brought in for the Ogaden refugees. Difficulties arose at local level, where food handouts destroyed the market for rural producers and created a strong dependency on foreign assistance (Bastlund 1994). Thus, in the 1980s Somalia ceased to be a 'banana republic', but became virtually dependent on refugee aid (Lewis 1993). By the end of that decade, difficulties arose in keeping up with repayment schedules and the country had to obtain new loans. This left the Somali government in a position where it had to accept the economic policy reforms set by the World Bank and the International Monetary Fund (IMF). The IMF's policy maintained Somalia's role as producer of primary agricultural products, with accompanying poor terms of trade, and may have had the effect of increasing poverty and destroying the livelihoods of sections of the population.

Insecurities During the War

The gradual ruin of Somalia has been explained by various analysts in many different ways. An important explicating factor often mentioned are internal Somali (clan) politics. But the war was also seen to be caused by colonial policies, international aid dependency and regional Cold War political strife. The USSR and the U.S.A. both tried to establish a military presence in the Horn of Africa because of its strategic location near the oil-rich Middle East. This strategic interest gave the Somali state considerable advantage to manipulate the superpowers and gain substantial economic and military assistance. In the final degeneration towards civil war, the end of the Cold War and the withdrawal of the international aid regime from Somalia has been indicated to play a major role. Since various studies provide analyses of these and other factors that eventually led to the Somali war[7], my main focus here will be on the consequences of, and responses to, the war by Somali citizens.

First Signs of War

In trying to understand the gradual escalation of pre-war 'normal' insecurities into outright war, I asked a number of refugees in the camps when and how they first noticed that the security situation was worsening in Somalia. Dahabo told me:

> I first noticed signs of war in 1988, when I was pregnant with our first-born. There were rumours that some roads had been blocked because army people were capturing one area after the other. The food aid at that time also decreased instead of increased. And I saw that the first agency workers were going; a few of them were leaving town already. That is when I suspected that the conditions were worsening. *Shifta* started laying ambushes on the roads to highjack cars, in which they would travel to Mogadishu. They left the owners on the roadside after stealing their money and valuables. They took everything from them… they even took the gold and the clothes that the girls were wearing. That is how I realised that war would soon begin. I believe that these *shifta* were the same people who later became militia. They started just as bandits

and they would only come at night to loot, but later they were ambushing on the roads even at daytime, looking for the cars to come. The problems really began when some men who were working for the government stopped their work and went into the bushes to fight the government. They then mobilised other government employees to stop their work and join them.

When I asked about the specific reasons behind the war, many people gave similar answers: It started off as opposition to the government, but later it turned into a clan-based conflict. This further increased the level of insecurity, because every Somali became a target simply by belonging to a certain clan. Ayaan Moxamed explains:

When the war in Somalia started, it began as a political issue against the government. But when it reached Mogadishu, it changed to focus on clan issues. At first it seemed as if all Somalis were against the clan of president Mohamed Siyad Barre. But it was impossible that only one clan had caused all the problems, and neither could one clan protect itself against all Somali. Later, it changed into a war of clan against clan, subclan against subclan. Very big tribes like the Hawiye and Darod started fighting against each other as well as internally. The situation was worsening and I did not even know my clan details. The biggest problem we faced in our family was that we did not understand the meaning of clan or tribe in this way. It was not our culture. The character of our family has always been that we do not ask people about their clan, since we do not need to know. Anybody who we can understand as a person is a brother or a sister or a friend. When the war started, our main problem was that we had to fear people because they were of a certain clan while we had never known this meaning of clan. We were never even taught the full genealogy of our own.

Although this may sound hard to believe at present, Ayaan was not the only one who told me she was not familiar with her full genealogy by the time the war started. It seems to me that there was a group of people, particularly amongst the elite, who held beliefs opposing the clan system and thus did not pass this information on to their children. Yet, it was very essential to know which clan one was from by the time the civil war escalated. All Somali were looking for the protection of their own clan or subclan, and flight was mostly in the direction of the 'home area' of that (sub)clan within or outside Somalia. Dahabo eventually decided to come back from Kismaayo, where her husband's family lived and various Darod subclans are situated; and move to Mogadishu, where the Hawiye have their origin. She talks about the clan-based pattern of fleeing: 'we experienced problems but I cannot say that we were the only people targeted. Instead, all Somali were targets. It would be surprising if it were only us who experienced these problems. In reality, everyone was running in all directions. Some people were going towards the fighting, others were running from the fighting. Everybody was looking for their own clan, their own family. We were not surprised about what was happening to us, because we saw that all people were in the same position. We were also just running'.

Economic Insecurity: Poverty and Hunger

Fighting was fierce in the riverine area in particular, from which most of the refugees in Dadaab originate. The United Somali Congress (Hawiye) and the Somali National Front (Marehan), two of Somalia's many fighting factions, used the region as a battleground. Severe structural damage occurred, and many people lost their lives in assaults and massacres. There was a complete breakdown of law and order and continuous violence (Brons 2001: 217). The war affected everybody; not only endangering people's lives directly but also disrupting agricultural production at critical moments. Levels of cultivation diminished because of security risks: farmers had to delay planting at times and abandoned far-off small-holder lands for fear of *shifta* and minefields. Likewise, good grazing areas became inaccessible. Looting was widespread and led to the loss of essential assets that guaranteed a livelihood, such as livestock and land, but also to a direct loss of cultivation yields. This was not necessarily a side effect of war, but also formed part of deliberate strategies. Food insecurity is not only beneficial from a military perspective, but also for the commercial elite. Merchants who had a business interest in famine, for example, sponsored the blocking and looting of relief food to safeguard prices (Keen 1993).

Most of the military campaigns caused massive loss of human life and also virtually destroyed all bases for life. As a consequence, famine occurred. In 1991, settled people relied on famine food for their survival, and levels of malnutrition were high (Menkhaus 1991). Because of their hunger, it was very likely that farmers would harvest the crops planted before maturation. Also, whatever small yields they could obtain were not safe from looters: Those in the possession of guns ensured their survival simply by taking it from others by force. In Nairobi I talked to Hassan Jamaac, who reluctantly admitted that he had also been involved in such activities. I asked him how he was able to sustain himself in Kismaayo, after fleeing from Mogadishu by himself. His initial answer was that he was not able to talk about life in Kismaayo, but my translator wanted to know why. Hassan said that he could not talk about it because it was not a human life; it was the lowest life possible. I insisted and asked him how he was able to find his daily bread if life in Kismaayo was so extremely difficult.

At that point, Hassan's friend Noor Ali, whom he had invited to join us, laughed and told us that Hassan did not want to talk about it because he went there as a soldier, carrying a gun. He got his daily bread through plundering, stealing and grabbing from other people. Hassan opened up after his friend gave him this push and admitted having looted money and valuables from people. 'But we did not take from members of our own clan', he added. Noor again was ready to correct his friend, saying that they would even take from their own mothers: if people fled from their houses, that was the time they would come in and take everything. Indeed, those who still possessed some resources to feed themselves were not safe from anybody with a gun and there were plenty of people with guns in Somalia. But even carrying a gun did not guarantee a sufficient livelihood, since food was often simply not available. Due to war and drought, seed stocks had been consumed, herds were minimised and agricultural activities were abandoned. With a loss of assets and a short-age of seeds and tools, most of the already scarce options that existed before the war were no longer available.

It is not uncommon for the Somali to go hungry during certain periods of scarcity. CARE Kenya carried out a livelihood security assessment in Garissa district and found that, on average, nomadic households consumed less than two meals a day for nearly seven months a year (Collins 1999). This is a clear indicator of food insecurity. De Waal (1989) stresses that 'famine' arises from the ordinary operation of society and he shows how idioms of famine are used to express ordinary social relations and experiences. But what happened in Somalia during the war went much further than the relatively normal food insecurity people commonly experience. Noor talked about the hunger: 'People were eating the carcasses of dead animals that they would find on the street. At times, these carcasses would smell terribly and they would only get the paws and the head. Those people later developed terrible swellings on the arms and the legs. Then, they would get many cuts near the mouth, until they died. At one time, we were in the bushes and so hungry that we decided to eat leaves. We were with a group of people and two men ate leaves from a wrong tree that was poisonous. They died right there'. At that point, Noor fell silent and I did not ask any further questions.

Physical Insecurity and Trauma

Most of the refugees I spoke to did not give me such detailed information about the terrible things they had experienced, but talked in quite general terms about atrocities. Still, I could sense that talking about the war and what happened to them was emotionally highly charged. Mostly, I did not want to push things too far because I felt that I was in no position to deal with people's pain, except as a human being. Since I am not a professional psychotherapist, I did not want to induce people to talk about traumatic events and then just leave them with the consequences of recollection. After my interview with Hassan and Noor, I wrote: 'The stories of hunger and inhumanity are horrendous. The whole scene has had a great emotional impact on me; I witnessed Noor retreat inside himself after he had talked about some of the things that happened in Somalia and had listened to his friend talk. He was clearly affected, his eyes depicting such an endless depth of sadness and despair. At that time, I was left wondering what to do. Should I continue asking questions? And would it be possible to stop in the first place? It seemed to me as if Hassan and Noor had told me their story without any pressure from my side, as if they wanted to tell me. They needed to tell me'.

No matter how carefully I approached the topic and how little was actually said, I did get an understanding of people's fear and the uncertainty they had to cope with during the war. Maybe even more so because of what was not said, than because of what was. Dahabo explained her daily uncertainty in a very clear manner to me:

> From morning to evening, I was thinking about whether I would survive the afternoon, or whether I would survive the night. And if I survived the night, I would still wonder whether I would survive the next day. I was worried because people were losing their lives so suddenly. Even if I would have cooked very good food, I would not have been able to eat it because of worrying too much. I was too worried to sit, to eat something, to chew because I feared that people might come and kill me. At that time, I preferred to just drink milk or water quickly. Then I was off, I would ask what is happening, who is coming, where have they reached, what is the latest news. I was always after information. We were talking too much both during the day and at night. I just wanted to hear any rumour, and I wanted to see everything that was happening. From morning up to evening I did not get tired of carrying the children. My mind was too occupied with what was happening and I would ask people a lot of questions. But had those problems not been there, carrying a child even for one minute would have made me feel tired.

Ubax Abdi was a twelve-year-old girl when the war in Somalia erupted. She assured me that she could still remember everything very clearly, and talked freely about a variety of topics. Her father was a soldier of some rank during the reign of president Barre, so when the war started, militiamen came to their house to look for him. In anticipation of these problems, her father had already fled 'into the bushes' and fortunately the militiamen left his wife and children alone after only a few slaps. Ubax explained:

> They were looking for all those who had worked for the government, even if you were only a soldier. They would beat you, they would kill you; they did not care as long as you were working for the government. There were some people who pinpointed those who used to work for the government, even the women. A neighbour of ours used to work for the government; she was a policewoman. They came to our hall and raped her; they tortured her and beat

her badly. They asked her where the property of the government was, even though she was just a policewoman! In Somalia, the policewomen used to wear the same clothes as the men. They took her clothes, the trousers, from her. Her husband was also a policeman and they took his clothes also. Then, they raped her in front of him and just left her on the ground. She was seriously injured.

It was me who brought her water after they had left. My mother told me to go and take some water to our neighbour. Everybody was inside the house and we could see her. They had first gone to my mother and asked about my father. They slapped her twice before they went and met with our neighbour. They beat her and she was there crying, oh, the way she cried... She called my mother, but my mother said that she could not go because there were too many bullets flying around. She said she could not go, and then she sent me. As if the bullets were not a problem for me! Every now and then, I ask my mother 'Did you not care about my life? You just cared for yourself, not me'. I took the water, I ran and I came back immediately. A lot of fire was being exchanged.

After listening to Ubax relating this story, I asked her whether she had seen the woman being mistreated. Had she witnessed everything? Then she told me that they were doing it in front of everybody. 'They did not care about that; there were quite a number of people'.

What happens to an individual when he or she witnesses such violence, and how can they grasp the most horrendous in mankind? Ubax at the age of twelve was trying hard to understand, but could not fully grasp what was happening:

I remember sometimes asking my mother why the people were fighting. She told me that it was because of the land. And I asked her why, why this land? What does the land possess? She laughed because I asked her why are they fighting over this land that has nothing? I was old enough, because I was twelve. I could hear the fighting and I understood it well. I can remember the war from the starting point up to the end. I remember the places we passed; I remember the villages and the people we met. But exactly why they were fighting, I could not understand.

It was not only a young and innocent girl like Ubax who was finding it difficult to understand what she had witnessed. At one point, Hassan and Noor were talking about the beast-like character of people when they start killing. It was never stated, but I sensed that they were talking about others merely in order to relate their own experiences. Hassan told me the following:

They kill one, they kill two, and by that time it no longer touches them; by then they are losing their morality. Some, however, wake up at night screaming or talking; they are haunted by the killings that they have done. Many are on drugs, *bhang* (marihuana), whatever... And everybody is in danger: someone may sit next to you and have in mind that you are going to kill him. Simply because he has been killing as if it was a small thing, he now believes that you can do the same. With that idea in mind, he may decide to kill you before you kill him. And you die while you are not even aware of anything! During the war in Somalia, people made good what is *xaaraam* (prohibited in Muslim law), they made legal what is illegal.

Social Security: Past Ways of Coping

Because the ecological and political environment in Somalia is highly variable and largely uncontrollable, economic activities are characterised by low productivity and uncertain yields. Choices of livelihood are also limited and, as a consequence, there is a strong focus on creating security. The basic rules of nomadic life are 'safety first' and 'risk aversion' (Braun 1992: 113). Economic strategies are geared toward not only current production needs, but also long-term security concerns (Aronson 1980). They are mainly based on three methods. First, the social network is something that is invested in greatly for it can provide people with long-term security guarantees and protect them in times of contingency. Second, mobility is very important to a large part of the Somali population, because it enables them to be highly flexible and thus avoid risks. Third, diversification of investments over different livelihood strategies, activities and/or people is essential for a 'safety first' attitude. Social security mechanisms like this function both to protect people in contingent situations as well as to promote their standard of living: for both insurance and development purposes (Leliveld 1994).

The exact nature of people's social security choices is not only determined by the opportunities available, but also by their norms and values. Decisions are not just based on the best technical option, but take place within sociocultural frameworks. Amongst the Ogaden refugees in camps in Somalia, for example, it was found that adaptation and change were not solely determined by survival functions, but also by a judgemental dimension which was influenced by cultural values and past experiences (Kibreab 1993). Yet, norms and regulations do not merely *constrain* possibilities. There is always a certain normative and regulative plurality that structures and influences, though it does not determine, social practices. This plurality offers options for choosing between or accumulating different constructions of social security, and different rights and obligations (Benda-Beckmann and Benda-Beckmann 1994). Flexibility is rooted in a plurality of cultural understandings, a concept referring to the cultural means that people employ to deal with insecurity. There is a need to have control in life, but control may be achieved not only through actions but also through thinking. Cultural understandings provide an alternative means of control, a mental and normative one, as they provide people with options to tackle problems, a sense of purpose, a framework to understand the world and a sense of identity (Bruijn and Dijk 1995).

Social Networks

In a situation of scarcity, the best way to guarantee security for both a group and an individual is to cooperate. According to Barnes (1954, quoted in Leliveld 1994: 87), there is a difference between social networks that depend on kinship and those depending on neighbours and friends. Kin relations are theoretically very strong; they have a high level of solidarity. Then, they are durable because blood relation is for life. Furthermore, they are composed of a broad range of people of differing age, sex, socio-economic status and geographical location. On top of this, kinship relations provide a strong normative insurance. When it comes to neighbours and friends, cooperation is mainly social and economic and often more intensive due to proximity. The operation of these kinds of networks depends on their normative insurance, which can be strong because of severe sanctions. If neighbours do not comply with expectations, they are punished with gossip, social isolation and eventual expulsion. Relations are based more on trust than on being 'natural', defined by birth. This means that more of an effort will be required to cultivate them. Overall, these relations are looser and offer more opportunity for negotiation and detachment.

Many authors have pointed to the fact that kinship ties are the strength and weakness of Somali society. Traditional mechanisms rely heavily on cooperation and support between family and clan members. The evocative power of kinship as the axiomatic 'natural' basis for all forms of social cooperation and as the ultimate guarantee of personal and collective security is deeply and pervasively rooted in Somali culture (Lewis 1994: vii). A blood relation or *tol* (clan, tribe, descent group) binds individuals together, providing them with their primary group identity and an elastic range of solidarity. Ultimately, a person's security depends on the strength and goodwill of his clansmen and not on his possession of wealth. Thus, loyalty to one's kin through the carrying of responsibility of clanship is more important than personal gain. After all, wealth can easily be lost, as Dahabo's story clearly illustrates. As the foundation of social cooperation, kinship is a feature of all transactions between and amongst individuals. Various forms of social security, such as support to families in times of crisis, natural disaster, drought, death of animals and harvest failure, are derived from the *diya*-paying unit within the Somali clan system (Brons 2001: 121). Research amongst the Ogaden refugee population in camps in Somalia also identified a system of social obligations inside extended lineage networks (Zitelmann 1991). This caused a channelling of a flow of information, goods and services that went across national borders, including ethnic Somali in the Ogaden region.

A social network functions as a system for the transaction of information, services and resources between individuals. Networks of people first engage in communication in order to transfer information, establish social norms and create a degree of consensus (Scott 1991). The transfer of information is not only important for people's functioning in everyday life, but may also be essential for the establishment of (a sense of) security, as Dahabo's account illustrates. Through her search for information during the war, Dahabo tried to reduce uncertainties, defined by Göbel (1998) as 'situations in which actors are insufficiently informed about the socio-economic conditions they face'. Collecting information did not prevent her from being at risk as such, since risks are 'unpredictable fluctuations in ecological and economic conditions' (Göbel 1998), which cannot be reduced by mere information gathering. During the war in Somalia, everybody was affected and most of the things that happened to people were quite unpredictable. Nevertheless, the gathering of information through communication within the social network was essential for a reduction in people's uncertainties and to give them the feeling that they were in control as much as they possibly could be.

A second function of the social network is the transfer of services. Relatives and neighbours assist each other in productive activities such as planting and harvesting crops, or herding and watering stock. Shukri Hassan, for example, explained to me that her neighbours would help her to plough, plant and harvest the land, as she was not able to do the work all by herself. Moreover, relatives and friends in many contexts are vital for the development of other livelihood activities, as they often assist in business and trade, finding jobs, migration, developing political power and the like. This was certainly the case in Somalia where, despite official policies, one needed the aid of relatives and clanmembers in order to get anything done. Furthermore, services are provided in the form of care activities, such as temporary or long-term care for children. In Somalia, the children of drought-affected pastoralists may stay with their relatives in town for a couple of years, or even permanently, and town children can be sent out to their nomadic family during the rich rainy season (Brons 2001: 122). It is also very common for children from a rural background to stay with relatives in town throughout their education.

Thirdly, social networks help to facilitate the transfer of resources. This is particularly essential in a climate of scarcity, as 'starvation is the characteristic of some people not having enough food to eat; it is not necessarily the characteristic of there not being enough food to eat' (Sen 1981). What is important for people is that they have entitlements in times of need: when a crisis occurs, they should be able to fall back on their social networks in order to obtain resources. The responsibility or even obligation to assist is deeply entrenched in Somali culture and Islam. As Muslims, Somalis are always expected to assist those in need: 'Devout is he who gives possession, out of love for Him, to relatives and orphans, the needy, wayfarers, beggars and for the ransom of slaves' (Sura 2, 177). There is a responsibility to assist destitute neighbours, and the zakat obligation similarly requires Muslims to give a percentage of their wealth and income to the needy. But these religious obligations closely interact with cultural responsibilities, in which relatives and clan members play an important role. Both Lewis (1994: 128) and Nunow (2000: 158) noticed that amongst the Somalis, Islamic obligations are often fulfilled between related households. Thus, even though Islamic rules are set up to protect the most destitute, if deprived Somalis do not have well-off relatives, they commonly face problems.

Within kinship borders, the ethics of reciprocity and support are paramount and rich people are expected to assist their poorer kinsmen. Those who are absent on business or are employed in town or overseas are supposed to send regular remittances to their clansmen in the interior. Kinship entails a sharing of resources and profits and commitments increase with the individual's wealth (Lewis 1994: 128). Dahabo, for example, mentioned how in the 1980s, her family's situation gradually improved, partly because her brother was sending remittances: 'At that time, my brother was working in the sugar factory in Marere. He had an important position and was earning a lot of money. He sent remittances to our mother through the *xawilaad* system instead of sending it via a person, as the money could be looted on the way'. Assistance not only occurs through a transfer of money, but can also be in kind. There are a number of traditional patterns of assistance amongst Somali pastoralists, involving loans and gifts of animals and their products (see Collins 1999). In all cases, the strength of kinship responsibilities is crucial, and poor relatives must be provided for even when reciprocity is not possible. The endurance of this responsibility lies in *nasiib*, in the unpredictability of life. After all, *'maanta waa aniga, berina waa adiga'*.

Mobility

Mobility has been an important way of dealing with insecurity in that it means people move away from hardship and that family members spread out to different places and engage in different activities thereby reducing the consequences of contingencies. Nomadic pastoralism in this respect is well adapted to the harsh and highly variable conditions of the Somali environment. Households with significant numbers of camels and cattle are reliant on movement to support their herds, given the arid and semi-arid nature of the area. It includes established travel practices such as 'scouting', where a few individuals are sent by the community to look for a new (temporary) residence, evaluating grazing and water, other liveli-hood opportunities, physical safety and sociocultural aspects. Migration forms the cornerstone of pastoral economic security in accordance to cus-tomary rules, in response to seasonal change and as a coping strategy in periods of natural disaster. The areas that nomads occupy are ecological-ly heterogeneous in both space and time, so movements are motivated by the need for good grazing and water, attempts to avoid epidemics and areas where raiders operate and the wish to coordinate pastoral with non-pastoral activities (Aronson 1980). Amongst sedentary communities, on the other hand, the migration of entire families is generally a last resort because it entails selling possessions as well as stress and hardship for the vulnerable members of a household. Yet, when everything else has failed, it does provide a hope of access to new opportunities (Dreze and Sen 1989: 77).

The Somali also have an ancient history of movement for the purpose of trade and are a community of businesspeople. In the southern region, trade has a long tradition and stretches far into present-day Kenya and Ethiopia. The northern Somali coast has for centuries been linked com-mercially with its Abyssinian hinterland and with Arabia and the Far East. Historical sources reveal the existence not only of local and intra-regional exchange but also of external trade as early as the first few cen-turies A.D. (see Lewis 1994: 113). Muslim Arab and Persian settlers devel-oped a string of commercial coastal centres. Originally, the main export products were myrrh and frankincense; later it changed to hides and skins and livestock. The trading networks have undergone slight alter-ations and adaptations to new political circumstances throughout the cen-turies, but are still functioning and make up the basic economic reality of the region today.

This trade system was given a considerable boost with the employment of Somalis in the British Merchant Marine as stokers in steamships as well as for manual work in the Gulf States. Labour migration was crucial to providing local Somali merchants and traders with access to hard curren-cy for the purchase of foreign goods. The muscle-drain assumed unparal-leled proportions in the 1970s and 1980s both in terms of the number of workers involved and in terms of the money that was sent by the Gulf workers. As the number of migrants increased with the oil boom, Somali traders began to collect hard currency from the migrant workers, using this to purchase commodities for sale in Somalia. The equivalent in Somali currency, or goods, was then handed over to the migrants' fami-lies and kinsmen. Annually, the remittances that were transferred through this so-called 'franco valuta' system tended to amount to two or three times the Somali Republic's export earnings (Lewis 1994). The money remitted remained largely outside the official banking system and was distributed along kinship lines. Thus, it forms the prelude to the present-day *xawilaad* system that is described in detail in chapter 4.

But migration was far more than a mere survival strategy. It has also always presented a way of life, enabling both individual growth as well as community development. As the majority of Somalis are Muslim, travel is important to them for religious reasons. Muslim doctrine explicitly encourages certain forms of travel, such as the obligation to undertake the pilgrimage to Mecca (*hajj*) and the obligation to migrate from lands where the practice of Islam is constrained (*hijra*). Visits to shrines and travel in search of knowledge (*rihla*) provide further examples of religiously inspired travel (Eickelman and Piscatori 1990: 5). In Somalia, travel is considered to be a learning process and a source of wisdom not only religiously, but also in a wider sense. Young men, and to a lesser extent women, are encouraged to travel in order to gain education and life experience. Migration is a popular form of investment since often, the material and nonmaterial gains that migration brings to the individual combine to benefit the larger community as well.

Another common form of mobility in Somalia was from rural to urban areas, a pattern that is widespread in Africa and elsewhere. Rural–urban movement may be both proactive and reactive: it may be an individual's deliberate choice to maximise advantage, or a response to a situation that has severely constrained his or her options (Richmond 1993). It is a common response to food scarcity that when drought conditions intensify, pastoralists and farmers search for a temporary livelihood in town. At the same time, household members (with or without their families) move to town in search of better education and employment opportunities. In Somalia, on the eve of independence in 1960, there was a migration wave to Mogadishu. Most of the formal jobs at that time could be found in the civil service sector or with foreign aid organisations, both of which were overrepresented in Mogadishu. In addition, Mogadishu possessed a modern educational system, unlike elsewhere in the country. As a consequence of the large number of people entering the city, Mogadishu underwent rapid urban growth. During the 1970s, it developed into a truly multiclan town and by the 1980s Somalia had one of the fastest growing urban population in Africa, accompanied by a growing urban and educated middle class (Gardner and El Bushra 2004: 8).

Often, the relocation to the towns does not involve the whole household but rather, household members disperse to maximise the chances of success and build a wider social network. Whereas the movement of the whole family is only a last resort as far as farmers are concerned, the migration of single adults in search of employment does provide an early response to the threat of starvation (Dreze and Sen 1989). This is a strategy that may lead to remittance sending and that, at the same time, brings immediate resource relief. Although nomadic pastoralists may find it less problematic to move with the whole family, they also often divide family members and animals into a strong and a weak group. The strong group, consisting of young men and camels, is highly mobile and covers large distances. The weaker group, on the other hand, is quite sedentary and usually settles close to a settlement or trading centre. Remittances are expected to flow from the strong group to the weak (Nunow 2000).

In this situation, it is not uncommon for some members to be settled in an area where they can find external support from either the government or NGOs. This happened, for example, with the government settlement schemes for drought-stricken pastoralists earlier mentioned. Once climatic conditions had improved, the family heads moved back to their home area, leaving behind their families in the settlements. It gave them a lee-way to rebuild their original livelihood without having to provide for the more vulnerable members of the family. A similar situation occurred when ethnic Somali fled across the border from Ethiopia into Somalia during and after the Ogaden war. Family security strategies often dictat-ed that wives and children should be safely looked after in refugee camps while the men continued fighting, trading or herding, crossing back and forth over borders (Brons 2001: 105). The opposite pattern of migration linked the refugee camps in Ethiopia and the Isaaq areas of Somaliland after 1988. Refugees were well informed about conditions in Somaliland and men were likely to leave their dependents in the camps while trying to re-establish their livelihood back home (Ryle 1992: 165).

The decision to migrate and the actualisation of that plan is not an indi-vidual project, but one in which a larger group is involved. In times of catastrophe, it is mostly the extended family that helps its members to leave an afflicted area. Resources are needed both for the actual migration and for the settlement process. Patterns of migration are often determined more by clan distributions than by formal borders since it is much easier to move to a region where relatives can be found and assistance will be provided. The geographical allocation underlying the clan structure exist-ed long before international borders were drawn, and cross-cut these bor-ders. According to Nunow (2000), people's options reduced greatly when colonial borders were drawn. Others argue that the Somali have never relied on networks that function within the framework of a nation-state. International borders are not taken into account in the day-to-day eco-nomic and trading activities of the Somali, reflecting their characteristic disregard for externally imposed concepts of territoriality (Brons 2001: 84). I agree with Brons' observations, although it is of course also true that strictly applied border controls and regulations do obstruct people's options. In the Horn of Africa, however, these types of border controls are very difficult to implement.

As a consequence, migration within the region often takes place along kinship and thus clan lines. At the same time, assistance from relatives or clansmen is needed even more urgently in the case of migration outside the region, for example in the case of Somali labour migrants to the Gulf or students going to the U.K. Overseas migration requires high investments, which are mostly covered by a network of relatives. They may pool resources so that one person is able to go, hoping that the initial migrant can save sufficient money for someone else to join him or her (Choldin 1973). Often, it is only through kinship links that people are able to gain the necessary capital and contacts to go abroad. Lewis (1994) observes that in Somaliland people's access to kinship networks has long been of central importance to their ability to migrate. This starts from assistance in kind at the local level, for example the practice of *gaadiid*, which involves the borrowing of a beast of burden to allow a family to move from one place to the next. The assistance extends to international level, where migration requires considerable funding and contacts, which often cannot be provided by the migrant alone. Various authors have studied kinship and migration patterns, and the fact that kinship plays a central role in enabling migration is widely acknowledged. For Somalis, this has been true in the past as much as it holds true at present, as I will illustrate in chapter 5.

Assisting family members in the migration process is not only of benefit to the migrant, since it also supports the vitality of the kinship network as a whole. Access to overseas countries may bring the migrant and his or her relatives remittances, prestige, knowledge, the 'cultural capital' of having been abroad, and the ability to be a patron or sponsor of others. Also, the proceeds generated while abroad can be used to invest in other activities such as marriage, construction work, business or education. The migratory process thus brings forth a chain of transactions of information, services and resources that does not necessarily bring greater wealth, but primarily establishes more security. Overseas migration does not really alter existing socio-economic structures, though a few studies have observed a change in power relations between different groups of people (see e.g. Haas 2003). It is mostly those who are already prosperous who can take up the resource of migration easily and use it to solidify their wealth against insecure factors. Still, there are also indirect benefits to processes of migration that may assist those unable to send a family member. When, for example, the 'muscle drain' from Somalia to the Gulf States was at its height, the outflow left some families short of manpower for herding tasks. This prompted men with a limited number of livestock to work as hired herders for better-off kinsmen, providing them with an additional source of income.

Especially in times of war, mobility is of utmost importance since it may make the difference between life and death. During the Somali war, nomadic pastoralists in that respect had an advantage over sedentary farmers because they were not tied to land or property and could move relatively freely with their herds (Menkhaus 1991). They were in a better position to evade looting since they could move with their livelihood resources, whereas farmers largely would have to leave their harvest and seed stocks behind. Farmers were more prone to looting and assault because they did not want to move from their land and property (Lehman 1993). The decision whether, when and where to move was not only made on the basis of the security situation but also depended on the availability of necessary resources, whether important assets had to be left behind and whether family or clan members could offer support at the new destination. The refugees I spoke to taught me that, though flight seems an immediate and radical response to acute danger, it still entails some form of choice.

Although the Somali move with relative ease, migration is a conscious and carefully weighed-up decision. Dahabo, for example, explained how she discussed flight from a conflict zone with her husband or her mother, until they decided to go. The same conscious decision-making also occurred when she was given the option to reunite with her husband.

> Nuradin communicated to me and I was informed that he was living in Hagadera. I sent him a message that we were all alive and staying in Mogadishu. The second letter that he sent to us included his photograph. I saw on the photograph that he was very black, very ugly and very thin. So I was asking myself: 'Can I really go to the place where my husband became like this?' And I decided that it was better for me to stay with my mother and work by myself. For two years, I thought about refugee life. I kept asking myself whether it would be possible for me to go to Hagadera, where Nuradin had become thin and ugly. It was impossible to imagine, because he was very rich and brown when he worked for the UNHCR in Beled Weyne. What kind of life was he living in the refugee camps? But after two years, some people from Hagadera came to Mogadishu and they told me that Nuradin was working with CARE. They told me that he had no problems and was in good condition. Receiving this information boosted my morale and I decided to go to Dadaab.

Diversification of Options

In an environment where insecurity is paramount, spreading risks is important. Thus, Somali social security strategies consist of a mix of various arrangements. Because of the diversity of situations that people come across, they need to be able to choose from various options, while basing their decisions on day-to-day observations. Within an extended family, it is common to find pastoralists, farmers and businessmen who will be able to assist each other when necessary. Also, those following a certain livelihood diversify their choices. Somali pastoralists follow a mixed-herding strategy and their livestock provides security in times of duress. Sheep, goats, cattle and camels offer different benefits in respect to drought security, milk yields, herd growth and cash incomes. These characteristics can be utilised to reach the objectives that a pastoralist may have in any given situation. After a drought for example, it may be advantageous to convert the surviving animals to small stock to benefit from their high reproduction rates and rebuild the herd within a relatively short time span. Camels, on the other hand, are far better equipped to live without water for a long time, and therefore stand a much greater chance of surviving a serious drought.

Within agricultural production, diversification strategies are also very common. Farming techniques are characterised by minimising risks and searching for opportunities to overcome drought years. Intercropping and planting a wide range of crops in different locations help farmers to reduce the consequences of a single crop failure. Farmers in Somalia distinguish between fast-maturing, drought resistant and standard varieties of the same crop. This knowledge serves to determine which seeds to plant, taking into account the urgency of the need for crops and the prospects of drought (Ahmed 1994). Agricultural communities can resort to various strategies in stable years, or in anticipation of a crisis. A few examples are the diversification of crops and herds, the exploitation of geographical complementarities in the ecosystem, the pursuit of 'symbiotic exchanges' between the different communities (e.g. pastoralists and farmers), the development of patronage or reciprocal gift-giving, the recourse to complex dietary adjustments and the storage of food or body fat (Dreze and Sen 1989: 71–72). This can at least reduce the negative effects of a period of drought or other crises.

During the war in Somalia, the grazing and planting strategies that people followed were adapted to meet their needs, although this was not always possible and in some cases starvation did occur. Because of the highly unstable war front, the Somali continued to use risk-averse behaviour in their production, commercial and security strategies. Pastoralists moved away from areas of severe fighting with their herds, and farmers adapted their agricultural techniques to overcome difficulties. Whereas they would normally rely on flood-recession agriculture in the minor rainy season, they now tried to practise rain-fed agriculture as well. Instead of using far-off land, some farmers also used the land of abandoned, large-scale, mechanised farming schemes (Menkhaus 1991). While those who were very mobile moved away from the war zones, those who were more closely tied to their assets instead tried to reduce their movements.

As mentioned before, though people may identify themselves primarily as nomads or as farmers, this does not imply that their only activities are related to animals or crops. Rather, the household as a production unit tries to spread risks by diversifying the activities of its members, and the same is true at the level of the extended family (Hjort af Ornäs 1990).

Pastoralists mix pastoral production with selected nonpastoral employment in other sectors of the economy (see e.g. Aronson 1980; El Hadi El Nagar 2001). Other activities they may engage in are the sale of charcoal and firewood, petty trade, labour migration and part-time fishing or farming. Farmers also engage in multiresource economies, investing money in nonfarming interests such as owning a small shop or producing a commodity. For example, camel power can be used to grind simsim (sesame seed) into oil that can be sold in town. These activities are part of a complex microregional economy, in which rural and urban areas are highly interdependent.

Another important way of maximising options is related to the social network. People generally have security mixes that are based on a plurality of social relationships (Benda-Beckmann and Benda-Beckmann 1994). There is a complex network of human relations within which individuals and small groups try to survive through negotiation and shifts. For many Somalis, the clan system is important for building and rebuilding coalitions continuously. Somali society is a complex of interwoven and interdependent strands in which clan affiliation is the dominant but not necessarily the decisive security network (Brons 2001: 113). For many Somalis, their kinship relations are most important in providing a general sense of security, but which specific relations can and will be used depends on the circumstances. In acute situations of danger or hunger, for example, it may not be possible for relatives to provide assistance and neighbours may play a central role. In other instances, the assistance of 'external' bodies like a government or NGO becomes crucial for people's survival. In the following chapters, I will present a variety of cases that illustrate the ways in which an individual can maximise the assistance and security provided by his or her social network in combination with international aid.

When a situation of crisis affects a whole region, a necessary way of diversifying options is by making use of assistance from outside the local community, as communal aid may no longer be available. On the other hand, this type of aid is based on principles that may lead to a loss of social and individual esteem. Relief food, for example, is presented as charity or gift-giving of which beneficiaries must be deserving (Harrell-Bond et al. 1992). Qualification is based on their level of destitution. These kinds of moral transactions that never expect any type of reciprocity unmistakably determine the unequal status and power relations between giver and recipient. It is not the first strategy people resort to, and it is definitely not the only one. In fact, relief is mostly combined with the pursuit of other livelihood strategies and therefore serves to give people an additional option. This was clearly the case in Ethiopia, in the camps for the refugees from Somaliland. These camps were incorporated into the seasonal pattern of movement so that members of pastoral families could recover in the camps in the dry season when pasture is hard to find (Ryle 1992: 163). The availability of the food ration became part of people's survival strategy; the camps became part of their ecology. Another way of combining relief aid with other livelihood strategies, is when the most vulnerable members of the family are left in refugee camps with the aim of releasing the burden on the household as a whole (see e.g. Harrell-Bond 1986; Kibreab 1993).

In Conclusion: How Resilient are Somali Social Security Mechanisms?

Relief food has become a permanent aspect of survival strategies for quite a number of Somali in the Horn of Africa.[8] In the past, 'begging' or receiving relief used to be frowned on (Nunow 2000). Even in 1969, many pastoralists in Garissa district still declined to apply for assistance despite conditions of severe drought. According to some authors, the shift in responsibility for coping with drought from the household and community level to the national government and international organisation level came about in part because of the failure of the traditional system to respond and adapt effectively to changing conditions. Collins (1999) states that, while this is a symptom of the structural vulnerability of the pastoral livelihood system in general, the provision of relief food has, in turn, exacerbated the erosion of traditional methods of coping and created an unsustainable dependency on external assistance. Although I do not fully agree with these observations, as will become clear throughout this book, it is important not to uncritically assume the resilience of Somali social security mechanisms under all circumstances. Some cautious remarks seem to be called for.

First of all, people's coping mechanisms may have damaging effects. The level of harm depends on whether a certain strategy is employed before, or as a response to, a crisis; whether it involves a smaller or bigger commitment of domestic resources; and whether it is more or less readily reversible (Keen 1993). When, for example, collective risks are experienced, strategies become severely constrained and are vulnerable to sudden changes in the security environment. When options become less freely available, strategies may be used that will jeopardise future production or involve significant suffering and health risks. For example, one of the strategies that people employ to respond to a crisis is the sale of assets to purchase food (Dietz et al. 2001: 6). This is likely to be done at a time when large numbers of other households are doing the same and when, therefore, the terms of trade are very unfavourable. In particular, the sale of productive assets that were not held as a form of insurance against famine can lead to destitution and lasting vulnerability to future

famines. Other strategies that may be preferred over the selling or con-
suming of productive assets are related to acquiring, preparing and con-
suming food. One way of reducing food insecurity is by eating wild food.
This is, however, labour-intensive and may entail physical insecurity.
There is also a risk of being poisoned if the necessary knowledge is not
available, as Hassan Jamaac's story illustrated.

Secondly, existing social security strategies do not necessarily provide
security for everybody and at all times. As Madimba Muse remarked:
'Some of the methods the Somali used and are still using to cope with
insecurity are based on injustice'. The unequal treatment of many of the
ethnic minorities in Somalia may lead to a situation where the coping
mechanisms of some may negatively affect the chances of others. On top
of that, in crisis conditions, the traditional system of assistance for the
most vulnerable within the community is likely to deteriorate. There is
greater general destitution, which leads to a decline in assistance and a
rise in the number of people needing assistance. Besides, a common
assumption exists that shifts in values may occur. Moxamed Suleiman, a
Kenyan Somali who works for the UNHCR, told me about the changes he
observed amongst the Somali in their perception of assistance. He
described this in relation to the *xiirso*, a system of contributions through
which vulnerable community members and travellers used to be assisted:
'People would bring milk, a goat or whatever they could do without and
those items would then be redistributed amongst the most destitute. Only
people who were absolutely needy would accept such contributions. It
was truly a great shame to live off the *xiirso*. Nowadays, however, everybody wants to get the most, no matter what they have already. People take
whatever they can get and it is considered normal to be dependent'. This
idea of increased voluntary dependency is very common amongst policy
makers and implementers as well as amongst some scholars, but my
research results do not justify such a conclusion, as I will argue in the next
chapter.

Many academics and professionals have claimed that nomadic pastoralists like the Somali are no longer adequately adapted to current conditions and will gradually have to give up their way of life. The assumption is that nomads are highly vulnerable in the contemporary world system and that, in response to crisis and changing conditions, their traditional social security mechanisms will decline. Others assert, however,
that nomadic pastoralism is the only viable livelihood option in the (semi)
arid regions inhabited by pastoralists. Pastoralists are organised to change
rapidly and decisively and have adapted continually over the years
(Aronson 1980). They are receptive to change without this meaning that
they lose their former way of life. Although I find it important not to take
the resilience of the existing Somali social security mechanisms for granted, research in Kenyan refugee camps has not provided any reason for me

to accept a doom scenario. Forced migration does not necessarily lead to a breakdown of social networks and patterns of assistance. When Somali refugees came from Ethiopia in the late 1970s, there was clear evidence that the refugees' social support networks in the camps and settlements were still in place and were far from breaking down and being replaced by formal structures (Kibreab 1993: 343). The same is true in Dadaab, where Somali refugees to a large extent continue to rely on social networks, mobility and diversification for their daily survival, as I will illustrate throughout this book. Experiencing crisis and scarcity does not necessarily alter that, since '*Labadii wax yar wada cuni, wayda wax badan ma wada cunaan*': If you do not eat the little you have together, you cannot eat together in times of plenty.

Notes

1. Literally, this Somali proverb means 'Today it is me, and tomorrow it is you', which refers to the fact that the conditions of life are unpredictable and what may happen to you today, may happen to me tomorrow. Consequently, I will assist you today and you will assist me tomorrow.

2. Nuradin's family belongs to the Darod (Ogaden), whereas Dahabo's family is Hawiye (Abgaal).

3. The 'q' sound is technically known as a voiced uvular plosive (Orwin 1995: 4). One can try to make this sound by saying 'k' and then moving the back of the tongue as far back as possible.

4. Others would rather consider Rahanweyn to be the overall term for the two agropastoral clan lineages of Digil and Merifle (see e.g. Gardner and El Bushra 2004: 7).

5. It should be noted, however, that figures vary greatly. Brons (2001: 76), for example, disputes such high estimates and finds that 52.5 percent of the population are nomads, 19.9 percent are settled farmers and 27.6 percent are nonagricultural. According to her, the pastoral base of Somali society has always been exaggerated in an attempt to propagate the nomadic as the national identity (Brons 2001: 89).

6. Paying *diya* is a common practice amongst all Muslims, as it is an aspect of Sharia law.

7. See for example: Gersony (1990), Samatar (1992), Makinda (1993), Bastlund (1994), Samatar (1994), Brons (2001).

8. According to Helland (2001: 56), the same image exists of other pastoralists in eastern Africa, who are assumed to have become permanent beneficiaries of various famine relief schemes.

3

Refugee Life in the Camps: Providing Security or Sustaining Dependency?

Hajir Aden, who works as a headmaster in Hagadera, once gave me a very clear and striking description of his life in the camp: 'By now, personally I have adapted to the life here, to being a refugee, to being spoon-fed. But the problem is that we have stayed in refugee camps for ten years, with no hope of getting citizenship or at least equal human rights. We are not allowed to earn the same amount of money as Kenyan citizens, our movements are restricted and we cannot settle anywhere in Kenya. After disintegrating and collapsing due to clan conflicts, my country of origin, which belongs to the Third World, has demoted me to the Fourth World of being a refugee'. This 'Fourth World', as Hajir calls it, is a world in which a large number of institutions play a role. Because refugees are (temporarily) outside the national order of things and cannot simply claim their citizenship rights, various forms of security are provided by the 'refugee regime'. This concept refers to the national and international body of institutions, law, policy and practice that exists to deal with refugees or forced migration (Van Hear 1998a: 342). The main actors within this regime are the UNHCR, host governments, implementing agencies and donors. Relationships between these different actors are highly complex, as will become clear throughout this chapter.

The refugees in Dadaab face insecurities of a physical, economic and existential nature that at times are similar to those they faced before and during the war in Somalia. The confined and artificial environment of the Dadaab camps is likely to affect the choices that Somali refugees are able to make in dealing with these insecurities. Whereas the ultimate raison d'être of refugee camps may be the existence of a population that requires assistance (Harrell-Bond and Voutira 1994: 3), the question arises of whether, in the end, the camps indeed provide security to the refugees who are supposed to live in them, or whether they rather force these refugees into a dependent position that only leads to further insecurity. This chapter will provide an answer to that question by describing the various economic and physical insecurities that refugees face because of living in Dadaab. The following section then examines simulated and real dependency amongst refugees, after which the role of the refugee regime will be analysed. Historical factors, as well as present-day interactions, tremendously complicate the task of providing security to African refugees in regional camps, and may combine to lead to policies that encourage their sustained dependency. Yet, as argued earlier, the structural properties of social systems, while seemingly operating independently and decisive, only exist through the actions of individual agents (Giddens 1984). It is not refugee policies as such but the actions of policy makers, government officials and practitioners that make a difference to the lives of refugees. Furthermore, it is important to acknowledge that the refugee regime does provide security for refugees who have insufficient means of income and are not taken care of by the community.

Dadaab Camp Organisation

Before 1991, Dadaab was a small and insignificant town in the region, with about five thousand inhabitants. Ifo was built first, and Dagahaley and Hagadera followed in March and June 1992. The camps attracted pastoral communities who were interested in using the water sources, purchasing food at low prices and selling cattle as well as milk. The town of Dadaab started to change and is now connected to an electricity supply, has a running water system, a slaughterhouse and health facilities for its population (Perouse de Montclos and Kagwanja 2000: 210). The camps themselves have also brought an important infrastructure compared to the rest of the region, with an educational system and health facilities. The areas have developed to become urban enclaves in the sparsely populated and economically underdeveloped Northeastern Province. Researchers are divided on the issue of the economic impact of refugee camps, but the presence of the refugees in the Dadaab area has had both positive and negative effects on the local communities. The refugee camps have stimulated trade, created new jobs and attracted humanitarian aid. However, the refugees have also consumed natural resources such as firewood and water, used the local infrastructure and attracted increased *shifta* activity.

Refugee camps are often seen as temporary settlements (Fig. 3.1), but in many places around the world, they have existed for decades and have become virtual cities (Perouse de Montclos and Kagwanja 2000: 205). In Dadaab, there are signs of urban planning, especially in the two camps

Figure 3.1 *Housing in Hagadera.*

that were set up later, after the initial emergency phase. Ifo, the first camp in the region, consists of seventy-one blocks, which are divided over three main sections, whereas Dagahaley is neatly cut into eight lines and three cross-cutting avenues. Hagadera consists of two big compact groups. The first is divided into eight sections and three cross-cutting avenues and the second divided into three sections and one cross-cutting avenue. All sections and blocks have section- and blockleaders, who are elected to function as brokers between the refugees and the agencies. According to Wilson (1992: 232), it is normal for authorities and relief agencies to require refugees in camps to organise in artificial structures to facilitate communication with the community. These official leaders are not necessarily the people who have traditionally functioned as leaders, and occupy quite visible and highly politicised positions. Besides these elected leaders, elders play an important role within their clan structures, and many of the religious leaders also occupy important sociopolitical positions in the camps. Furthermore, a new group of people in relatively powerful positions are those working for the agencies. Due to preference for English or Swahili speakers and gender-sensitive hiring, this group includes a disproportionate number of young people and women.

To a certain extent, the Dadaab camps function according to the prototype refugee camp situation that Harrell-Bond and Voutira (1994) describe. The organisational structure of the camps is mostly top-down, with a hierarchy of authority and a specific division of labour between the different parties. Whereas commonly, host government officials administer a camp, in Kenya this responsibility has been ceded to the UNHCR and NGOs. The UNHCR's primary role is one of supervision and coordination, whereas international agencies, mainly subcontracted by the UNHCR, are in charge of delivering specific services. CARE International is the leading agency in the region and operates in the fields of community services, education, water and sanitation and logistics. Whereas CARE carries out the distribution of food and nonfood items, WFP (World Food Programme) is responsible for providing food. Medical services are provided by MSF (Medicines sans Frontières), while GTZ (Gemeinschaft für Technologische Zusammenarbeit) is concerned with environmental activities like the distribution of firewood and the conservation of the local environment. On the receiving end are the refugees; the direct benefits from any of the activities of the various agencies for the local population are only limited.[1] All parties involved in the organisation of the camps are highly heterogeneous, and it is therefore quite difficult to form a unified and coherent system of communication at the intergroup and intragroup levels (Harrell-Bond and Voutira 1994). The main link that binds the different actors together is the aid itself.

Living in the Dadaab Camps: Insecurities Faced

Refugee camps exist in order to provide refugees with protection and assistance. Yet, they are often situated in areas that are neither safe nor offer a viable livelihood, while the assistance provided is insufficient and declines over time. This section describes the main economic and physical insecurities that the Somali refugees in Dadaab have to deal with. The survival of 135,000 refugees in Dadaab region is currently only possible because of regular food distributions, but the rations by themselves are insufficient. Some alternative livelihood opportunities are provided by the activities of the refugee regime, while others are sought independently. But when a refugee is not able to invest sufficient capital in income-generating activities, the activities that they can engage in offer only minimal returns and may not be safe. The security situation in and around the camps is generally problematic, with instances of rape, armed attacks, clan conflicts and personal intimidation occurring quite regularly.

Economic Insecurity

Living in the Dadaab refugee camps, Somali refugees find themselves without freedom of movement, with few economic or educational opportunities and with almost no prospect of a timely solution to their problems

(Crisp 1999b). Whereas international assistance is focused on care for the refugees, far less attention is paid to providing them with opportunities to become self-sufficient. On the one hand, this approach is related to the fact that the Kenyan government assumes that the refugees will eventually go back to their own countries. Regardless of their location and length of stay in countries of asylum, refugees in Africa are treated as temporary guests (Kibreab 1999: 399). Thus, the government of Kenya also prefers to see the refugees confined in camps and penalises any initiative by refugees to invest or settle outside the camps (Perouse de Montclos and Kagwanja 2000: 220). The fact that they are not integrated into the local economy in terms of benefits or obligations substantially limits their options as regards securing a livelihood, since success with livelihood strategies requires refugee access to markets and resources (Wilson 1992: 230). Policies or local political factors that limit refugee integration therefore threaten refugee well-being.

On the other hand, the 'handout approach' is related to the bureaucratic division between those organisations and institutes dealing with humanitarian assistance and those dealing with development aid. The institutional, financial and conceptual distinctions between the UNHCR and the UNDP (United Nations Development Programme), replicated in many of the UN member states, served to separate development issues from refugee assistance. The consequences of this bureaucratic division are felt in most refugee-hosting situations and, for decades, attempts have been made to bridge the gap in order to approach humanitarian assistance from a developmental perspective, so far with quite limited results (see Crisp 2001). In Dadaab, it has led to 'temporary and technical fixes' that have only provided short-term and inadequate answers to the real need for investment, infrastructure, education and training and long-term income-generating opportunities for the area (CASA Consulting 2001: 289). As a result, economic opportunities are scarce and in high demand in the region, not only amongst the refugees but also amongst the local population. Although views on costs versus benefits of refugee camps differ greatly, it is certainly true that the establishment of refugee camps often breathes new life and dynamism into the regional economies of a refugee-hosting area (Kibreab 1993: 340). In the case of Dadaab, the camps attract local Somalis who are looking for rations, jobs, trade and small-scale business openings. Thus, the refugees have to share available opportunities with locals, who at times have more advantages due to their higher (certified) level of education and English skills.

Due to the scarce economic opportunities in the region, combined with policies of care and maintenance rather than self-sufficiency, the refugees in Dadaab have, from 1991 until now, largely been dependent on rations provided by the international community. According to Verdirame (1999: 67), the institutions that force the refugees to depend on rations are obliged to ensure the distribution of sufficient food. However, this is far from the reality in the camps. In 1994, when a large number of Kenyan refugee camps were closed down and Dadaab experienced an influx of refugees from these camps, the following items were distributed per person every fifteen days: 6.75 kg cereal, 450 g pulses, 300 g sugar, 375 g oil, 75 g salt and 750 g cereal-soya blend (CARE 1995: 7). This is a quite common diet for African refugees, who in general only receive cereal and somewhat erratic supplies of pulses and a fat source (Wilson 1992: 227). Nevertheless, this diet is insufficient not only in terms of calories but also in terms of micronutrient content. Besides these nutritional objections, the handouts do not provide any variety and also do not correspond to Somali food preferences. The direct delivery of food aid to recipients, which is the model for assistance in refugee camps, is rarely sufficient and often inappropriate for tackling people's needs (Dreze and Sen 1989).

Another threat to the diet is the policy that full rations are only needed during the emergency phase, which WFP presumes to last no longer than two years. This is purportedly to encourage self-reliance and avoid dependency on aid, neglecting the reality of life in Dadaab, where it is impossible for most to supplement their incomes by keeping animals or growing food (Verdirame 1999: 68). Others relate the change in kind, quantity and quality of food aid to 'donor fatigue' (see e.g. Kibreab 1993). Whatever the reasons, the reductions in rations seriously affect the livelihoods of refugees in the camps. In 1991, Nadar Moxamuud, whose husband had died of shock after *shifta* looted their livestock, arrived in the El Wak camps of Mandera district. She described to me how, initially, life in the camps was better than the nomadic life she used to live: 'When we arrived, they took our pictures and presented us to the agencies. When those agencies saw that we were suffering, they came to give us cards for food. One distribution we were given rice; the next time it would be cereals or wheat flour. If we were given greens once, then the next time we would be given beans and porridge. We were receiving the new ration before we had even finished the food we kept at home'.

When I asked Nadar whether the conditions in the El Wak camps were like those in Ifo, she told me: 'There, it was much better. Women were safe in El Wak, and the rations were double the amount we get here. I lived in those camps for one-and-a-half years, before we were taken to Ifo by the agencies. We were not expecting this place, because El Wak was so much better. We even used to get milk and meat at times. Ifo was a hard place to us'. In fact, the situation only deteriorated from the time Nadar arrived in the Dadaab camps. In 2000, I witnessed distributions of only three kilograms of maize for months in a row, though the refugees were supposed to get three kilograms of maize, three kilograms of wheat flour and a cup of oil. And even these full rations only lasted for approximately ten days rather than the fifteen days it was supposed to last; providing for 65–70 percent of a family's most basic needs.[2] The refugees are forced to sell a portion of the food distributed to them in order to purchase the items that they lack. They spend a great deal of time and effort seeking ways to diversify their diet, in search for greens, animal protein and condiments to accompany the starchy staple (Wilson 1992: 227). But they also need to exchange part of their food rations to obtain nonfood items such as firewood, shelter and clothing. The rations are a necessary condition for survival in Dadaab, but they are certainly not a sufficient condition.

Since it is not easy to survive on the rations provided in Dadaab, other sources of income are in high demand. The presence of the international regime not only secures food distribution, it also provides job opportunities. The activities of NGOs in Dadaab provide more than two thousand jobs, of which 24 go to expatriates and 383 to Kenyans (Perouse de Montclos and Kagwanja 2000: 218).[3] For example, CARE employs more than one thousand refugees, thereby contributing considerable purchasing power to the camps. Refugees are employed in a variety of jobs with different levels of responsibility and work as teachers, loaders, CDWs, nurses, secretaries, school inspectors, cooks, doctors and so on. But whatever the weight of their position, the payment continues to be no more than an incentive, varying between 2,200 and 4,000 shillings a month. 'Incentive' refers to the money paid to refugees employed directly by the UNHCR or by one of its implementing partners in the camps. Such incentives do not correspond to salaries paid to Kenyans for the same job, because it is said that in that case, refugees would require a work permit from the Kenyan authorities (Verdirame 1999: 66).

This situation at times causes frustration, especially when refugees compare their work with that of regularly paid (Kenyan) staff. *Macallin* Hajir Aden was a well respected headmaster in Hagadera, up to the point where he, at times, even acted in practice as education supervisor, although this position had never been designed for refugees. I assumed that such a sign of respect and trust would make a difference to him because it gave him a challenging opportunity to learn and gather experience in a situation where such opportunities were very scarce. By assuming this I may have very naively overlooked the hardships of life in Dadaab. Hajir told me:

> I am currently responsible for well over two hundred people, including the teachers, *askari* [soldier, guard, policeman; in this case guards] and some carpenters, but the 3,700 shillings that I get paid every month by no means reflects the responsibility I have. I do not get any satisfaction from my work, because of my pay and knowing what a Kenyan citizen would earn in this position. My wife is at home waiting for money to buy clothes and food. We do not have children yet, but we are responsible for my wife's family: her mother and a number of her siblings live with us and they do not have any other source of income. So they all live from my meagre earnings.

Although the incentive is small and the number of positions available is quite limited, for the families involved having a job with any of the agencies really makes a difference. Rashid Ibrahim had worked in various positions in the different subsectors of CARE, and therefore knew his way around the refugee regime. He was staying in the camp with his parents and five siblings and explained the relative importance of his income for his family:

> My family depends for about 60 percent on the rations with the other 40 percent being provided by my income. That is 3,200 shillings, but 200 shillings disappear in small contributions here and there. Of the remaining 3,000 shillings, 2,000 go to the family and 1,000 are mine. I use this amount to buy clothes, assist my friends and so on. My mother uses the 2,000 to operate a small business. She has a table in the market from which she sells items. That enables her to recycle the money instead of only spending it on food. She did the same in Liboya, from the extra food we used to receive there.

In a later conversation, Rashid told me that he had built a house and was now trying to make a door for it. The Logistics department had provided him with the iron sheets, and he also found timber through the agencies. This made me realise that an NGO job might not only offer an income, however small, but also provide other benefits to the incentive worker and his family. This may be in terms of direct material benefits, but also in terms of getting the right information or occupying strategic positions (see also Turner 1999).

Since only few incentive jobs are available, the large majority of people cannot benefit from being on an agency's payroll. Nevertheless, most families do have a source of income to supplement the rations, however small it is. But the search for a livelihood is complicated by two factors. First, the Somali refugees are forced into the 'informal sector', because their economic activities are considered 'illegal', given the fact that they are not granted work permits. This reality is contrary to Articles 17 and 18 of the 1951 Convention, which provide that refugees should be allowed to engage in wage-earning employment and in agriculture, industry, handicrafts and commerce. They should also be allowed to establish commercial and industrial companies (Verdirame 1999: 69). Secondly, their location in the Dadaab camps complicates the attempts of the Somali refugees to secure a livelihood. It is common for refugee populations to be concentrated in camps that are located in ecologically marginal areas. This has negative consequences for their welfare because refugees usually rely heavily on natural resources to meet their basic livelihood needs (Wilson 1992: 229–230). In and around the camps, it is difficult for them to find adequate building materials, firewood, gathered food or productive agricultural land. For those who are not employed and do not have the resources to guarantee sufficient investments, life in Dadaab entails gaining an income in the margins.

CARE and other NGOs have tried to promote income-generating activities such as mat- and basket-weaving, soap production and shoe making, but these projects have a rather limited impact. According to Wilson (1992: 232), it is probably more effective to support refugees' own institutions. One way of doing this is through providing small loans and it seems that this has indeed assisted refugees in Dadaab. From August 1997, CARE provided cash and materials for small-scale refugee initiatives that enabled groups of refugees to start up a small business or craft activity. Within the community itself, 'money-go-round' systems exist, mainly among women, which similarly provide an individual with enough money to invest in any income-generating activity. Within a group, every individual woman will, for example, pay one hundred shillings a month, or contribute one kilogram of wheat flour or one cup of oil after every distribution. The collective resources rotate amongst the women so that each individual contributor benefits after a certain period of time and is able to try to make some profit. Some of the income-generating activities that the women undertake are baking bread or sambuusi to sell in the market, or starting a small business. The business competition with local Somalis is intense, however, and many of the refugees have adapted to a market of less well-off customers by selling goods in smaller quantities such as individual packets of detergent and single tea bags and cigarettes (Perouse de Montclos and Kagwanja 2000: 214).

There are also income-generating activities that do not need any form of financial investment at all. Some families send their young daughters to work as maids for others, which earns them about three hundred shillings a month. Bantu women go to fetch water for wealthier Somali families and Bantu men construct houses or pit latrines for the Somali refugees. The Bantu residents in Hagadera at times work as casual labourers, at a distance of ten to fifteen kilometres from the camp. Because of the distance and the fact that the area is only used by the Abdalla and Abdwak subdivisions of the Ogaden, not many Somalis farm there. They may instead be engaged in herding activities for other refugees who own cattle. Every morning very early, large herds of up to two hundred goats are collected and taken out to graze by men or young boys. They are brought back to their owners in the evening, who pay some small monthly fee for the herding services. The returns on this kind of labour are typically low, but the precarious situation of the refugees demands that they engage in these activities (Wilson 1992: 228).

Some women go into the area surrounding the camps to collect firewood for their own consumption or for sale, although this brings very little profit and involves great risks. In Dagahaley, I interviewed Abshiro Siyaad, who used to live as a nomad in the Afmadow region. She now lives in the camp with her six children, ranging from one to fifteen years old. Her husband is often away staying with his relatives in Afmadow. I asked Abshiro whether her husband was able to bring some income when he visited the camps, but Abshiro sounded a bit cynical when she told me:

> My husband often goes to stay with his relatives who keep cattle, in order to drink milk and eat meat. He does not work there, or in the camp and usually cannot bring anything. Last time when he came he did not even bring me a cloth. His close relatives have nothing and are therefore also unable to assist him. If God gives him something, he will bring it for me. If not, what can I say? He will come to produce more children and I will accept the situation. What choice do I have?

I asked Abshiro how she could manage to sustain her family and she pointed to a strong rope that she was weaving from the fibres of an old UNHCR food bag: 'I will use this rope to tie the firewood that I collect in the bush. Besides, I sell half of our "family size seven" rations [food rations for a family of seven members] to buy things that are not provided by the agencies, such as sugar. Moreover, my sister who lives in Ifo has a milking cow, from which at times I can get some milk for my children'.

Physical Insecurity

Besides economic insecurity, Somali refugees in Dadaab face various types of physical insecurity. The underlying reason behind this is that, ultimately, there is no proper legal basis for protecting refugees in Kenya, and they are expected to remain in refugee camps. The refugees lack a clear legal status and do not have identity cards (Crisp 1999b). The UNHCR can issue them with a 'protection letter', which is an A4-sized sheet of photocopy paper with a passport-sized photo of the 'asylum seeker'. In reality, the government has not officially recognised this document and it is essentially devoid of any legal significance (Verdirame 1999: 58). Thus, Kenyan police often treat the letter issued by the UNHCR with complete disregard whenever refugees are found outside the camps. But inside the camps, it seems that human rights are also very difficult to uphold. In his research in Kakuma and Dadaab, Verdirame (1999) found that the camps represented a legal anomaly because they are in practice - albeit certainly not in theory – beyond the scope of national law and subject to an informal legal system established by the agencies that run them. On top of this, within the camps, the refugees are vulnerable to forced repatriation attempts and the UNHCR has already had to intercede several times to prevent a government decision to oust the refugees from Kenyan soil. All of these factors combine with the location of the Dadaab camps in an area that has only recently stopped being under emergency law and that has a long tra-

Figure 3.2 *Women collecting firewood.*

dition of *shifta* activity: both in opposition to the Kenyan government as well as in the form of regular banditry with a criminal motive. Therefore, occurrences of rape, armed attacks by *shifta*, clan conflicts and individual threats are rather common in the Dadaab area.

When a refugee is not in a position to make any financial investment, attempts to acquire an income can be a risky undertaking. By collecting firewood in the bushes around Dadaab (Fig. 3.2), women, and even children, run the risk of encountering *shifta* and being raped. The CDW who introduced me to Nadar Moxamuud informed me that this had also happened to her. When Nadar explained how different Ifo had been from El Wak, I realised that she was referring not only to the rations, but also to the security situation. I found it difficult to bring up the issue, more so since at that point Nadar's responses became very brief. She had told me that she had not expected Ifo to be such a hard place, because when she went to collect firewood in El Wak the situation was peaceful. In Ifo, however, 'if a woman went into the bush she would meet a man with a gun'. I asked her whether she had ever personally experienced this and Nadar said: 'I have faced this problem because I could not buy any sugar for the children. I went into the bush to cut firewood that I would sell so that I was able to buy sugar for my children'. I asked her whether she had been collecting firewood for a long time, and Nadar replied: 'I was not doing it for long. After I was only getting sugar for my children for a short period, those men in the bush got me and I was raped. I cannot go back into the bush because I have experienced those things. I stopped selling firewood, and my children are suffering'. I cautiously asked her: 'So if you do not mind, can you tell me what exactly happened?' Nadar replied: 'I was raped by five men, and they damaged me so much that I was bleeding for three months. My blood was flowing for three months and I did not get the help I needed. I never went back into the bush'. I decided to leave the topic at that though, of course, I could have asked a lot more questions. Nadar seemed highly uncomfortable and reluctant to talk about the experience.

It is difficult to get a good idea of the exact nature and magnitude of rape and other forms of gender-based violence in and around the camps. Incidents are very often not reported because of stigmatisation and shame, and because women do not feel safe enough to report them. Many women have been threatened by their assailants and told that if they report or divulge information about the incident or the identity of the assailant, he will come after them again. The police are often seen as part of the problem, rather than the solution: 'police inaction or complicity with bandits and rapists has been cited by refugee women as a main reason for not wanting to report to the police' (CASA Consulting 2001: 254). Ubax Abdi once confessed to me that at times she advises the rape victims whom she counsels not to report the case to the police. She explained her reasons as follows:

> There is a woman who recently identified one of the six men who raped her in December last year. She just saw him in the Hagadera market, and reported this to the police. The man was caught and brought to Garissa, but that same evening, the other men who had raped the woman were seen looking for her in the camp. And five days later, the man who was caught was already back in Hagadera. Now, the woman sleeps in a different block every night, away from her husband and children.

In this climate of fear, it is very problematic for all parties involved to take action in order to reduce rape occurrences. Crisp (1999b) explains that bringing suspects to trial, especially in cases of sexual violence, is problematic due to a number of factors: there are no effective witness protection arrangements, people fear revenge attacks and the victims of rape are ashamed of what they have gone through. As Affi (1997: 444) notes: 'Unfortunately, the stigma of making a claim based on rape or sexual abuse in Somali society is so great that few Somali women have done so, although some would no doubt qualify'.

Rape is a common experience for refugee women in camps, which often provide them with little protection. In Dadaab, measures were taken through the 'Firewood Project', carried out by GTZ and funded by the U.S. government (Fig. 3.3). It entailed regular firewood distributions with the main goal of diminishing rape during firewood collection while at the

Figure 3.3 *The Firewood Project.*

same time reducing environmental degradation and local conflicts. A recent evaluation found that there was no clear evidence that rape occurred less as a consequence of the project (CASA Consulting 2001). Firewood collection is only one of the occasions that facilitate rape and while rape numbers related to firewood did go down in periods of distribution, at the same time rape in other areas went up. Rape and other forms of abuse do not only occur outside the camps, carried out by *shifta*. In addition, a lot of the violence experienced is actually inflicted upon refugees by members of their own family and community. Domestic violence, normally involving the physical abuse of women, children and adolescents by adult men, seems to be a common occurrence within the camps, although the exact scale of the problem is unknown (Crisp 1999b). Various researchers have related the increase of domestic violence to the fact that refugee men in camps have largely lost the responsibilities, work, property and status they used to have (see e.g. Schrijvers 1997). A number of these men cannot deal with the frustrations this leads to and take to substance abuse and gender-based violence.

Women are not the only victims of violent attacks in and around the camps. According to Crisp (1999b), the *shifta* that operate in the Dadaab area have four other principal targets: refugees, especially those who have a business or a cash income; aid agency facilities; vehicles travelling in the region; and *qaad* or *miraa* (a narcotic plant) dealers. During my stay in

Dadaab, quite a number of refugees became the victims of armed attacks. When I was in Hagadera at the end of August 1999, for example, a number of incidents occurred within the space of only ten days. First, a refugee businessman who owned a truck that transported maize and wheat between the camps and Garissa was robbed of 60,000 shillings. A few days later an additional 60,000 shillings were stolen, this time from four different people in one block. During a third incident, a large group of *shifta* came into the blocks and the shooting could be heard through the whole of the camp, although they took only little. That whole week, the 'midnight music' was the topic that I heard people talk about wherever I went and many refugees were clearly worried about the increasing banditry in the camps.[4]

When Ubax Abdi came to my temporary home at the CARE compound for her afternoon computer lessons, she was able to tell me more about the four families who had been attacked. She told me: 'Bandits came to the block and took 23,500 shillings from a woman who owns a shop in the market. They also looted from a woman working at the butchery and two other families a total amount of 60,000 shillings. They did not rape anybody and it is only the second time that I have heard of a case where *shifta* attacked the blocks and left without raping a woman'. I asked Ubax how the *shifta* knew that these refugees had so much money. 'They know', she said. 'The bandits live in Dadaab and in the blocks, so they know which refugees are working and where everybody goes to and comes from. The bandits have associates standing near the bus station to be able to recognise exactly who is leaving and who is coming to Dadaab and what those coming to the camps are carrying. If a refugee comes with the bus from Garissa or Nairobi carrying something that might be of interest, he can generally expect "visitors" the same night. If someone receives money from the *xawilaad*, the bandits will soon be at his or her doorstep'.

Then Ubax explained what had happened the previous night, involving the heavy shooting that could be heard throughout the camp:

> Yesterday night, I was very afraid. Although my block is far from where the noise came from, I feared that my relatives or friends would get hurt or that people in the blocks in which I work would be killed. My whole family sat outside last night. This morning, I rushed to the blocks for a social report. I was told that a group of twelve men had entered the camp and had scared people in the blocks from their sleep. A mother, who wanted to protect her son from being mistreated by the *shifta*, was seriously beaten and strangled. She was just an old woman and she has been admitted to hospital because of her injuries. They only took a couple of things: all they found was 8,000 shillings, some mattresses and mats, two UN plastic sheets and a golden necklace.

Listening to Ubax and others talking about the incident, it was clear that everybody had been very afraid. Many had sat outside, some worrying about their own lives and others worrying about the lives of the people under attack. I realised that these kinds of incidents greatly increase the feeling of insecurity that the refugees in the camps already have.

From the previous descriptions, the conclusion could be drawn that physical insecurity stems from a high level of violence in general, affecting every refugee in Dadaab to an equal extent. Yet, there are indications that the attacks are, at times, clan related. Rape can be used as a weapon of war between fighting clans and statistics show that minority groups are affected relatively often (CASA Consulting 2001). Some of the armed attacks in the camps are related to clan conflicts as well, as Rashid Ibrahim explained. He told me of a clan-based conflict that occurred in Hagadera in 1999:

> In February there were clashes between the Sheikhal, who belong to Hawiye, and the Aulihan, who are part of Ogaden. Six young Aulihan boys were killed. Their attackers were difficult to trace because they went into the bush and were able to cross the border in no time. Initially, the Aulihan suspected a subclan of the Ogaden with whom they were not on good terms. However, later on, one of the attackers was found and turned out to be Sheikhal. At that time, I learned what was going on from close by because I went into the Aulihan blocks where the fighting had occurred. They did not suspect me because of my clan links with the Aulihan. I saw how the Aulihan were preparing themselves with clubs and the like to attack the Sheikhal in the camp, even though there were only a few Sheikhal families in Hagadera and these were not the ones who had caused the problem. Still, they were beaten badly. But at the same time, the Sheikhal were feared because they live at the border, close by. The local community could easily come to assist the refugees.

These kinds of clashes have their origin in occurrences in the camp, like fights over grazing and watering rights, or in events that happen in Somalia (Crisp 1999b: 21). Because radio transmitters keep the refugees informed of the latest developments in their home areas, this can easily incite tensions between the refugees in Dadaab. Thus, incidents that occur in Somalia can have an effect on the lives of refugees in Dadaab, further complicating the provision of security to African refugees in regional camps.

Refugee Dependency?

The conclusion that can be drawn from the above is that the Dadaab camps do not naturally provide economic and physical security to the refugees who live there. On the contrary, the camp organisation itself serves to exacerbate feelings of uncertainty and insecurity (Knudsen 1991: 23). These insecurities are partly caused by the fact that the refugees are confined in an area where they remain dependent on international assistance. Some authors have argued that keeping refugees in camps for substantial periods is damaging because it fosters a dependent mentality. This 'refugee dependency syndrome' is characterised by the acceptance of handouts without taking any initiatives to attain self-sufficiency, accompanied by symptoms of excessive and unreasonable demands, frequent complaints, passivity and lethargy. A healthy independence involves the capability to adopt responses that rely on traditional social support systems, coping mechanisms and organisational and technical skills, and that enable the refugee to achieve not only sustainable material well-being but also nonmaterial advancement (Kibreab 1993). When refugees are 'diagnosed' as suffering from the dependency syndrome, on the other hand, this entails their inability to achieve economic self-sufficiency, even in the presence of enabling interventions or opportunities. I will briefly look at some of the theoretical assumptions behind the concept, before examining in greater detail the related images of refugees as 'cunning crooks' or 'vulnerable victims'.

The Refugee Dependency Syndrome Explained

In the literature on the dependency syndrome, various explanations can be found for its existence in reality, or as a concept. Here, I want to discuss three theories that explain the syndrome in terms of the actions or ideas of the refugees themselves; whereas the next section deals with the role of the refugee regime in sustaining dependency. One theory stems from a psychoanalytic perspective that situates the syndrome in the minds of the refugees. There are interesting similarities between the symptoms associated with refugee dependency and the concept of 'learned helplessness' that was developed by Seligman (1975). Seligman describes a cognitive, emotional and motivational disposition that favours the appearance of a passive reaction rather than initiative or the search for a solution to stress and danger. The theory assumes that human beings will refrain from action when they have been exposed to a number of uncontrollable events in their lives, even in situations where their response would prevent a negative outcome (Seligman 1975). Indeed, control over one's life is a basic human need and yet refugees often find themselves in situations that are beyond their control. However, Seligman's theory does not seem to apply to the Somali refugees in Dadaab, as Dahabo's account in the previous chapter may have shown. When trying to explain things beyond human control, the Somali frequently refer to *nasiib*, but this leads to an acceptance of the conditions of life without causing apathy and dependency.

Another perspective on the dependency syndrome stresses the influence of cultural factors on labelling dependent behaviour: people may be expressing other attitudes or socially normative behaviours when they behave in ways *others* label as dependent (Hansen 1991). In many soci-

eties, it is quite normal to expect others to meet the needs of people temporarily unable to provide for themselves. There is a responsibility to take
care of those who cannot take care of themselves in most sociocultural
and religious systems across the world. What this perspective would
imply is that the norms of charity and gift-giving that dominate beliefs
about aid are highly inappropriate and should be replaced by standards
of rights and responsibilities. The provision of assistance to refugees
needs to be understood within the context of the full cultural meaning of
the gift for the recipients (Harrell-Bond et al. 1992). Somalis are often seen
as arrogant refugees by agency staff around the world because they take
assistance for granted or even seem to demand it at times. Yet, it is essential to study the meaning of assistance within the Somali community, in
order to understand behaviour labelled as dependent. Assistance provided by the international community may need to be examined in light of
Somali norms of assistance provision to those in need.

Another theory that can be found in the literature is that the dependency syndrome stems from the instrumental behaviour of refugees; they
do not really suffer from it, but are merely simulating dependency.
Refugees simply try to achieve their own objectives by acting out role
behaviour (Hansen 1991). Kibreab would support this view, finding it
'entirely rational under highly uncertain circumstances to exhibit simulated traits of poverty or dependency in order not to lose rations' (1993:
332). So in fact, this perspective would deny the existence of the syndrome
and rather say the opposite: that refugees are highly capable actors who
utilise the opportunities open to them in the best way possible. The
assumption that refugees undergo fundamental adaptational changes in
response to receiving handouts is an oversimplification, because adaptation is determined not solely by survival functions but also by cultural
values and history (Kibreab 1993). The Somali in Dadaab, who were surviving relatively independently for decades, lost their basis of sustenance
due to war and displacement and became dependent on others for their
survival. But this change did not automatically change a culture of independence into one of dependence. Rather, the majority of refugees try to
survive independently despite the restrictions that their life in the camps
brings about in this respect.

Cunning Crooks?

The line between simulated and real dependency is thin, as is the line
between refugees as agents and refugees as 'cunning crooks' or 'vulnerable victims'. Because they are often in really dependent and vulnerable
positions, refugees need to maximise the assistance possibly available to
them by showing their deservingness, which at times requires exaggera-
tion or simulation. The same actions that can be seen as acts of agency can

easily be interpreted as sheer manipulation or powerless desperation. In fact, the three may largely overlap. But no matter the difficulty of making clear distinctions, the way refugee actions are interpreted by, for example, policy makers or agency staff will ultimately determine the way they are treated. A UNHCR field officer who interprets everything that refugees do as stemming from their cunningness will approach them very differently to an agency staff member who sees all refugees as vulnerable victims of circumstances. Whereas the first person may hardly take the words of any refugee seriously, expecting to be cheated at all times; the second may try to assist a refugee even if it is clear that he or she is not telling the truth or not following the rules of the refugee regime. That is how perceptions make an enormous difference in the lives of refugees.

Although the rations that are distributed in Dadaab are insufficient to sustain the refugees, they do form an essential part of the resources available in the region. Thus, they also constitute an important stake in the refugees' attempts to build a livelihood in the camps. There are various ways by which additional rations can be obtained. First of all, there are refugees who have lived in the camps and went back to Somalia, or moved on to Garissa and Nairobi. Often, they leave their ration card with their relatives in the camps so that these people can consume or trade the additional food. Sometimes, those who move to Garissa arrange for their family members in the camps to send part of the ration to Garissa by bus and keep part for personal consumption. Those who may not have close relatives back in the camps can decide to sell their ration card at the local market. There, refugees can buy a card for prices ranging from five hundred shillings to two hundred dollars (depending on the family size and time remaining until the next revalidation). Similar practices have been found in other refugee camps, for example, in Malawi amongst Mozambican refugees (Callamard 1994). Callamard also mentions that in some households, people who have died are still registered on the ration card, and other families are able to obtain additional rations because their family members are involved in the food distribution process. Yet, it is important to take into account that not all refugees have the same capacity or opportunity to manipulate the advantages of the aid system (Harrell-Bond 1986: 111). Rather, the factors determining this ability should be studied on a case-by-case basis.

Agency staff members are largely aware of the fact that 'card games' are being played in the camps. Duncan Odhiambo, who is a CARE staff member working for Logistics, told me:

> The number of cards in the camps does not coincide with the number of refugees actually living here. At times, we find some people carrying a bunch of cards to the distribution. Many of those cards belong to their relatives outside the camps: people who went to other areas in Kenya or back to Somalia.

Sometimes, they also belong to those who have gone overseas. Besides, there are people who have cards although officially they do not have the right to refugee assistance since they are locals.

Peter Njoroge, who also works in the Logistics Department, explained to me:

> Of the forty-five thousand refugees in Ifo, maybe eleven thousand are Kenyans. I do not have a problem with that, because the government has not been assisting those people. We are here in a semi-arid region, with no opportunities for survival and on top of that there are frequent droughts and famines. Yet, no assistance is provided for the local population. Thus, I really do not mind whether I am feeding Somalis or Kenyans.

Duncan does not completely agree with him, arguing:

> Sure, those people are also in need, but it is not the task of the UNHCR to deal with them. It is not fair to assist Kenyans, because those resources were not meant for them, and are taken from the real needy people. Kenyans should be assisted by NGOs in cooperation with the government of Kenya, as recently happened in Turkana, for example.

A UNHCR field officer in one of the Dadaab camps talked about the buying and selling of ration cards as if it was very common: 'Ration cards can be bought at the local market. This is not a problem, since people may be in need of those cards. As long as the refugees know the details that go with the card they bought, they will be able to keep it'. In my eyes, however, the question should be why people who 'may be in need of those cards' have to buy them. There are many families in the camps who have more than one ration card, which may be a strategy to acquire some additional resources to supplement the insufficient rations. But not all refugees have extra cards totalling more than the actual number of people in their household. It is often the case that a number of family members are not included on the 'genuine' card, for example because they did not arrive at the same time or because they were born after registration in the camp (Harrell-Bond et al. 1992: 216). Others are still waiting to get a card, or have had their card confiscated unjustly by an overly active UN employee during a revalidation exercise. Yet others will have family members who have opted for resettlement or repatriation, for which UNHCR requires them to hand in the ration card, even if some family members remain behind in the camp.

The buying and selling of ration cards does not necessarily imply cunningness on the part of the refugees, but can also be interpreted as a creative response to the rigidity of the refugee regime. Ubax Abdi explained to me what happened when her mother decided to be repatriated to Ethiopia, where she is originally from: 'When my mother left for Ethiopia, she took our "family size eight" ration card with her. She had to take it because the UNHCR did not want to split our card and when someone is repatriated through the UNHCR, he or she has to hand in the card. Thus, we arranged for another family of "family size seven" to join her, so that the card was not lost'. Rashid Ibrahim explained what happened in the case of his own family: 'In Hagadera, we initially did not have enough ration cards because there were six of us when we arrived but later my father joined us from north Somalia, accompanied by my brother and his family. Again, another sister of mine arrived with one child from Ethiopia. We were only given a "family size six" ration card and we later bought the remainder in the market'.

Indeed, the registration bureaucracy is quite slow and displays a high level of suspicion towards the refugees. The problem partly lies in the dispute between UNHCR and WFP over numbers, with WFP alleging that those individuals that UNHCR counts as new arrivals are actually 'recyclers'. Both organisations have different interests, and WFP sets its 'planning numbers', which cannot take into account new arrivals throughout the year (Verdirame 1999: 68). Thus, UNHCR may register them but this does not automatically lead to additional rations. In the end, the refugee community bears the responsibility of feeding them. Bishar Moxamuud came to Ifo from Kismaayo in 1996 and told me how he found the camps to be very basic when he first arrived. I asked him how he managed to adapt and Bishar told me: 'It was possible for me to adapt, because I could do nothing else. I went to the UNHCR gate to get a card and we waited there day after day. But for three years, I did not get a card or rations. They only registered me in August 1999'. I asked Bishar how he was able to survive without a ration card for three years and he replied: 'I was living with Somalis and the Somali help each other. If you go to someone you know he will give you tea. Even though I do not have relatives in Ifo, and my clan is very small here, I was always helped. But I was not going to the same place all the time and besides I am alone. I would go to a certain house one day, and the next day I would go to another house'.

In the 1999 registration of 'new arrivals', in which I participated, Bishar was finally registered. Some of the new arrivals had indeed arrived recently as a consequence of the renewed fighting in Kismaayo from April to July that year. Others, however, like Bishar, had come years before but had never been able to obtain a ration card. A total of about eleven thousand people were registered during the exercise in the three camps. Early 2000, I was talking to Yasiin Hussein, a CDW in Dagahaley, who told me that the registered people were still not entitled to collect food. According to Yasiin:

> There are real problems with the rations at the moment and they surfaced especially from the time that large numbers of people came from Kismaayo some months ago. Imagine a refugee family in the camp with a ration card of 'fami-

ly size four'. All of a sudden, this family would find their relatives fleeing from Kismaayo to Dadaab, living with them on the same ration card. And the new arrivals are not provided with their own cards since the government and UNHCR are still fighting over the issue. Meanwhile, people in the camps suffer really badly. The *baahanay* (needy, destitute) have been taken care of by the community, but for the last couple of months the rations have been seriously reduced. It is no longer possible to assist.

When individuals or families are not assisted through the refugee regime, the Somali community will mostly assist them, as both Somali religion and culture requires people to take care of the needy. But, of course, the aid providers need to be in a position to share, which with the current trend of reduced handouts in Dadaab is becoming increasingly difficult.

It is important to analyse refugee behaviour that might be interpreted as cheating, such as the unendorsed use of ration cards, in order to understand that behaviour. However, as Abukar Hassan commented during a participatory workshop, this should not lead to the conclusion that all refugees cheat:

> This is a very common assumption amongst the agencies working in Dadaab, who do not seem to trust the refugees. It is indeed important to recognise the fact that refugees in Dadaab do have problems. When observing the reality of life in the camp, it is easy to assume that all refugees cheat about everything. The rations are insufficient, so some refugees cheat about their numbers in order to get enough food. Others may want to appear vulnerable so that they will be given additional assistance. But it is essential to distinguish between the genuine cases and the cheaters. Not all refugees cheat!

I agree with Abukar that, in general, there is a great level of suspicion amongst UN and NGO staff towards the refugees. The direct system of aid delivery in refugee camps implies stratified control, which generates an atmosphere of distrust between the different parties. Besides, those who have worked with refugees for a long time run the risk of becoming cynical. They repeatedly hear the same stories and discover 'falsehoods' on a number of occasions.

Yet, this again should not lead to the conclusion that all agency staff distrust refugees. In the course of my fieldwork, I slowly learned that it is also important to distinguish between agency staff members who do believe that all refugees cheat, and those who do not. Initially, I only noticed the rather negative ideas on refugees of those working within the aid regime. A UNHCR field officer in one of the Dadaab camps represents an extreme case.

> The best thing that the international community can do to the Somali, is to stop giving assistance. They are very capable of assisting themselves and have just become refugees out of profession. Somalis are very cunning and will try, try

and try again. I have worked with them for a long time and I am fed up with their manipulations. I have faced cases where a child even does not know the name of his alleged father, or where a girl who is said to be a recent arrival opens her mouth and says '*mimi?*'.[5] In order to perform well in one's job, it is necessary after some time to stop working with the Somali, or even with refugees in general.

Moxamed Suleiman, whom I interviewed at UNHCR Nairobi, gave me many examples of colleagues who had become equally cynical about their job. But he also told me that even those who were just starting their career with UNHCR may already have a very negative attitude towards the refugees.

Those who come straight from university and start working as lawyers in the UNHCR office, without ever having done emergency work, are likely not to regard refugees as human beings. The only thing they think about when hearing people's stories, is 'you cheat here, you lie there'. But even if a refugee does cheat, it is important to understand what made him or her do it, instead of being personally offended. I always try to find out the reason behind the lie and have learned that it is often the system that makes people act in certain ways. We can understand so much more by simply talking to refugees. It is amazing how open and honest some refugees are about why they cheat. Thus, it becomes much easier to understand them, and realise that nothing is ever black and white.

When I talked to a staff member of the Joint Voluntary Agencies (JVA) in Nairobi about these issues, I realised how difficult it might be for those working with refugees to deal with the many layers of truth their work entails. She told me the following.

All refugees will try to take the opportunities that are there and we would do the same in their position. The Somali, however, are experts. I have never seen refugees manipulating the system as ingeniously as they do. Their stories leave you completely confused and they never match. We just try to check their truthfulness and, throughout the years, we have gained quite a lot of experience on that as well as having good and up-to-date information available to us. But, in fact, I would prefer for someone to get through the system who should not have, rather than someone failing who deserves to be assisted. Not all refugees cheat and in the end it may be to their own disadvantage. I have come across instances in which the applicant had a very convincing and deserving story, but when he was asked whether he had applied before, he was frank and said yes. I had to turn the request down.

Vulnerable Victims?

In the camps, food and other resources are distributed equally and the principal value of being labelled as a refugee is to have access to these handouts. But this homogenising label leads to the development of additional and more precisely defined categories (Zetter 1991: 49). Compartmentalising the refugees into these categories is a bureaucratic way of fulfilling a set of managerial objectives. Aid is seen in terms of charity and it should go to the most deserving. Desert or merit is therefore construed in terms of absolute destitution on the part of the recipient (Harrell-Bond et al. 1992: 207). Since it is bureaucratically complicated to determine the level of destitution of every individual refugee, categories are used to identify groups of people likely to be most destitute. These change over time according to the priorities of donors. By 1990, for example, a growing sensitivity existed within the donor community regarding the issue of unequal opportunities afforded to women in refugee assistance programmes (Ager et al. 1995: 266). As a result, specific groups of women, such as widows or single mothers, were included in special programmes for 'the vulnerable'. But the disadvantage of the selective, group-based allocation of resources is that it leads to a rather problematic commoditisation of NGO-defined categories. The response of some, mostly 'more able', refugees has been to simulate vulnerability in order to qualify for certain benefits. At the same time, these programmes hardly take the community-based forms of assistance operating in Dadaab into account.

In most refugee camps nowadays, UNHCR and its implementing partners have various programmes to promote women's livelihood possibilities and their influence on decision making (Turner 1999). This is certainly also the case in Dadaab, where there are general attempts to improve 'gender awareness' as well as more specific programmes to assist the most vulnerable, including women. The main categories of vulnerable people that have been identified are: widows, divorcees, orphans, rape cases, needy cases and the disabled. Within the CARE Community Services sector, there is a department called 'Vulnerable Women and Children' (VWC), which deals with various issues related to the vulnerability of these specific groups. According to its coordinator, the programme exists because

> all refugees are vulnerables. They have lost everything: the townspeople left behind their houses and possessions, the nomads lost their livestock, and all refugees lost their dignity and pride as human beings. As a consequence of their circumstances, refugees are vulnerable. But then, within the refugee community, there are some who are more vulnerable than others. Those are the people that VWC assists, in order to enable them to assist themselves.

The VWC department deals with a combination of physical and economic insecurities, especially since, as Nadar's account has shown, the two are intrinsically linked. The various programme elements provide counselling for rape victims, additional handouts of food and nonfood items for the most needy, training and income-generating opportunities. A database has been developed of all vulnerable people, who are identified by VWC with the assistance of the CDWs. The VWC Coordinator then personally visits every individual in order to conduct an interview and observe her or his situation. On top of that, those identified can visit the VWC office in the event of specific problems and a number of them have been coming to the office for years, on a frequent basis. In 1999, the opportunity arose to extend the scope of the programme when UNHCR received funding from the Ted Turner Fund. The allocation to Dadaab camps was specifically for prevention and response to sexual violence. It was decided that the best way to reach this goal was by providing the women with loans in order to carry out income-generating activities. Some of the business activities the women are engaged in are selling cereals, firewood or milk, running teashops and weaving baskets or mats.

During one of the initial meetings held with a first group of 'vulnerable women' selected to benefit from the Ted Turner Fund, I became very aware of the politicised nature of categories that compartmentalise refugees in order to provide them with assistance. A group of about one hundred women were being addressed by representatives of the various agencies that were involved in the implementation of the project. After they explained the purpose and content of the project, the women were invited to pose questions. One woman stood up and asked a question in Somali. Even before her words were translated, Raxmo Abdulahi, a CDW who was at the same time a women's leader, told her to be silent and give Adoy Hassan the opportunity to speak. And Adoy, who is one of the senior women's leaders in Hagadera, started speaking. The translator informed us that she had two comments and one question, when Carol Kavagi of Community Services interrupted and said: 'There are two groups of women here: those who will benefit from the project, the vulnerable women, and the women's leaders who represent the women in all manner of situations. Though I welcome the last group today, we have organised this meeting particularly for the vulnerable women. So let us listen to them now'.

Very soon after, Raxmo walked out of the meeting. However, she returned rapidly in order to chase all the women out of the hall, screaming 'Go, move, get out!'. She expected them to obey, yelling 'I am your leader', but when some of the women did not respond to her order, she even used force, pulling some of them out of the building. Later, when most of the women were indeed outside, I witnessed how she slapped the woman who had tried to ask a question in the meeting. The woman fought back and bit Raxmo. What seemed to be at stake was a challenge to existing power structures, both by the agencies as well as by some of the women. Some of those who remained in the hall were women I had met before in the blocks who had no relatives and were rather isolated within the community. They were not assisted and lived in the worst conditions, so there was not much they risked losing by not obeying the women's leaders. Others who remained were Somali Bantu women, who are less affected by challenges to Somali leadership, living rather separate in their own communities with their own leadership structure. The incident made me more aware of the complications of trying to target the most vulnerable and the delicate position the agencies are often in when dealing with community leaders.

I was also interested in projects that targeted 'the vulnerable' because I object to the explicit use of the term – inviting refugees to see or at least present themselves merely as 'vulnerable'. Such an approach goes directly against my own focus on human agency, as I realised during an appraisal session for the Ted Turner group loans that I attended. In order to screen the women as regards their eligibility for a loan, they were literally asked 'What is your vulnerability?' which was mostly translated as *Dhibkaaga waa maxaa?* – 'What is your problem?' When the woman was not sure what to answer to this rather broad question, she would be assisted with some examples: are you a widow, a divorcee, disabled? Again, translation could cause confusion, because the Somali word that was used, *garoob*, means both widow and divorcee. If the word was translated as, for example, widow, this caused the appraiser to be suspicious, since his forms indicated that the woman was a divorcee. There was a lot of distrust towards the women and at times, I found they were approached rather rudely. When a woman said that she was abandoned because her husband had left her six months ago and she had not heard from him since, the appraiser bluntly told her that six months was not exceptional and the husband might even be back by the next day. I found the whole approach of forcing people to argue their vulnerability, and thus eligibility for assistance, rather degrading.

The above does not prevent me from seeing the importance of providing additional assistance to those in disadvantaged positions. I agree with Kibreab (1993: 347) that there are people who need the assistance of the international refugee support systems, since they are (temporarily) not capable of living an independent life and their community is not in a position to meet their needs. This group is relatively overrepresented in refugee camps precisely because of the kind of assistance that is provided there. At times, they have been placed in the care of the international community in the camps by relatives who are not able to take care of them (see also Harrell-Bond 1986), or who send them occasional remittances from regional towns. When a refugee who is, for example, chronically ill or too old to take care of himself or herself, stays in the camps without relatives, the handouts provided or the remittances sent are essential for his or her survival but will not lead to self-sufficiency. But the question remains of who the most vulnerable are, how to identify them and how to make sure that they are indeed the people who benefit from special programmes.

When I asked Adoy Moxamed, who was working for VWC in Ifo, to specify who, according to her, were the most vulnerable people they were assisting in her department, she told me:

> Many of them belong to minority clans and most are nomads. There is a large number in block A11, for example, who are Galaajo. They are Hawiye who lived in Lower Juba region and were robbed of all their possessions when the war started. When they lost their animals, they lost their way of life: they had never done anything else. Many are widows, many of them have undergone rape, and some are still facing psychological problems. They are depressed and feel despised and useless in their own community. They need a lot of counselling but, in fact, there is not much we can do since CARE has no resources. The UNHCR has hardly ever assisted someone we referred to them for resettlement. In reality, you need power, connections or money. In that system, the real vulnerables will always lose out since, by definition, they do not have any of the three.

Adoy's description highlights many elements of vulnerability. The group she mentions has lost all economic as well as social resources and suffers from psychological problems. She tells me that some of the women do not even leave their house and they never come to the agencies except in order to collect their rations. Thus, they do not know anything about what could be available to them. This stands in sharp contrast to those who have the 'power, connections or money' to know what assistance can be obtained and what are the conditions for acquiring it. The argument that assistance should be targeted on the poorest is unlikely to be controversial, but the major question is of how aid can be differentially distributed to make sure that those most in need are given priority (Harrell-Bond 1986). Similar to the situation in Dadaab, Harrell-Bond has found that agencies dealing with Ugandan refugees relied on conventional definitions of the vulnerable, like the physically disabled, elderly, widows and orphans. According to her, these general categories are not very satisfactory because the real disadvantages that refugees face are determined by individual circumstances. The characteristics that, according to her, clearly distinguish the vulnerable are: a low physical mobility, a lack of even the most basic economic assets and the absence of relatives near enough to offer support (Harrell-Bond 1986). This list would be very applicable to the case of the Somali in Dadaab, since it closely matches the 'nomadic heritage' that I argue still offers security in the camps. Only the idea that relatives must be living within a certain distance in order to offer support to refugees in camps may not be accurate, because in the Somali case, support reaches the camps from as far away as the U.S.A. or Australia.

Abukar Hassan commented on the problematic nature of existing definitions of vulnerability during a participatory workshop:

> The agencies are more on the women's side, with programmes for vulnerable women and the like. This enhances their chances but it is not fair considering the fact that there are also vulnerable men in the camps. I know an elderly man whose wife died and who is now taking care of four young children since he does not have relatives who could assist him. He is the one who has to fetch water, stand in line for rations and get firewood in order to cook for them, despite being old and sick. No one can assist in his case, simply because he is a man. But that does not seem fair because he never chose to be a man.

I informed Abukar about Turner's (1999) study, which addresses similar issues, and we discussed the problems related to determining who the real needy are. In my opinion, fixed categories of 'vulnerable people' can never determine the precise vulnerability of an individual refugee. A solution would be a far more case-based approach, though current bureaucratic systems clearly prefer approaches based on categories of people. Deciding which individuals require special assistance is difficult and frustrating, especially considering the limited resources available. But generalised approaches may not be fair either and can cause a lot of frustration amongst those who do not fall within a target group as well as amongst the aid distributors.

Community-based Forms of Assistance

While NGO programmes that aim to assist the vulnerable members of the community are important, at the same time many such initiatives exist within the Somali community. During food distributions there are collections amongst members of the same clan. Rashid Ibrahim explained to me that his 'uncle' (of six generations back) is a member of the committee within his clan that collects the rations:

> 'After every distribution, there will be a kind of *zakat* amongst our clan. During these collections, the committee will receive one or two kilograms of maize or wheat per family. It is most likely that the families with a ration card of "family size ten" give something, since they get more food. Besides, in a family of ten, chances are higher that at least one of them is earning an income. The food is collected to give to needy families, but it can also be sold and the money kept for special cases'.

The clan contributions that Rashid describes here are based on *qaaraan*, a practice that is widely known amongst Somalis. *Qaaraan* is a Somali word that can be described as 'the collection of money or livestock for the needy'

(Zorc and Osman 1993). Madimba Musa informed me that *qaaraan* stems from the Arabic word *gharaama*, literally meaning 'shared expenses'. Collections are held to which people are expected to contribute, at times to assist the needy periodically, and at others to assist those in need of assistance due to a contingency. Rashid gave another example: 'The money is also kept as part of the *xeer*, which is agreed upon by families within the larger clan. We usually deal with disputes through customary law and this involves compensational payments. These payments are usually too much money for the family to pay, so the clan members will be asked to contribute'.

Another community-based form of assistance I found to be common in Dadaab was *ayuuto*, which in Italian means 'help'. According to Madimba and others, the system it describes was originally known in Somalia as *shaloongo*, which is a Bantu word. The settled farmers, who were mainly Somali Bantu, were the first to exercise *shaloongo*. They used a savings and loan system within a group of people, whereby each person would periodically contribute a certain amount in money or kind, with one person receiving the total amount each time. Soon, the principle became popular amongst city dwellers, who called it *ayuuto*. The reason for its popularity was the unreliable banking system in Somalia; *ayuuto* functioned as an alternative form of saving. It was mainly practised amongst women, as many of the money-go-round systems around the world commonly are (Ardener and Burman 1995). Muslima Abdille, a Somali Bantu woman who worked as a CDW for CARE, told me how she engaged in the system with three other woman. After every distribution, they would contribute one kilogram of maize flour and one cup of oil: 'Every time, someone else gets those communal resources. I sell the flour and oil at the market and I try to make some more profit with that money. I usually buy material for making mats and baskets. When I come home from work, I tell the children to cook dinner. Then, I work for half an hour on a mat and half an hour on a basket'. By pooling their resources and then investing them wisely, these women were thus able to supplement the rations.

Whereas I originally assumed that amongst Somalis, assistance was mainly provided between relatives and clan members, I slowly learned that neighbours also played an important role. Adoy Moxamed told me that the Somali have a general culture of assistance: 'If your neighbour does not have anything, you should yourself not eat. If you put sugar in your tea and your neighbour does not even have anything to cook tea from, you will have to share. That is the Somali culture'. According to Adoy, those who are able simply have the cultural and religious responsibility to assist those who have less: 'The Qoran says that if someone who lives close to you suffers, he or she should be assisted before you assist a relative who is far away'. I asked her how she experienced this personally, given the fact that everybody in her block was aware of the fact that she worked for CARE. Did many people come to her for assistance? Adoy said that this was indeed the case and if one of her neighbours asked her for sugar and she had some she could not refuse. She added:

> In my block, there are three incentive workers: there is a woman who works as a Community Health Worker (CHW) Coordinator for MSF, one who works as a teacher, and myself. We pool our resources together and then decide to whom to give the money. Every month we identify three families in our block to assist. During the recent *ciid*, when it is common to contribute to people with problems, we came together to discuss what to do. We identified five of the most vulnerable families and bought them clothes for the children. That is our obligation as Muslims.

My next question to Adoy was whether everybody in the camp fulfils that obligation, given the fact that there are some people in the camps who are clearly wealthy as opposed to others who have absolutely nothing. Adoy told me that people are different and not everybody fulfils the obligation of giving to those who do not have anything:

> In my block, there is a woman who is quite wealthy since she has a son as well as some other relatives who live overseas. She receives remittances every month, but she does not assist anybody with that money. It is just like in Christianity: some people follow the religion, whereas others do not. But the *sheikhs* do warn the people to follow their religion, and they also set the example. I heard that last Friday there was a man from Garissa who prayed in the mosque in Ifo. He ended up in the camps with no money to continue his travel and no relatives in Dadaab, but he received the money to buy a bus ticket from the religious men in the mosque.

A number of refugees contrasted these various forms of assistance within the Somali community with the aid provided by UNHCR. During a women's group discussion in Ifo, Ebla Awas commented on the assistance that one might expect from neighbours or family members in the camps: 'The difference is that your neighbours and relatives live with you day in, day out and know what you have. They know your situation and they know your problems. The UNHCR does not stay in the blocks, so they do not know our problems'.

A Harmful Concept

The concept of the dependency syndrome is problematic for a number of reasons. First, blaming the refugees harms the relationship between refugees and agency staff. If those who work with refugees believe that the refugees are in part to blame for their lack of self-reliance, commitment to refugee participation in programming can be undermined. This may lead to a situation in which refugees are powerless and not allowed to make choices, despite a policy on paper of restoring refugees' agency. Also, NGO employees who believe in the existence of such a syndrome disregard the vulnerable position of a number of refugees, especially those who have to survive without economic or social capital. These employees diagnose the problem to be in the head of the refugees instead of in the structural position in which some refugees find themselves. Besides, it is neither fair nor helpful to blame refugees for not attaining independent livelihoods, when they were never given any options to attain that independence. If the camp environment is unfavourable, the goal of self-sufficiency can remain remote and unattainable, no matter how committed the refugees might be to principles of independence and self-sufficiency (Kibreab 1993: 332). This is certainly also the case in Dadaab, where livelihood options are extremely limited.

Secondly, the term 'refugee dependency syndrome' is damaging because it implies that refugees' thinking and behaviour is maladaptive, which disregards the existing community-based initiatives to deal with insecurity in the camps. Besides, the actions and thoughts of refugees that may indicate vulnerability might also be viewed as rational and adaptive, considering a system that rewards dependency. The concept leads to a wrong diagnosis of the cause of the problem and thus to wrongly directed aid projects: instead of seeking a solution for sustained dependency on international assistance in refugee camps at the level of the refugees, we should look for ways to change the system (Harrell-Bond 1986). Why is it that the refugee regime has been unable to provide the large majority of refugees with durable solutions? Why are most refugees kept in camps for considerable periods of time, when the belief exists that camps cause dependency? Why have policies that were deemed unsuccessful for decades still not been replaced by more efficient ones? Though I do not want to imply that I have a simple answer to these major questions that others have posed before, I do believe it is essential to analyse the role of the refugee regime in order to acquire a better understanding of why humanitarian aid programmes for refugees in developing countries have largely been unable to provide security.

The Role of the Refugee Regime

Life in Dadaab is shaped by the fact that the refugees 'inhabit an institutionalised world of NGOs, intergovernmental agencies and governments' (Zetter 1991: 40). Although the combined task of these institutions is to provide security to refugees, it is clear that the Somali do face various economic and physical insecurities in and around the camps. Besides, they are still highly dependent on external aid even after having stayed in Dadaab for over ten years. This can partly be explained by examining the past and present situation of the refugee regime itself. The relationships between the governments, implementing agencies and donors that constitute the regime are highly complex and often problematic. Harrell-Bond (1996: 54) poses a relevant question in this respect, wondering whether 'the combination of the political interests of states, the competition within the refugee regime for funds, together with the demands of donors, may have converged leading to a situation in which the bureaucratic and political interests of humanitarian agencies and states have unintentionally taken precedence over the interest of refugees'. This section describes the nature of the interests of these different parties as well as their interactions within the refugee regime; so as to understand how this may affect the security and independence of life in refugee camps like Dadaab.

The UNHCR: A Compromised Position

In order to put present-day complications of providing security to refugees in perspective, it is important to look at the conditions under which the refugee regime came into being. Although involuntary migration has taken place throughout history, refugees have existed only since the twentieth century. With the rise of states in Europe, and the conflicts this involved, passports and visa requirements became an instrument to restrict the entrance of noncitizens. Thus, it may be said that the root of the refugee problem is, in fact, restricted immigration (Skran 1992). This meant that people who were fleeing their home country for whatever reason, now had difficulties re-establishing themselves. After the Russian Revolution, European states tried to prevent these problems through the League of Nations. The Russian refugees were provided with the Nansen passport, which permitted free movement. The emerging international refugee regime operated within a highly politicised context, in which governments supported refugee assistance programs for security and foreign policy reasons as much as humanitarian ones (Loescher 1993: 39).

Then, in the aftermath of the dislocations caused by the First and Second World Wars, governments recognised that their power to control international population movements was limited and that the global refugee problem far outstripped their individual capacities to manage. Thus, measures were taken mainly to serve the interests of governments and to facilitate both burden sharing and the coordination of policies regarding the treatment of refugees. When the world community set up the UNHCR in 1951, it was given little authority and even fewer resources (Hathaway 1995: 290–91). The UNHCR initially was intended as a temporary body with a three-year life span, supplied with resources for administrative costs only. But the political upheavals in Eastern Europe that followed added to the numbers of refugees. During this Cold War period, the eastern Europeans were seen as a welcome confirmation of the failures of the communist system (Harrell-Bond 1996). Thus, reasons for the continued existence of a refugee regime were mainly political again.

At that time, refugees were believed to be a European problem although, of course, the problems were not restricted to Europe alone. Others were a consequence of European action, against which anticolonial struggles followed. With some reluctance, the refugee definition was extended to include the people who fled these upheavals, although they were expected to return to their country, unlike the 'victims of communism' in Europe. The 1967 Protocol removed the time- and place limitations of the Convention, which was meant to be applicable only for pre-1951 events within Europe. Yet, in practice, the refugee definition remained Eurocentric and Western states were determining the agenda. Despite objections, especially from developing countries and socialist states, the Protocol still only acknowledged civil-political rights, leaving the condition of individual persecution on specific, civil-political grounds intact. Natural disasters and civil or internal war were not added, even though in the South, these factors cause far greater numbers of people to flee than individual persecution. Furthermore, socio-economic reasons were still excluded, whereas such motives are easily presumed and very difficult to disprove when someone moves from the South to the North (Hathaway 1991: note 52). As such, though regional restrictions were formally lifted, the refugee definition still entailed a de facto exclusion of large groups of forced migrants, mainly from developing countries.

African states responded by developing a more inclusive, regional agreement through the OAU in 1969. This agreement accepts the Geneva Convention definition and obliges states also to provide protection to those who are forced to flee abuse as a result of a loss of authority by the government due to external factors. This refers to the need to look at a claim from the perspective of the de facto rather than formal authority structure in the country of origin (Hathaway 1991: 17). Furthermore, the agreement provides for group determination and acknowledges the need for protection of those who flee in circumstances of general danger; thus including victims of any manmade or natural disaster. Finally, it acknowledges that the basis of harm may be indeterminate, thus not demanding that the applicant demonstrate individual or group motives justifying flight. As long as the general conditions in the country of origin are gravely disrupted, it is up to the individual to decide whether he or she wants to seek refuge elsewhere. Finding it difficult to fulfil its mandate in Africa using the individualist 1951 definition, UNHCR activities are largely based on the OAU agreement.

Thus, a clear distinction was created between refugee admission policies in Western states and protection in the region; even though this protection was largely funded by the same states. Levels of assistance and protection likewise greatly differed. In the 1980s and 1990s, new developments were taking place that confronted Western states with refugees from Africa and other developing areas. Although the causes of forced migrations were similar to those at the beginning of the century, technological developments intensified their results. All over the world, ongoing conflicts and wars produced increasing numbers of refugees. The West was faced with more and more refugees from non-Western countries because of developments in transportation technologies, even though the vast majority of refugees remained in developing countries. Throughout the 1980s, the policies of the international refugee regime came under attack and since that time, UNHCR has faced increasing difficulties in funding and maintaining its services (Harrell-Bond 1996: 56). Western countries are attempting to close their borders and use the refugee regime to contain refugees in developing countries. The UNHCR is increasingly asked to bear more responsibility and leadership, but this development is being accompanied by a reduction in funds.

The refugee regime rapidly became overwhelmed by the unprecedented refugee crises and was ill equipped to address either the causes or consequences of the problems (Loescher 1993: 129). However, its current limitations can largely be ascribed to the initial intentions with which the regime was created. The problems are due in part to the constraints placed on it by the founders, who conceptualised refugee assistance as a temporary project (Skran 1992: 18). In addition, these founders were not ready to give the UNHCR any real power. The most significant institutional weakness of the UNHCR is its dependence on voluntary support and contributions to carry out its programmes. It has to seek the support of states in order to guarantee asylum, for it has no shelter of its own in which to provide protection to refugees (Hathaway 1995). Furthermore, it has to petition its wealthier member states to donate funds each year, which creates a dependency on a small number of developed states. Less than 5 percent of the UNHCR's budget is covered by the UN regular budget, while the rest comes from voluntary contributions, mainly from national governments (Loescher 1993: 131).

But the problem of voluntary contributions is not merely economic. It is also related to the contradictory role the UNHCR plays in refugee affairs today: it must confront states on politically sensitive protection issues while, at the same time, asking them to contribute to its budgets and to permit aid programs to operate within their territories. The UNHCR's dependence on voluntary contributions forces it to adopt policies that reflect the interests and priorities of the major donor countries. Politics and foreign policy priorities cause donor governments to favour some refugee groups rather than others as demonstrated, for example, by comparing the budget available in Kakuma with that of Dadaab. Whereas there is considerable funding for a wide variety of projects in Kakuma, Dadaab faces budget cuts and severe financial constraints to its programming every year. According to refugees as well as staff members in Dadaab, this difference is not in any way related to a discrepancy in the level of needs in the respective camps, but rather reflects a religious bias. Whereas Kakuma largely hosts Sudanese, of whom many are Christians fleeing an Islamic regime, Somalis are almost all Muslims. At times, UNHCR is critical of its donor states, but this is often met with threats to cut funding (Loescher 1993: 138). In the last decade, Western governments have continued to override UNHCR protests and disregard widespread criticism as, for example, the government of Australia did in 2001 in a conflict over a group of boat refugees.

Effective protection requires operational independence, but the UNHCR is ever more tied to donors by increasingly dealing with relief assistance. Setting up camps, generating assistance efforts and raising money necessitate dependence on national governments. This severely limits the UNHCR's opportunity to deal with protection, which is even more remarkable considering the above-mentioned restriction of the 1951 refugee definition. Whereas refugees are only considered deserving of protection when they have fled for civil-political reasons, they are mainly provided with socio-economic assistance. When I talked to Moxamed Suleiman of UNHCR Nairobi, he presented an interesting view of these issues:

> UNHCR as an institution, like all other UN organisations, is restricted by many conditions. When we compare the three main players in the camps – the refugees, the international community of donors and governments and the UNHCR – it is the UNHCR that is most vulnerable. That is because it cannot plan the movements of refugees, and is dependent completely on governments since it has no independent funding of its own. It is the dependency on contributions from the various countries that makes UNHCR so vulnerable and powerless, since these are the same countries that create and control refugee movements.

Moxamed presents a very debatable vision here, yet his comments do point to the need to acknowledge the mutual dependency of the various actors within refugee assistance programmes, instead of only focusing on the dependent position that refugees are in.

Problems in Practice

But again, this is not the whole story. Although it is important to understand the institutional restrictions that complicate UNHCR's work, these restrictions do not provide an explanation for every aspect of UNHCR policy and practice. In Dadaab, I talked to a UN staff member who explained to me how at times she had to 'play politics' with the Somali refugees: 'When I want a certain leader to mobilise the community, at times it can help to provide him with empty sacks. But the person may also demand that he be given a plastic sheet, because he feels that he has the right to it. You need to go along with it, because you need the support of the community. If they do not cooperate with us, our job becomes impossible'. In a resource-poor area like Dadaab, it is inevitable that the distribution of food, firewood and nonfood items is highly politicised. To distribute it means having to deal with various stakes and pressures from many sides (CASA Consulting 2001: 5). Although it might be understandable at times to favour certain refugees for the sake of politics, considering the importance of refugee cooperation, the step beyond 'politicised aid' is quite small.

It is quite difficult to obtain adequate information on corruption cases, more so to write about them with sufficient substantiation, unless they have been dealt with officially. During my fieldwork, there was one such case in Dadaab, although I heard many more allegations. A number of staff members and refugees told me about the firing of Moxamed Ibrahim, who worked as a UNHCR clerk for many years. Duncan Odhiambo was the first person to inform me about the case:

> Moxamed has three plots in his home town, Garissa, with fully self-contained houses on them. On top of that, he managed to send two of his brothers and one sister abroad. In the meantime, he might only be earning 20,000 shillings. Even though Moxamed has been sacked, he is still comfortable, having assured himself a good pension. You know, one of the things the clerks do is write cards for nonexistent people, and then get refugees or locals to collect those rations for them. They sell them in Garissa and are paid well since the price of maize and wheat in Garissa is about double what it is in the camps. The problem is that they can just go ahead, since the system is corrupt from the lowest up to the highest level.

One major weakness of the UNHCR is the lack of accountability for its programmes. Its interest in ensuring survival to refugees seems to be sufficient to legitimise its actions without a critical mechanism for determining efficiency and refugee satisfaction (Harrell-Bond et al. 1992: 220). But we should not forget that aid creates employment opportunities and other economic benefits for both locals and expatriates. Its latent functions diverge from the manifest aims and, in the final analysis, an essential purpose of the aid regime is self-perpetuation (Harrell-Bond and Voutira 1994). This is something that agency staff in Dadaab confirm. Martin Ndereba of CARE once told me that he was employed by the agencies that I accused of 'labelling refugees'. According to him, labelling was done with a primary self-interested motive: 'The main objectives of the agencies in Dadaab are twofold. The first is to keep the agencies there and the second is to assist the refugees. Seventy-five to eighty percent of the work that we currently do is not what we originally came for. We have moved on in order to continue benefiting, just like the refugees have'.

Such issues are much analysed within the literature on humanitarian aid, and similar observations can be made when analysing development aid (see e.g. Schrijvers 1993).

Many of the complexities surrounding refugee assistance may be explained by the common motives for this type of aid. A number of authors have pointed to the fact that refugee aid is often motivated and perceived in terms of humanitarianism (Harrell-Bond et al. 1992; Malkki 1996; Chimni 2000; Schrijvers 2004). It is based on the principle of providing relief to human suffering: people deserve to be assisted because they are conceptualised as the 'vulnerable victims' of extreme circumstances. In the process, this type of aid dehistoricises and depoliticises the situation it addresses as much as development aid does (Ferguson 1990). Relief aid to refugees purports to be based on a moral kind of 'doing good' that denies the fact that refugee creation and assistance is always determined by international historical and politico-economic factors. Underlying causes of a specific refugee-creating situation and the reasons for providing assistance are hardly dealt with. Instead, interventions in the region are mainly presented in terms of technical solutions to refugees' basic needs problems; assisting underdeveloped countries in alleviating poverty and reaching 'modernity'. As a consequence, European UNHCR officers can freely 'advise' African governments on how to deal with refugees arriving in their countries, for example pleading for integration of African refugees, while simultaneously their own governments are closing borders to refugees and refuse their participation in society.

Related to this perception of refugee aid as charity, another main flaw in UNHCR practice in Dadaab is that it operates in a rather nonparticipatory and hierarchical manner; both towards the refugees as well as towards its implementing partners (see also Schrijvers 2004). Whether the refugees, for example, agree with the kind of food they get and how it is being distributed, seems to be of no significance. There have been a number of instances in which the refugees have refused to collect their rations in protest, but always to no avail. Shamsa Abdulahi, who is a regular CARE employee, recounted:

> Recently, the refugees refused to take the handouts because of the poor quality and type of food provided. They organised a strike since they were only given yellow maize, and yellow maize of the worst quality. There were rumours that there was good quality maize in stock but WFP wanted to finish the bad quality first. Until August, there will also be no wheat flour in stock. When the refugees informed us of the strike, the UNHCR in Dadaab told CARE Logistics people just to be in the 'Rubb halls' [portable warehouses] (Fig. 3.4), even if no refugee would come. For some days, no one came, but eventually those who really have nothing had no option but to come since they depend on the rations.[6] The UNHCR maintains a very authoritarian position: it does every-

Figure 3.4 *Rubb Halls in Jfo.*

thing by force and seems to prefer a status of refugee dependency. The organisation maintains considerable distance from the refugees, so that it is not confronted with the consequences of the measures it takes, for which CARE staff have to account.

In Dagahaley, I talked to Nurudiin Moxamed, a 71-year-old refugee who lives in the camps with his wife, eleven of his thirteen children and six relatives. Nurudiin was rather critical of agency policies in the Dadaab camps.

The rations we get here are only very small and unsuitable. If they give me maize, wheat and oil, what am I going to feed my one-year-old son with? Though African refugees do not receive the same level of assistance that European refugees get, it also seems as if a lot of the money that the Western countries do send to Africa never reaches the refugees. For example, if the UNHCR assists refugees from Dadaab with repatriation, these people are only given a very small amount of money, with which they cannot rebuild their lives at home. At the same time, the UNHCR pays an awful lot of money to charter a plane to transport those people. Why do they not just leave the plane and give the refugees five hundred instead of fifty dollars and let them find their own way home? That is because not only the pilot will benefit, but also UNHCR itself.

A CARE staff member at the Financial Department fully agreed with this criticism, telling me that UNHCR wanted to cut a number of activities 'in the name of an insufficient budget'; whereas, according to him, the actual reason was the uneven allocation of money directly spent on the refugees, compared to the money that was used for support activities. During my stay in Dadaab, refugees and agency staff voiced a lot of similar criticisms as well as interesting ideas on how to improve the situation. Unfortunately, the UNHCR, as an organisation and as local staff, never truly asked for or listened to the opinions of refugees or NGOs.

Despite their importance, NGOs are not at the heart of the decision-making process, but rather serve as the volunteers who implement the relief decisions made by others (Gorman 1985). This at times causes frustration amongst staff members who find their efforts being complicated by UNHCR practices. During my fieldwork in Garissa, I met Khadija Ali of CARE, who was accompanying two aged Somali refugee women who had appeared as witnesses at the trial of their rapist. When we met, the court case had taken place and she was fuming:

> The UNHCR staff are not representing the refugees like they are supposed to do. They do not care and I wonder whether they have any morals. They drive around in town in their air-conditioned cars, go shopping and disappear to the camps again. Every year the budget for legal representation goes back to Nairobi unused, but these 65- and 80-year-old women who were raped by a serial rapist from Dadaab were not even assigned a lawyer! They had to present their own case, in a highly politicised environment. Can you imagine that the file disappeared and the accused was aware of that? When our doctor came with his personal copy of the file, the accused stood up and asked where he got it from. We are putting ourselves in danger; even I have received threats from the rapist. But this time, we are going to insist. With all this talk about a 'human rights approach' within CARE, we should finally have the guts to speak out against UNHCR.

A factor that further contributes to the tensions between UNHCR and its implementing partners is related to their respective financial status. As donors increasingly prefer NGOs as the conduit for aid, these aid agencies have become important competitors with the UNHCR for funds (Harrell-Bond and Mahmud 1996: 5). Both face uncertainty about the coming year's budget, and this leads to regular retrenchment in staff and a great level of discontinuity in the refugee assistance programme. Another highly problematic feature of some of the donor funding is that the funds that are provided, need to be spend and produce tangible outcomes within a one-year period. Thus, decisions have to be made on a short-term basis, with the aim of finding technical fixes with fast (though temporary) results. Donor funds tend to be earmarked only for relief and not for development programmes and this leads to a bureaucratic interest in keeping affected populations dependent, inhibiting the search for permanent solutions (Harrell-Bond and Mahmud 1996: 6). At times, the UNHCR or NGOs try to raise the profile of certain parts of their programme in order to make it interesting and thus fundable for donors. Projects are often highly politicised and phrased in value-laden terms that do no justice to the reality in the camp. An example is the concept of 'life-line distribution' that the UNHCR uses to describe the distribution of firewood in the Dadaab camps, while this distribution only provides a small percentage of the actual need for firewood (CASA Consulting 2001: 212).

Donors visit the camps during evaluation missions, which in practice are often still carried out in a rather top-down and nonparticipatory manner, even though standards in guidelines and manuals would suggest otherwise (Kaiser 2002). While I was in Dagahaley, I was able to observe two such evaluations. The evaluators were interested in meeting with 'the beneficiaries', so they drove into the blocks and started talking to the refugees. I got out of the car and followed a WFP staff member, someone from the U.S. Embassy and two staff members from UNHCR Nairobi. We sat crammed in a hut, all eyes fixed on the refugee and his wife. Meanwhile, I was wondering whether the refugee family was from Somalia or Kenya, since the man used a number of Swahili words to answer the questions being asked. He told the group how he had had to flee from Somalia as a nomad and he denied any form of livelihood options besides the rations. He was asked whether he had any livestock left, whether he could contact any relatives who were better off than him or whether he could find an income-generating activity in the camps. His main message was that life in Dadaab was very hard, the family was extremely vulnerable and they needed assistance. This did not surprise me, since I was told similar stories during my first few weeks in the camps. Above all, it should be expected that 'beneficiaries and others function as strategic actors, and may strategically omit to tell assistance providers what they believe would make them withdraw support' (Kaiser 2002: 23). Thus, it might be rather impossible to gain significant information based on an evaluation of a few hours in each refugee camp, without having a considerable prior understanding of the refugee population.

The group that I had joined visited a number of refugee households in one block. It seemed as if the representatives of UNHCR and WFP wanted to avoid criticism directed towards their own organisations, since they reacted to complaints and questions of refugees by immediately asking new questions instead of answering. Some of the questions being asked by the team were rather judgemental; such as why the men were not collecting firewood, what they usually did and why they had to spend so much time at the market. A woman was asked why she did not send her children to school and she said that she had been told to pay ten shillings, which she could not afford. I had never before heard of any refugee being asked for money to enrol his or her children, and it sounded like she was inventing the answer to avoid being blamed by this senior group of people. Nevertheless, the matter was immediately acted upon, which made me realise how powerful, but at the same time ad hoc, this kind of evaluation could be. Thus, I fully agree with Kaiser's recommendation that 'there will be a need to re-define evaluation processes as collaborative and constructive rather than intimidating and judgemental for programme and project staff' (Kaiser 2002: 4). The current situation contributes to the fact that staff will try to prevent donors hearing the criticism of refugees that is addressed towards their own organisation, since evaluations have been used before to cut funding and judge agency performance.

The Position of the Kenyan Government

The expectations and requirements of donor states are not only affecting UNHCR and its implementing agencies in Dadaab, but also the government. Kenya is not in a position to deal with the large numbers of refugees within its borders without external resources, and thus depends on the international community for assistance. Generally, donors do not trust host governments from the developing world, because their institutions are seen to be too weak and their personnel insufficiently trained and corruptible (Harrell-Bond 1986). The impression exists that outsiders are needed: donor states prefer the factual administration of the refugee camps in Kenya to be in the hands of the UNHCR and international NGOs. The government is held accountable for those few tasks given to it, mainly related to providing physical security to refugees and agency staff. Then, it is expected to approve whatever the international regime does on its territory; for the sake of providing humanitarian aid. In fact, the government is often seen as an obstacle to the free exercising of charity. The major argument for donors to bypass governments in Africa is based on the assumption that they are corrupt, nondemocratic and that the problems are so great that governments cannot do everything alone (Harrell-Bond and Mahmud 1996: 6).

The government is soon forced into a position of economic dependence and becomes an observer of what happens in the camps. The UNHCR acts accordingly, viewing the camps as spaces in which it is entitled to exercise a form of sovereignty (Verdirame 1999: 70). Although no legal basis exists for this, the UNHCR determines whether visitors are allowed to enter the camps, has taken over refugee status determination in Kenya and has opposed attempts by the government to impose taxes on the refugees in Dadaab. The government's response is to take the position that, as a result of the suspension of status determination by its authorised body, Kenya is now a 'transit country', where refugees are allowed to remain, provided that they receive assistance from the UNHCR in camps (Verdirame 1999: 58). It seems that the response to a forced taking of sovereign space from Kenya by the UNHCR has been to denounce any responsibility for the refugees. Marginalising Kenyan authorities from refugee affairs has not only led to the loss of the experience that the government of Kenya had acquired in the past; it has also created a sense of resentment on the part of Kenyan government officials (Verdirame 1999: 57).

It is clear that there are strong institutional interests in Africa and elsewhere to maintain refugees as separate populations (Wilson 1992: 230). The question could be why host governments in the developing world subscribed for so long to policies that neither uphold the rights of refugees nor serve the interests of their economy. One of the common justifications from the side of the government for segregating refugees in camps is that they represent a national security threat (Harrell-Bond 1996: 57). There is a general trend in relation to refugee protection that has seen the language of 'burden sharing' being transformed into a language of the threats to the security of states. Refugees are now seen as threatening the host country's security by increasing demands on its scarce resources or threatening the security of regions by their sheer presence (Chimni 2000: 252). This is certainly the case in Kenya, which has historically had a problematic relationship both with the Somali and the Somali state. The latter has challenged Kenyan territory in an attempt to accomplish the pan-Somali dream, whereas the Somali citizens of Kenya supported that move. The Somali and their country are treated with suspicion in the media and the government contributes to the negative image by blaming the refugees for various ills in society in a rather polemic way. I talked about this with the father of Moxamed Farah, who worked for Community Services in Hagadera and assisted me a great deal with my work there. Farah Abdinoor found it understandable that problems within the Kenyan society were readily attributed to the Somali people or state: 'Since all other neighbouring countries at least have a government, the safest and easiest move for the government is to blame the Somali for everything. There is no government that the President might need in the future, so there is also no one he might offend with his remarks'.

At the same time, the main task that is left with the government is the provision of individual security to the Somali refugees. The question arises of why the refugees cannot be protected against the various types of insecurities that I earlier described. In and around the camps, security issues are primarily in the hands of the Kenyan police, with the army stepping in only in rare cases of acute emergency. Each camp has one police base with about forty officers and Dadaab has two posts that deal with the town of Dadaab as well as the roads that connect it with the camps. The main tasks of the police consist of containing *shifta* activity in and around the camps, providing escorts to the agencies travelling between Dadaab, the three camps and Garissa, controlling or settling disputes between refugees and taking action against any person violating Kenyan law. These tasks are carried out with limited resources and limited manpower in an area where quite a number of policemen have lost their lives already and both the local population as well as the refugees are suspicious towards the police. Cooperation with investigations is minimal and often *maslaxad* (community-based arbitration between the two parties) is preferred to Kenyan national law. Thus, providing protection to the refugees is not an easy task. But, at the same time, Kenyan police are accused by refugees, researchers and human rights organisations alike of further contributing to the refugees' insecurity through negligence, corruption and even harassment and abuse (see e.g. African Rights 1993; Human Rights Watch 1993).

In Kenyan society as a whole, the image of the police is quite negative. They are seen as highly corrupt, harassing citizens with requests for *kitu kidogo* ('something small', bribe); as well as undisciplined and badly behaved, ready to abuse citizens rather than assist them. In Northeastern Province, these general stereotypes combine with the highly problematic relationship between Somali citizens and the Kenyan state. The Kenyan Somalis were, for decades, blamed with threatening Kenyan national security; whereas the state, embodied by policemen and military on the ground, is seen to be extremely brutal and repressive towards its Somali population. Refugees, in addition, are accused of threatening state security since their arrival would lead to the spread of firearms, increased levels of crime and social unrest (Crisp 1999b). Thus, providing protection to refugees has to be seen in the light of the preoccupation of the Kenyan government with the security of the state. Since September 11th 2001, this situation has only intensified. Currently, there is not only a national preoccupation with security, but also an international one, as the Somali refugees in Dadaab are suspected of having links with Al Qa'ida.

The available literature refers to a lot of related causes for the lack of security in the camps. For one, the police in Kenya are notoriously underpaid and thus refugees, and especially Somali refugees, may be regarded as an additional source of income (Verdirame 1999: 73). On average, a police officer in Dadaab earns about 5,000 shillings a month, which is not much more than the better-paid incentive workers receive.[7] The UNHCR supplements the police wages as well as paying them bonuses for escorting and food-distribution duties, as Crisp (1999b) points out. However, it is not uncommon for these extras not to end up with the officers, since the system suffers from a 'trickle-down' syndrome. Thus, extra income may instead be acquired via *matatu* (Swahili: minibus) services during regular escorts. Also, policemen may 'tax' refugee business activities in the camps such as the operation of *taar* (which is illegal in Kenya) or video shops.

Furthermore, business operations between Somalia and Kenya are lucrative sources of income for local policemen. Other reasons that could explain why UNHCR support to the police has not necessarily led to improved security are that the police force is too small, unmotivated and unprofessional, while the judicial system they depend on for prosecuting criminal offenders is weak (Crisp 1999b). Motivation is at times a problem because most policemen have to leave their families for many months in order to live in a highly isolated and risk-prone environment where their work is scarcely appreciated. Several officers based in Dadaab have seen colleagues and friends die in the area. At times, they have to participate in missions that cause them to witness the worst kinds of atrocities. These are not necessarily things that a normal police officer is trained to do and the level of special training received is insufficient. It is therefore not surprising that a number of officers, though certainly not all, are suffering from low morale and may not be willing to risk their lives in order to protect refugees.

Individual or System?

The refugee regime faces quite a number of restrictions and has its own limitations. These may be ascribed to the system as a whole, affecting all individuals who constitute the regime. Indeed, from the viewpoint of refugees, agency staff and government officials mostly serve as representatives of the camp organisation, responsible for controlling them (Knudsen 1991: 24). Thus, a situation arises where those who are categorised as 'refugees' similarly reduce those who are assigned to assist them to a single category. Moxamed Suleiman pointed this out to me when I was mentioning the tendency of the international regime to label refugees. He described the different stages in the relationship between the refugees and UNHCR employees:

> In the emergency stage, the refugees are very happy with the UNHCR presence. At that time, the refugees are still most trustworthy and honest. They follow the ideas of the UNHCR staff since they do not know anything in their new environment. But when the situation starts to stabilise, the refugees develop new, different needs. They are past the need for food alone and develop other needs that concern their future. They then want durable solutions. Or they simply want to visit a friend in town or something of the sort. That is when they start seeing UNHCR staff like an obstacle in the way of getting something. They may become angry or very demanding and approach UNHCR staff like an abstract figure instead of a human being.

What Zetter (1991) argues in the case of refugees may be extended to any other group working with them. In Dadaab, groups of people are often defined in convenient images by replacing individual identities with stereotyped identities, shorn of variety and uniqueness. This is part-ly related to the hierarchical structure common to refugee camps that makes communication difficult and leads to a reciprocal attitude of dif-ference between 'us' and 'them'. Initially, I rather shortsightedly assumed that anybody functioning within a system like that of the UNHCR would fully agree with its policies and practices and act accordingly. In one of my discussions with Moxamed Suleiman, however, I realised that he did not always agree with the organisation's policies and practices. We dis-cussed the topic extensively and Moxamed stressed that it really depends on the people as to how the job is carried out:

> At first I also thought it was the institution that was deficient, but I found out that is not necessarily true: it is the people making or breaking it. I was on the point of quitting twice, but the realisation that it is not UNHCR but its staff that is creating inhumane situations made me stay. Many of my colleagues are cyn-ical about the work and the refugees, or they are just there to make money. The kind of work we do entails this risk, since we hear similar stories constantly and are lied to often. There are those who take the job as a mechanical process and who play with figures between the four walls of their office in a way you would do when managing a factory. But you cannot do this when dealing with human beings, since they react to your policies, unlike the products produced in a factory. But then, there are also colleagues who are very humane, from whom I can learn much. I decided to stay because I am able to make a human difference.

The policy and practice of certain organisations are directly related to particular individuals and to their training, value system and compe-tence, even though, of course, those individuals are selected and limited by the system in which they function. What happens on the ground is much more the result of individuals' decisions and personalities than of the applications of standards and procedures (Verdirame 1999: 54–55). In this respect, Moxamed told me:

> In emergency situations, you cannot just be a robot following the expected poli-cies. It needs your life involvement: you have to act, be innovative and move beyond the fixed structures. You cannot just say that the UNHCR does not have the budget to feed refugees when you meet five thousand people who are dying of starvation. You should even go into the local community to lobby for assistance. Whether it is part of your mandate or not, what matters is that those people need to be assisted. That is how working with refugees has greatly enriched my life: in my opinion, living entails struggling. It gives depth to one's life to struggle, to have worked for something. If you have a farm, it gives great satisfaction to toil the land and see a mango grow. You learn to appreci-ate that growth, you learn to see that things are not just there. You do not take them for granted.

With this simple metaphor, Moxamed challenged me to mirror my views on the harmfulness of labelling refugees. Labelling those working within the refugee regime is just as easily done, leading to a similar denial of their individual agency. But the larger structure of the refugee regime, while seemingly operating independently and decisive, only exists through the actions of individuals, who work towards either reproducing or changing it.

Notes

1. Before 2003, benefits were mainly in the shape of a few jobs and contracts for the delivery of local building materials and firewood. In 2003, CARE Dadaab started the Local Area Project (LAP) in order to reduce the gap between assistance provision for refugees and that for locals, thus initiating a first, very careful attempt to integrate relief and development programmes. Still, livelihood opportunities are hardly addressed in either.

2. Of course, those basic needs are not the same for all families and may depend on the family composition and consumption patterns of individual members. The rations are, however, distributed on the basis of all people being equal and having equal rights (Turner 1999).

3. Perouse de Montclos does not take into account, however, that although specific jobs are clearly earmarked either for locals or for refugees, quite a number of Kenyan Somalis manage to get 'incentive' jobs that were meant for refugees.

4. 'Midnight music' is a term used by the refugees for the armed attacks by *shifta* in the blocks at night and refers to the firing of guns during such attacks.

5. *Mimi* is a Swahili word and means 'I'.

6. In 1998, a similar situation caused violent clashes between the Bantu Somalis and the Somalis in Dagahaley; when the Bantu went to collect their wristbands despite a camp-wide boycott of a ration card revalidation exercise (see also Crisp 1999b).

7. Though in late 2003, the position of police officers greatly improved when the Kibaki government doubled their salaries. I do not know what effect this had on the corruption mentioned here, as the change occurred after my fieldwork period.

4

Transnational Livelihoods:
The Role of *Taar* and *Xawilaad*

'Walaalkaa xoolahiisa in yar baad ku leedahay'[1]

Refugee camps are often depicted as excluded and isolated areas with no connections to wider networks. This assumption denies the realities of life in many places, where, due to technological developments in transport and communication, people have become connected to other areas and receive money and information from elsewhere. Although Dadaab is certainly an isolated place, in terms of its geography and limited road network, this does not inhibit transnational connections. I will demonstrate that the strong social networks that enabled Somalis to cope with insecurities before and during the war are still present and play a vital role in people's livelihoods. Every Somali has demands firmly fixed into his or her mind as to the responsibilities to be borne by family members in the current crisis (Farah 2000). Being at a distance does not commonly negate these feelings of responsibility. Whereas refugees in the camps do provide assistance to each other, the camp environment, with its high level of economic and physical insecurity, provides only limited opportunities to do so. Mostly, relatives outside the camps are in a better position to send assistance to Dadaab, as the material in this chapter will clearly illustrate.

After I had been in the camps for about one month, I was quite dissatisfied with the limited progress I had made. I still did not know exactly what information I needed to obtain from the refugees in the camps, I did not know how to get it and I certainly did not know how to overcome people's reluctance to tell me the ways in which they survived in Dadaab despite the insufficient handouts. When I discussed my frustrations with Rashid Ibrahim, he suggested that I give him my research questions, so that he could go through them. A few days later, on Friday 20 August 1999, he came to my temporary home in the CARE compound of Hagadera, asked for clarification in instances in which the questions were not clear to him and started providing me with his answers. We talked for hours, until the discussions we had and the information he provided me with, was more than I could process. After I handed him my report of our discussion, he came to the compound that Sunday and again, we talked for three hours. We had to stop because we were completely drained, but the process was absolutely fascinating. On Monday, we used one more hour to close our discussions. Not only was this a breakthrough in my fieldwork, since it enabled me to reflect on that first month and determine my focus more consciously, it also made me realise the enormous potential of a truly dialogical research approach. Rashid and I immensely enjoyed the debates and discussions and, whereas I gained a lot of information about the Somali community in Dadaab, Rashid commented on how much he had learned from my knowledge in the field of social sciences and refugee studies.

One of my original research interests was related to De Waal's (1989) thesis that 'the experience of the threat to a way of life may be more real than the experience of starvation'. I wanted to know whether the social networks between Somalis were used mainly for physical survival or to retain a 'Somali identity'. When I explained this question, Rashid said that both were closely linked together and could not be separated:

> Islam teaches people to safeguard their social relations and especially those with relatives. When a Somali sends money from the U.S.A. to Dadaab, this may be done for many reasons, often combining both economic and cultural ones. When someone sends money every month in order to enable his or her brother to eat, an underlying reason may be that this person wants to make sure that the relationship between the two of them is good. When a Somali sends money for a sister's wedding, it is a financial support that she needs at that moment but the money also enables her to continue her culture and give her a distinct identity.

I asked Rashid what kind of identity that was: a refugee, a Muslim, a Somali or a clan identity? Rashid answered that it was both a Muslim and a Somali identity, since the two are interwoven, and he added: 'Being Somali as well as being Muslim entails a responsibility to assist those who have less'.[2] In this chapter, I will show how the cultural-religious responsibility to assist others is central to the livelihoods of Somalis in Dadaab, and that this is particularly determined by transnational connections. After introducing the topic, I will describe the function of the *taar* in facilitating regional connections. Then, I will move on to a description of the *xawilaad* system and its important role in enabling overseas connections, in order to arrive at a number of concluding remarks.

The Role of Social Networks in Providing Security

In a recent study in Dadaab, it was found that the main determinant of wealth in the camps is a household's connections (CASA Consulting 2001: 320). Those refugees who are 'well-connected' have access to remittances from outside Kenya, to relatives who have an incentive job or are involved in extensive trade, or to well off Kenyan Somalis. According to the study, these wealthier households assist their relatives in earning an income and increasing their wealth, particularly through giving them credit to operate a small business. Households without access to wealthier people, on the other hand, remain poor. Being interested in similar issues, I worked with participatory matrices to learn in which situations refugees needed assistance from others, and whom they would ask for that assistance. During workshops and trainings on data collection (Fig. 4.1), I taught participants how to use matrices by having them fill in and discuss one or two samples that simultaneously provided me with relevant research data. During a follow-up workshop with my research assistants in Ifo, I asked participants to complete a matrix with, on the one axis, occasions in which refugees needed assistance and, on the other axis, the people or institutions whom they would ask for assistance (see Table 4.1). After they had listed the occasions on which money could be requested and from whom, I proceeded by asking the participants to look at each occasion, for example, marriage or debt, and tell me the three most likely

Figure 4.1 *Participants during a training session.*

groups of people or institutions to ask assistance from. These were given three, two and one points, with the most likely group receiving most points. The exercise confirmed that kinship plays a very important role in providing assistance, though relatives are not the only people that refugees can fall back on in times of need.

Table 4.1 *Patterns of Assistance in Dadaab Participatory Matrix, Workshop Ifo, March 2000.*

From whom / Occasion	Neighbours	Clan	Religious Institutes	NGOs	Relatives[3]	Money Lenders
Marriage	1	3			2	
Death	2	3			1	
Robbery	3	1			2	
Travel		1	2		3	
Education			1	3	2	
Communication		2			3	1
Diya		3	1		2	
Sickness	1			3	2	
Debt		3	1		2	
No ration card	2	1			3	
Total	9	17	5	6	22	1

The ongoing discussions during this data collection process can generate highly relevant research material (Pretty et al. 1995). When analysing the matrix and the ensuing discussions, a number of things become clear. First, in all circumstances, relatives play a central role in providing security in times of need, and this includes both relatives who live in the camps and those who live elsewhere, who send money through the *taar* or *xawilaad*. Furthermore, clan members in the camps also play a major role in most circumstances; especially those that are clan-related such as life cycle and diya-paying events. Therefore, kinship is, in all respects, extremely vital to providing security in Dadaab, guaranteeing assistance when necessary. Secondly, neighbours play an important role in the livelihoods of refugees in Dadaab; particularly in life cycle events and after unexpected setbacks like illness or theft. Being neighbours, they observe the consequences of such calamities and have the responsibility to assist whenever possible. Thirdly, NGOs are mentioned as playing a major role in providing assistance for education and during illness, which is related to the programmes in these sectors that are operated by CARE and MSF in Dadaab. In addition, people in religious institutes like mosques and *dariiqoyin* (sing. *dariiqo*: sect, religious group) often assist travellers, largely going back to the important role of travel in Islam (see e.g. Eickelman and Piscatori 1990). Refugees do not like to ask assistance from the money lenders operating in the markets, because a loan entails the risk of losing a deposit, which is often the ration card. Loans are only taken when there are no other options and the refugee wants to invest in something that will almost certainly generate profit.

In most societies, social networks operate with a certain degree of flexibility and enable individuals to spread risks. There are many aspects of social relations, such as descent, kinship, age, gender or residence, that play a role in an individual's delineation of his own people (Bruijn and Dijk 1995). Whereas, as far as the Somali are concerned, kinship plays a central role in providing assistance, this is certainly not the only factor. There are situations when relatives are not available and neighbours or friends play a more important role in assisting, especially where daily life survival is concerned. On top of that, kinship itself cannot be seen as a fixed and clearly demarcated institution. Rather, it is used in strategies and moulded by circumstances, as Rashid explained when talking about an uncle: 'Well, we share a great-grandfather six generations back, but that does not really make a difference. I respect and assist him like a real uncle, because next time, I might be the one in need of help'. Whereas in Somalia, certain distant relatives may not have played any role in providing assistance, these relatives may now be counted upon by refugees who stay in Dadaab, for example when they live overseas. Social networks consist of complex human relations in which individuals negotiate and at times switch (power) positions, in order to survive. There is no single type of relationship that someone can always trust, even though certain types offer more security than others. That is why in most social organisations, people are involved in a multiplicity of social relationships along which goods and services for their needs can, or should be, provided (Benda-Beckmann and Benda-Beckmann 1994). Similarly, it is often a good risk-spreading strategy to invest in social relations amongst people who are based in different localities.

Transnational Livelihoods

The fact that people try to reduce their insecurity by investing in people and activities in different locations, is widely accepted within migration studies, but it is far less commonly applied to refugees. In the new field of transnational studies, not much seems to have changed in this respect. According to Vertovec (1999: 453), whereas many transnational communities have found themselves dispersed for reasons of forced migration, others have largely spread out in order to spread their assets, as if the first group could not engage in the second activity. There is much debate on the strict division between political and economic migration and dispersal strategies that lies behind this categorisation (see e.g. Black 1995). Therefore, these distinctions cannot simply be assumed within the current debates on transnationalism, especially since it obscures the fact that refugees do spread themselves for reasons of economic security, irrespective of the forced nature of their movements. Amongst the Somalis, there are many communication and assistance links between those who live in homeland areas, country of first asylum and resettlement countries. Other diasporic people similarly form strong networks, which enable transnational flows of people, goods, money and information (Van Hear 2002: 3). These networks and the flows within them are essential for determining the livelihoods of people in different places.

Transnational livelihoods can take many shapes and forms and have been studied from various perspectives. In the first place, family networks across political and economic borders provide the possibility for individual survival and, at times, social mobility in contexts of vulnerability and subordination (Glick Schiller et al. 1995: 54). This is not necessarily a new phenomenon, but one that has substantially changed character as a consequence of certain technological developments. Salih (2001b: 52), in research on Moroccan migrant women working in Italy, draws the conclusion that 'transnational practices such as transferring money, buying land and houses or investing in other signifiers of symbolic and economic capital in their country of origin have been a constant character of Moroccan international migrants who held a "myth of return"'. What has altered, in her view, is the level to which changes in technological communication, travel and financial services have favoured the maintenance of transnational relations, reducing imaginary and real distances. Similar processes of involvement between home and host country have been identified in the case of refugees. Koser (2001b; 2001a) for example describes how financial assistance from the Eritrean diaspora has been used by relatives to contribute to their daily lives and future investments as well as by the state for military and humanitarian purposes (see also Al-Ali et al. 2001).

Besides being essential for the livelihoods of individual families, remittances have become a major factor in international financial flows and in the economic well-being of many countries (Diaz-Briquets and Perez-Lopez 1997: 411). There are various benefits a country can profit from, even if, as is often the case for refugees, the government is not on good terms with its transnational migrants. For governments, remittances represent the quickest and surest source of foreign exchange. On top of that, remittance-receiving countries have a greater capacity to import capital goods and raw materials, gain a potential source of savings and investment capital, and increase the standard of living of recipients (Russell 1986). Thus, many governments have now acknowledged the important role that their 'transnational nationals' play in financial terms. Indeed, a great number of national economies today depend absolutely on monetary transfers of many kinds from 'nationals' abroad (Vertovec 1999: 452–53). As Adamson (2001: 156) points out, one of the ways in which transnational communities can have an impact on transformation is due to the fact that they mobilise and transfer resources directly to actors in the home country, thereby altering the local balance of resources and power. Werbner (1999) takes the argument one step further, drawing attention to the changing *international* balance of power and resources.

Yet, the effects of transnational flows on people's livelihood options and (inter)national politico-economic divisions are highly complex and contradictory. Critics have noted that countries depending on remittances are at grave risk since these financial flows are notorious for their volatility, being sensitive to fluctuations in economic conditions and political developments. According to Russell (1986), remittances also tend to give rise to dependency by replacing other sources of income and undermining traditional work habits. A number of studies have found that remittances tend to be spent on consumer goods and ultimately fuel inflation. It is assumed that, since they are private monies, they cannot be directed to development objectives as effectively as other foreign transfers of an official nature (see Diaz-Briquets and Perez-Lopez 1997: 414–15). However, remittance flows by far exceed global development assistance and, due to the face-to-face nature of the assistance, reach beneficiaries directly, as opposed to institutionalised aid. There is also evidence that they are used to establish small businesses, which is one of the more promising employment-generating sectors in various migrant-sending countries (Diaz-Briquets and Weintraub 1991).

Another negative aspect often mentioned in studies on remittance flows is that they are responsible for growing inequality between households that do or do not receive remittances and may contribute to tensions. Yet, the effects of this growing inequality are mitigated in Dadaab by the redistribution of resources. At a national level, remittances can contribute to both conflict and peace, due to the powerful position of transnational communities. The political role of the diaspora should not be underestimated, both as a force to assist in the peace process and rebuild the country, and as a destabilising force due to continued financing of the fighting parties. The financial weight of refugees in diaspora largely accounts for their political importance in the home area, besides the fact that many of those in exile belong to the elite and thus historically have played a political role. In the case of Puntland and Somaliland, the financial power of the Somali diaspora to a large extent explains their considerable role in the development of the constitutions of these regions, facilitated by the Internet. But simultaneously, remittances have also been used to obtain arms and other material to support clan militias. Similar processes have been observed in other areas, for example, in Eritrea and

Sri Lanka (see e.g. Koser 2001b; Van Hear 2002). The remittances that refugees send to their home countries not only guarantee the livelihoods of those remaining ('stayees') and support the peace process, but also contribute to the continuation of war by sponsoring the elites and warring factions. I will mainly focus on the role of transnational remittances and other flows in giving refugees a level of power and choice when determining their livelihoods, but it is important to take into account that these flows have a wide range of other effects as well.

The *Taar*: Facilitating Regional Connections

Since the ability to assist is quite limited amongst refugees within the camps, it is important to study networks of assistance beyond the bounded space of Dadaab. Somalis in the camps are linked to their relatives and friends in the Somali homelands, other parts of Africa, Kenyan cities and 'overseas' countries. This section describes the regional connections between the camps and the Somali homelands and, to a lesser extent, other African countries that can be reached through the *taar*. Then, a next section focuses on the overseas connections that exist from Dadaab. What is true for all regional connections, including those within Kenya, is that they are mostly facilitated by the *taar*. *Taar* is a Somali word that literally means telegram or cable, metal wire (Zorc and Osman 1993). The word is used to refer to the radio communication sets that enable communication in a relatively cheap and easy manner throughout the region. The sets are used both for communication and remittance sending, facilitating flows of information and money both to and from the camps.

Connecting the Somali in Dadaab with their Homelands

The introduction of the taar in 1998 in Hagadera and Ifo and in Dagahaley in 1999 resulted in major improvements in terms of communication. Zeinab Rashid made me realise just how important this shift was, although the conditions under which we talked were initially far from ideal. On 9 December 1999, I had arranged an interview with her in Dagahaley. When I arrived at her house together with my translator, a big group of children were following us. They were chased away by the neighbouring women, but these women themselves were also quite interested in our visit. While we were sitting in Zeinab's hut they came in one by one, until the small hut was packed with people staring at me. When it became too embarrassing, Zeinab told the women to go and they did, reluctantly. My presence there and then seemed quite unnatural in the kind of responses it created, and this was not the only time that this happened during my stay in Dadaab, although luckily such instances were rare. Despite the poor start, Zeinab provided me with many new insights. She told me: 'All my siblings are in Somalia and I do not have any other relatives elsewhere. I usually communicate to them through the *taar* and I have been doing that since January of this year. Before, when the *taar* had not yet been introduced in Dagahaley, I used to send letters. Now, I can just call my mother in Mogadishu and I also speak to one of my sisters in Afmadow through the sets. I last spoke to my mother five days ago and to my sister the day before yesterday'.

Surprised about how recently she communicated with people in Somalia, I asked Zeinab whether she communicated to her mother and sister frequently. Zeinab told me that the *taar* only cost one hundred shillings and that, at times, the owner assisted by allowing her to use it without charge. I asked what topics she usually talked about with her mother and sister and Zeinab told me that they mainly discussed the health of their relatives, the general condition in the camps and in Somalia and the security situation in both areas. When I enquired about the conditions of life for her relatives in Somalia, Zeinab said:

My mother has a small business, a table shop, and is doing okay. The current situation in Mogadishu is not bad, except for the bullets, the risk of being robbed or killed. But otherwise, my mother does not face any problems. My sister has a farm in Afmadow, where there is peace at the moment. She is just a poor farmer and used to stay in that area even when I had my own business in Kismaayo and my mother was in Mogadishu. None of us is in a position to assist the other. If I am faced by difficulties, I will have to rely on my husband's business; he owns a maize-grinding machine that he operates in the Dagahaley market. My sister has nothing to assist me with and she also knows my own situation as a refugee here, so she does not ask me for assistance either.

Even if they were not in a position to assist each other financially, due to the introduction of the *taar*, Zeinab was now able to be informed of, and involved in, the lives of her relatives.

The *taar* business has rapidly expanded in the Dadaab area. After the first one was introduced in Hagadera in 1998, the number grew to approximately twenty-five in the three camps in 2001. In September 1999, I conducted an interview with Bishar Abdirahman, one of the *taar* owners in Hagadera. Bishar explained that he was the first person to introduce the taar to the camps:

I brought a radio set to Hagadera in August 1998, together with Moxamuud Aden. At that time, we paid about 1,800 dollars and I needed a partner to be able to afford that amount. Because of the high price of the sets, it is quite common in the camps for two people to buy a set together. When we started, business was very good: at least twenty people came to make a call every day, and we hired a watchman to bring them in one by one. On top of that, we received around twenty calls a day, for which ten to fifteen people could be traced. We only make money when it is possible to trace people, because only then do the caller and the receiver have to pay. Nowadays, we also own a *taar* in Ifo but business has changed. As radio owners, we are facing a lot of problems. Nowadays there are eight radio sets in Hagadera alone, in addition to five in Ifo and four in Dagahaley. The market is flooded, and we may have merely ten customers daily, of which only three or four actually end up paying. Another problem we face is that we do not have a licence. I have been taken to court once and on another occasion I only just managed to avoid prosecution.

None of the *taar* owners has a licence, which is partly because these licences are very hard to obtain. Thus, their activities are illegal in Kenya. Still, they are usually not arrested since they pay a weekly 'fee' to the police. Ismail Abdi explained the situation to me in some detail: 'Kenyan Telecom is not happy with the operation of the radios in the camps and they claim they are losing a lot of money to the *taar*. In reality, many of the places we communicate to do not even have telephones and besides, the refugees would not be able to pay Telecom rates. Still, Telecom every now and then is able to sue us. We were taken to court in Garissa only recently for carrying out illegal operations, with seven people from Hagadera and three from Dagahaley'. I asked Ismail how the case was handled, and he told me: 'You have to know something about the operations of this state. Everything is possible, as long as you pay. Kenyans can be bribed and the Somali are known to have money: their relationship is one of giving and receiving bribes. To be released from charges every one of us had to pay 30,000 shillings. We already pay a weekly or monthly amount to the local police officers in order to be able to continue our activities without being caught. But when the boss orders those police officers to confiscate our equipment, we cannot do anything and have to pay again'.

Once a radio set has been bought, there are hardly any other costs for transmission and maintenance is barely required. Only batteries need to be recharged regularly, which can be done in the market for a small fee or alternatively the *taar* owner can decide to invest in solar panels. Furthermore, small costs are incurred for paying messengers who inform refugees of their calls. Customers are expected to pay two hundred shillings and nowadays at times one hundred shillings, both when sending and receiving a call. Besides, when sending remittances, 5–10 percent of the sum remitted is charged. *Taar* profits have gone down due to an increase in the number of radio sets, but the number of refugees using the radio sets is still increasing. Business varies from day to day and the sets are used particularly intensively when there is important news that affects all refugees in the camps. When card revalidation or resettlement registration exercises are expected, for example, relatives who have moved outside the camps are called back to be present during these occasions. At other times, such as when the borders are closed and trade is

Figure 4.2 Baafin: *Man holding a picture of his daughter in the Netherlands.*

negatively affected, profits are low. On top of that, a number of *taar* own-ers at times lose profits because they only charge small amounts or noth-ing at all to relatives and friends. Similarly, when a refugee needs to com-municate urgently but does not have sufficient money, he or she may be assisted. *Taar* owners spend a lot of time on *baafin* (Fig. 4.2), which literal-ly means inquiry or search, trying to trace relatives who have lost track of each other during the war. Often, this requires a lot of calls to be made, for which the customer does not pay anything unless the missing person is found.

When I asked with which places the *taar* usually connect the refugees, Bishar Abdirahman told me: 'Most calls are made to Somalia and Nairobi, but the radio sets have communicated to a wide range of places. I have, for example, contacted Uganda, Tanzania, Djibouti, Ethiopia, United Arab Emirates, Yemen, Zambia and South Africa. In Somalia, the places that are called a lot are Mogadishu, Kismaayo and other places in the Lower Juba region, like Doble, Bu'aale, Afmadow and Jilib. Incoming calls are also mostly from Somalia and Nairobi'. The information exchanged concerns, in the first place, the general situation of the relatives and the place in which they stay. But information is also exchanged with the specific goal of influencing the migration decisions of relatives. It is always important to know the opportunities and risks that exist in different places, especially when a refugee is considering returning to Somalia or moving from or towards the camps. In November 1999, I talked to Sheikh Hussein Bashir in Dagahaley camp and was amazed by his extensive use of the *taar*. He told me that the day before, he had communicated with relatives in Nairobi, Afmadow and Jamaame through the radio sets. After our interview, he went to the market to try to communicate with family members in Mogadishu and Kismaayo.

A number of Sheikh Hussein's wives and children do not live in the camps and he likes to keep in touch with them frequently. On top of that, the recent calls had particular reasons, as Sheikh Hussein explained: 'The purpose of calling my daughter in Jamaame was to inform her that her mother is sick and to ask her to come and take care of her mother'. Salih (2001a: 665) would argue that such arrangements are part of a 'transnational sphere of reproductive and care activities', mainly carried out by women.[4] Then, Sheikh Hussein called his son in Jamaame to tell him to come to Dadaab to get married. I asked Sheikh Hussein whether he had found a bride for his son, but he said that he would never force his daughters or sons to marry anyone he had chosen. However, since he has a good name in Dagahaley, his son could marry any of the girls in the camp: he would not be refused. Sheikh Hussein continued 'I want to speak to my son in Kismaayo in order to find out whether they still receive money from abroad. Because if they do not, I will advise them to come and live with their relatives. What is the use of living in a war area when they are not better off economically than their family members in a refugee camp? Then, they might as well come and stay with us. My son should only stay there if his situation is stable'. When I expressed my surprise at the frequency of his use of the *taar*, Sheikh Hussein told me that it was not just by coincidence that he had made a lot of calls the day before, and he was expecting to make more today: 'I am able to use the radio sets on a daily basis. I want to keep myself informed about the situation my children face, especially in terms of finances and security. Also, I hope to hear the voices of my grandchildren when I call. At the same time, I inform my children about my own situation here in the camps'.

The radio sets play an important role not only in providing information about the situation in various localities at family level. The owners of the *taar* also pass on important information to each other, for example, when fighting occurs. During my stay in Ifo in February 2000, I was informed about renewed heavy fighting in Doble the day after it started. Sahra Yusuf had come home after spending the afternoon translating for me, when she heard wailing in her block. Fighting had broken out in Doble between Moxamed Zubeir and Aulihan, two subclans of the Ogaden branch of Darod. It had left seven people dead and many more injured. In the block I used to frequent, one woman had lost her husband and another had lost her brother. One of the reasons why the number of *taar* was growing was precisely because they are also used to pass on important information about the war; information which should be kept within the clan. As such, due to the *taar*, whatever happens in Somalia may also cause tension within the camps, as Crisp (1999b: 21) suggests. Simultaneously, the *taar* can enable Somalis to move from conflict areas, when their relatives send them enough money to do so and provide them with the right information on where to go to.

Providing Assistance To and From the Camps

Besides enabling the exchange of information, the *taar* is also very important for sending remittances. It is not always clear whether conditions are better in the camps or in Somali areas and it is therefore not necessarily apparent who is in a better position to assist. Marian Issa, one of the four wives of Sheikh Hussein, had recently arrived from Mogadishu when I visited their house. I asked her to compare the situation in Mogadishu with the one she found in Dagahaley and she told me:

> First of all, security is better in Mogadishu. There, everybody carries a gun to protect himself and his family, so nobody can be attacked. Then, food and housing is also worse in Dagahaley. In Mogadishu, and more specifically the *Al Barakaat* market, business is flourishing and life is much cheaper than here. There are a lot of vegetables and fruits in Somalia, whereas in these refugee camps there is only staple food. *Al Barakaat* market is very well supplied and it is a safe place since the traders have hired security forces for protection. This makes it impossible for bandits to loot anything. The only thing that is better in the camps is education, since no proper education is provided in Somalia.

Not all refugees would agree with Marian's definition of security and opinions also differed about the economic conditions in Somalia compared to those in the camps. Indeed, during my stay in Dadaab I learned that money was sent both to and from the camps.

A number of refugees receive money or goods from their relatives in the region, most of whom live in Somali areas. The quantity of this assistance varies widely, depending on the position that those who send it are in. Fartun Yusuf, for example, told me that she had left their farmland to be used by her neighbours in Somalia. One of the crops they were growing was simsim, sesame seed, which can be ground into oil. During her stay in Hagadera, where she arrived in 1997, Fartun received oil twice after a good *simsim* harvest. Someone travelling from Kismaayo area to Dadaab brought it to her. In an interview report that was collected by Hassan Moxamuud, one of my research assistants in Ifo, there is also a reference to assistance through small farming activities:

Fatuma Noor is thirty-five years old and has fled from Jilib, a town in Middle Juba. She is a divorcee and lives in Ifo with her two sons. Fatuma gets assistance from her previous husband, who lives in a town called Marerey. He is a farmer and grows maize, tobacco, *simsim* and beans. Every three months after he harvests his crops, her ex-husband sends Fatuma some money that provides for their basic needs. But at times, she does not receive any assistance because of problems that destroy the crops. The river may overflow and wash away the crops, or pests and diseases destroy the harvest.

There are others who receive limited amounts from relatives who are just a little bit better off than them. Another report by Hassan Moxamuud mentions how a mother of five children receives some money from her husband, who works in Mogadishu as a mechanic: 'Khadija Hussein at times gets assistance from her husband, who works in a garage in Mogadishu. He can only send her a small amount, and only in the months during which he gets enough work in the garage. Khadija says that using the *taar* can be a problem because it is expensive and at times the sets disappear from the camps since they operate illegally'. Despite this risk, the radio sets do help a lot of refugees in the camps. Adoy Moxamed told me that sometimes her blind uncle in Mogadishu sends her family some money:

My uncle graduated from the Islamic University in Saudi-Arabia and when he went blind after that an Islamic institute provided him with a monthly allowance. He now stays in a room in Mogadishu because his own house is occupied by Hawiye and he cannot claim it back. They would kill him if they knew it was his house, so he stays in a room in the house of his Hawiye friend. It is only because his friend defends him that my uncle can stay in Mogadishu safely. Yet, financially, his condition is somewhat better than our own and that is why he assists us every now and then.

There are also a few cases in which relatives who live in the region have been in a position to send a considerable amount of money. Many refugees especially mentioned South Africa as a place of opportunities, where Somalis have done very well. A number of people told me the story of a man who went to South Africa in early 1999. One year later, when he heard of the drought that hit parts of Kenya, Ethiopia and Somalia, he sent 3,500 dollars to his cousin through the *xawilaad* in Dadaab. The cousin was then responsible for distributing the money amongst approximately thirty families; a few of whom lived in the camps while the majority were resident in Ethiopia. He delivered the money in person to the relatives in Ifo and Hagadera and sent the remaining amount through the *taar*. Since, at the time, there was no *taar* in Ethiopia where those families stayed, the money was sent to Ceel Berde, the nearest village on the Somali side of the border. He contacted a relative in Ceel Berde, an old man who then became responsible for taking the money to the remaining families. I asked how the man in South Africa could be sure that his relatives in Ethiopia would receive the money safely and was told that this was a matter of trust between relatives. Besides, it was made possible by the operation of *taar* and *xawilaad* businesses between Somalis.

Money is not only received but also sent from Dadaab, even though livelihood opportunities are extremely limited in the area. When I talked to Bishar Abdirahman, he told me that the refugees in the camps receive more money than they send, for example from South Africa. He added: 'But if someone in the camps is informed that one of his relatives in Somalia is sick, he may still be able to send some money'. Muse Omar, a young Somali Bantu man working as an incentive worker for CARE, at one point found himself in a situation where he had to assist his brother in Somalia in a 'contingency' situation. He was told to pay an equivalent of 1,300 Kenyan shillings because his brother had stolen money and would be killed if that money would not be returned, including compensation. When I met him a few days after he received this news, he had sold his watch and paid the money, but he had not heard anything from his brother or anybody else since. Muse explained to me: 'My mother contacts me regularly, usually at the end of every month. At that time, I also mostly send her some money. But my brother is a different case. He only called me once, last year, when he was in Mogadishu. My brother is not very good at keeping in touch and since he is moving through the country quite a bit, I cannot contact him myself. When I confronted him about this he replied that I had chosen to go to Kenya whereas he had chosen to stay in Somalia. That was his way of telling me to mind my own business'. Yet, despite this disagreement between the two brothers, Muse immediately sold his watch in order to assist his brother.

Whereas I was initially surprised to hear that someone in Dadaab was sending money to relatives elsewhere, I slowly realised that this was not uncommon. It happened in times of crisis or special need, but also when the person in Dadaab was in a relatively well-off position due to operating a business or receiving remittances from overseas. When I was in Dagahaley in November 1999, Yunis Axmed gave me another example. The year before, he had gone to Ethiopia and was assisted by his relatives in Dagahaley during the journey back to the camps:

The introduction of the *taar* has really assisted us here in Dagahaley. Last year, I went to visit my brother in Ethiopia for some time. On my way back, in Beled Weyne, I ran out of money due to unforeseen circumstances. I contacted my brother in Ethiopia through the *Dahabshiil* [*xawilaad* company], but after ten days, the money still had not arrived. I therefore decided to move back in the direction I had come from. Another relative of mine lived in the vicinity. However, on the way, I met someone who told me that the first radio set had just started to operate in Dagahaley. I contacted my brother there, since I knew he had recently received 250 dollars from overseas. My brother sent me 3,000 shillings and I was able to continue my journey. By the time I passed Beled Weyne for the second time, my brother in Ethiopia had also sent me money. I added his fifty dollars to the sum I had already collected and the total amount enabled me to reach Dadaab.

Advantages and Disadvantages of the Taar

As Yunis' story demonstrates, the introduction of the *taar* has had many advantages in the camps and elsewhere. At the same time, it has also had negative effects and entails risks. Through flow diagrams for impact analysis (Pretty et al. 1995: 244–45) and group discussions, I was able to get an impression of who was affected by the introduction of the *taar*, and in what way. The most important consequence of the introduction of the *taar*, in my view, was that it enabled many Somalis to trace their relatives and stay in touch with them. For example, Dheka Hassan told me that the radio sets had permitted her to communicate with her brothers and sisters in Somaliland for the first time. I asked her whether she had not been able to use other means of communication before, and Dheka told me: 'I could not send letters because the mail services are not reliable. And since most of my siblings are in Boosaaso, I also could not pass a message through people who were travelling there. Boosaaso is so far away that it is very unlikely that anybody from Dadaab will go there'. As such, the *taar* not only brought a different means of communication to the camps but in many cases it enabled the refugees to establish a connection with their relatives elsewhere for the first time. The *taar* plays a central role in strengthening transnational networks, but the refugees and other parties involved have also experienced the negative effects of the introduction of the *taar*.

Besides connecting those who were restricted in their contacts by limited communication technologies, the *taar* has played a major role in tracing *baafin*. Bishar Abdirahman explained to me how this works:

> There are two groups of customers who approach us: those who have the exact details of their relatives, and those who do not. The last group will want to trace a person whom they have left somewhere, for example in Mogadishu. When I receive such a request, I contact different radios in Mogadishu; I have the numbers of all the radio sets in the region. Then, the radio operators in Mogadishu try to trace the missing person, through the full clan details that I provide. If he or she is found, they will contact my *taar* and I will send a messenger to the person in Hagadera who tried to trace his or her relative. I only receive a payment when the two people manage to speak together.

Bishar removed a piece of paper that he kept in his pocket and continued: 'This paper has some names and numbers of a person for whom we received a call. A man in Somalia tried to trace his cousin, who indeed used to live in Hagadera but has now resettled in the U.S.A. I sent someone to the block and we found out his details. Then, I contacted the radio operator and was able to give him the person's telephone number in the States. These days it is very cheap to call the U.S.A. from Somalia, so the man who was trying to trace his cousin can now simply phone him'.

When relatives and friends are able to communicate with relative ease, important information can be exchanged fast and, when necessary, can be acted upon. Money can be sent in contingencies, as in the case of Muse Omar's brother. And when someone has died or a wedding is planned, refugees in Dadaab can decide to travel to their relatives or vice versa. In the Dadaab area, as well as in the wider Somali-inhabited region, the *taar* is ideally suited to bringing relatives, who live at a distance from each other, closer together, due to a number of practical advantages. First, the radios are portable and can be used anywhere, since they operate on a battery or solar energy and therefore do not have to be connected to an electricity supply. In most places, they are the only available means of communication. Secondly, once the radio set has been purchased there are little further costs involved in communication. Due to their relatively low costs, the *taar* are quite accessible to most people. Thirdly, the sets increase the safety of travellers because they do not need to carry money through insecure areas but can send it to their place of destination. Most business deals between the camps and Somalia take place in the same way, which increases the trust of both parties in a successful transaction. Thus, the introduction of the *taar* has led to economic development, as it has increased the flows of goods, money and people to even the most remote areas.

Yet, at the same time, there are also negative aspects associated with the functioning of the taar. First of all, as I mentioned earlier, the radio sets are kept and operated illegally in the camps, which entails a number of problematic consequences. A *taar* can only be operated by paying bribes and there is still a risk of confiscation. If that happens, it becomes impossible to send and receive information and money for an unknown period. Furthermore, those who have sent remittances just before the closure are not likely to be compensated for their losses. Another problem that many refugees mentioned was that the radio sets are not confidential. In order to communicate, it is necessary to speak loudly. Thus, when sitting in a place where a radio is operated, one can clearly follow arguments between husbands and wives or strategy discussions between businessmen. There is no privacy and there are people who visit them with the sole purpose of listening in on conversations. Parents send their children to get any interesting gossip and information about the war and *shifta* learn about who is to receive money or who is engaged in profitable business transactions. When money is collected from the *taar* and taken home, there is always the risk that bandits will come to claim it the same night. That is why many refugees believe that *taar* operations have increased the level of insecurity in the camps.

Another party that various groups of people mention as having 'lost out' as a consequence of the introduction of the *taar* is the Kenyan government. First, it is assumed that the *taar* has reduced the number of money orders and telephone conversations through the banks and Kenyan Postal and Telecom Cooperation. This would mean a loss of revenues for the Kenyan government, although it can also be argued that these Kenyan institutions do not operate in most of the areas to which the refugees communicate. Secondly, there are suspicions that *shifta* use the *taar* to pass encoded criminal information, which would be a threat to Kenyan national security. In Somalia, the radios are not only used to pass private information between relatives, but also for military purposes, when militias use them to exchange details on the ongoing war. Since the *taar* provide information about the conflicts in Somalia between clans that live together in the camps, this may spread tension in Dadaab as well. Besides, the Kenyan government fears that business activities between Somalia and Kenya using the *taar* include widespread arms smuggling. All of these factors combine to jeopardise Kenya's national security, which is another important reason why the *taar* operations are often closely monitored and at times obstructed.

Urban Refugees: Sustaining Links

Although refugees are supposed to stay in the camps unless they have explicit permission to be elsewhere, such as for medical reasons or educational purposes, many Somali refugees live in Nairobi. Somali refugees move from Dadaab to Nairobi for a variety of reasons. There are better means of communication in Nairobi and information provision from UNHCR and NGOs is also seen to be more accurate in town. Besides, refugees hope to gain better economic opportunities in town, as well as a better life in general. Looking for education, a job or resettlement, Somalis from Dadaab often require the assistance of others to establish themselves in Nairobi. At times, these others are relatives and friends who are already in town; at times they are family members who have gone for resettlement. Opportunities in the camps are limited, so migration to town is part of a family's livelihood strategies. Yet, city life is also hard: Eastleigh is filthy, insecure and expensive. Prices for daily living expenses are much higher in town than in Dadaab, and there is always the risk of being caught by the police. This entails further costs involved in 'buying freedom' because most urban refugees lead illegal lives, not having the correct documents to live outside the camps. It is clearly not easy for those who move to town to assist their relatives in Dadaab but still, many do, whenever possible. The husbands, daughters and sons who have gone to town with the specific goal of earning an income do manage to send money to their relatives in the camps. And even those who are in Nairobi for educational or other purposes economise in order to send a small amount to their dependents. The *taar*, especially, plays a very important role in remittance sending as well as communication. For a long time, it was the only means for refugees to connect from Nairobi to the camps directly, in a cheap and easy way. From 2004, this situation has greatly improved with the introduction of a repeater station in Dadaab, which has made mobile phone communication possible as well.

It is far more difficult to make an estimation of the number of Somali *taar* in Nairobi than those in the camps. Their number is much larger in Nairobi, and the *taar* are less visible there. In Dadaab, one can recognise the aerials on the roofs of the huts. But in Nairobi, *taar* are hidden inside lodges, behind guarded doors or in tiny rooms on the highest floors of residential blocks. According to Salad Abdinoor, who owned a *taar*, this did not mean that the Kenyan police were not aware of the operations of most radio sets. Though his *taar* was hidden from sight in one of the less busy streets of Eastleigh, with its main entrance locked by an iron door that had to be opened from the inside, the 'policemen on ground' knew of his activities. In fact, on the day of our interview in May 2000, I had to wait for him since he had just been arrested. When Salad arrived, he did not seem to be disturbed by the incidence at all. Laughing, he said that his arrest meant that he would have no lunch that day. When I asked him when the *taar* was first introduced in Nairobi, Salad told me: 'They first came with the sets from Somalia in 1994. The *taar* came with the refugees; they had not been used before that time. Radio sets are actually sold openly in town: there is nothing illegal about buying them, since they are also used on trucks and by NGOs. But the police refuses usage to the Somali refugees, so my business itself is illegal. Whenever the officers come, I will have to pay them something'.

The communication business is clearly lucrative in Nairobi. One of the radio sets I visited was situated in a room inside a dirty and run-down building. The small room was literally stuffed with Somalis, and people constantly came and went. Ibrahim Yassin, a refugee from Ifo who studied at a city college and had taken me to the *taar*, explained that in Nairobi, Somalis could afford 200 shillings to communicate: 'Often, they also pay the 200 shillings that the receiver of the call should pay. In the camps on the other hand, people do not make any money and thus 200 shillings is a lot'. According to Salad, the average number of customers he received a day was around ten to twelve. He told me:

But it varies from day to day. There are even moments when I have fifteen people in my place, all waiting to use the *taar*. Communication goes up when there are many business activities going on, like now that president Moi has reopened the border with Somalia. It also occurs in periods of drought or hunger, since that is the time when Somalis who stay in Eastleigh call their relatives in order to send them assistance. Most of the communication takes place between Nairobi and Somalia, with places like Mogadishu, Baidoba or Kismaayo. Recently, we also started communicating with Ethiopia. Then, there is extensive communication with the camps, both with Dadaab and Kakuma. Mostly these people call their relatives to send them money and exchange information about the health of family members, the general conditions and specific problems faced in the place they stay.

The better communication and economic opportunities available in town also benefit the refugees in Dadaab, as information and money are sent from Nairobi to Dadaab. When I asked Salad about the direction of the financial flows between Nairobi and the camps, he told me: 'Assistance is mainly sent from Nairobi, since refugees above all go to town to work for their families in the camps. The amounts cannot be compared to the amounts that we exchange in business transactions between Nairobi and Somalia for example, which often involve thousands of dollars. The money that is sent by refugees in Nairobi to their relatives in the camps is often no more than an equivalent of one hundred dollars; exceptionally they may go up to two hundred'. Dek Osman was one of the many who came to Nairobi in search of an income to sustain his family. He left behind his wife and children in Ifo, and when I asked him whether he was in touch with them, Dek told me: 'I communicate to them once or twice a month; not only through the *taar* but also by sending letters, which is cheaper. Besides, every now and then I go to Ifo and stay with my family for about ten days'. I then asked whether Dek was in a position to assist them, and he said: 'All the money I make from this job goes to my family: I am only here because of my wife and children. If there were an opportunity for me to make my living in the camps, I would not be here, away from them'.

But even those who had not come to Nairobi with the sole purpose of earning a living, like Ibrahim Yassin, did at times send money to the camps. He had left behind wife and children, aged four and two, in Ifo. He told me: 'I communicate to my wife every day, because my neighbour in Ifo has a *taar* and my wife is a friend of his wife. So I pass Salad's place every day, just to hear whether they are okay'. When I asked Ibrahim whether he was able to assist his family in any way, he told me:

> I get 7,490 shillings a month from Goal [an international NGO], in order to sustain myself during my studies. As soon as I receive that money, I send 2,000 shillings to Ifo, for my children. But the rest I really need for transport, food and lodgings in town. When I was working for CARE in Ifo I first earned 3,500 shillings, and later 4,000, and I managed to save 1,000 shillings every month. In Dadaab, you only need 40 shillings to make it through the day: food is provided, and there is hardly anything to buy in the camps. I continued saving until I had 40,000 shillings, but because my relatives were in need, the money reduced over time. Now, I still have 10,000 shillings in Ifo, and I am going to keep that money.

Despite his marginal income and limited choices, throughout the years Ibrahim has managed to save a considerable amount of money and is currently providing for his family, while simultaneously trying to improve his chances of better-paid employment by going to college.

Besides the many refugees who are in Nairobi to earn money and send it to those they left in the camps, there are also many refugees who come from Dadaab to Nairobi because they *receive* money. The first group often leaves behind family members in the camps, whereas the last group mostly lives in town with the whole family. When I tried to get an idea of the people in the camps who receive a monthly allowance from overseas, I was often told that I would not find many of such families in Dadaab. Those who receive money do not want to stay in the difficult conditions of the Dadaab camps, but will decide to move either to Garissa or Nairobi. After all, why should one live in an area with hardly any opportunities, when one can afford to do without the handouts that are provided there? Besides, due to security reasons, it is not safe to receive money in the camps. The main difficulty of life in town is that refugees officially are not allowed to stay there, except in special circumstances. Yet, living an illegal life is only truly problematic if a refugee is caught without the right documents and has no money or nobody to assist. Thus, many take the risk and shift to town.

Often it is through the suggestion of family members overseas, or at least with their consent, that refugees decide to move to Nairobi. Since it is not very easy to make a living in town, a monthly allowance becomes very essential to survival. During my conversation with Hassan Jamaac, I learned that it was mainly because of the *habar yar* (mother's sister) of Hassan's wife, Marian, that they now lived in Nairobi. After reuniting through the International Red Cross, Hassan and his wife stayed in Kenyan refugee camps for some time, but found the conditions unbearable due to shortages and insecurity. They decided to go back to Somalia, trusting that the circumstances in Mogadishu would have improved due to UNISOM's deployment. They stayed there for some years, though the situation was deteriorating. By that time, Marian's *habar yar*, who had never given birth and had taken care of Marian as if she were her own daughter, had gone to the U.S.A. When the situation got worse in Mogadishu, she contacted Marian and told her that they should move to Nairobi. She knew both places and promised that she would send them sufficient money to sustain themselves in Nairobi. This example clearly illustrates the fact that remittances improve the options of Somali refugees, and the *xawilaad* plays a vital role in this process.

Xawilaad: The Importance of Overseas Connections

Assistance amongst refugees in the camps and regional remittance flows between the camps and Somali homelands, other African countries or Nairobi are important for livelihoods in Dadaab. The majority of the Somali refugees do have relatives in these areas, and often can count on them in times of need. Yet, opportunities for making a living are not much better in Nairobi or Kismaayo than they are in Dadaab. As a consequence, although just a small minority of all Somali refugees live in Western countries, the remittances that these refugees send are very important for the livelihoods of refugees in Dadaab. Whereas in Western countries, (Somali) refugees also mainly occupy the lower socio-economic strata, living standards in the West cannot be compared with those in the Horn of Africa. Thus, it may even be possible for an unemployed refugee in Scandinavia to save hard and send fifty dollars a month to his or her relatives. Those who are better off may send two hundred dollars monthly, or higher amounts for specific occasions. Whereas these are relatively small amounts in the U.S.A. and Europe, in Dadaab such remittances enable the survival of many.

The Somali Diaspora and the Development of the Xawilaad

Nowadays, Somalis can be found on all continents and they constitute a considerable migrant group in a number of countries. But there is no specific information on the exact nature and magnitude of their dispersal. One of the problems encountered in identifying exact numbers is that Somalis who reside outside their home country fall under several statistical categories. There are those who migrated before the war, for education, job opportunities and a number of other reasons; who hold various types of residence permits or are now nationals of their new country. Then, there are those who fled after the war; some of whom are still registered as asylum seekers, others who hold temporary permits, others with full refugee status and yet others who are nationals. On top of all this, there is a grey mass of unregistered and illegal migrants. As a consequence, estimates of exact numbers vary widely. For example, Perouse de Montclos (2000: 3) has estimated that there are 75,000 Somalis in the U.K., as opposed to an estimate of 100,000 by Ahmed (2000: 380); whereas their official number (excluding preconflict Somalis) is 20,000 (Gundel 2003: 241). The difference is even greater in estimates of the total figure of Somalis abroad. Official figures indicate that by early 2002, an estimated 440,000 Somalis were registered refugees (UNHCR 2003), but their actual numbers have been estimated even at one to two million (Gundel 2003: 242).

As to the location of the Somali diaspora, existing networks of Somali migrants were important in shaping who was able to go, as well as how and where the later and much larger numbers of refugees went (Gundel 2003: 242). Migration to the Gulf States and Saudi Arabia by the time of the war had largely come to a halt and many of the workers had been expelled after 1991 (Perouse de Montclos 2000). Existing links did, however, enable Somalis to flee to Saudi Arabia, Dubai, Yemen and neighbouring countries. Then, before the war, a limited number of Somalis had migrated to the former colonisers of Italy and the U.K., as well as to the U.S.A. These early migrants were essential in providing the information and resources for others to be able to move to Western Europe and North America. Independent from this community-facilitated migration, resettlement programmes in the U.S.A., Canada and Australia also enabled Somalis to move to the West. Since the start of the war, the number of Somalis living abroad has risen almost tenfold, yet hardly 10 percent of them live in developed countries. The majority of Somali refugees can be found in neighbouring countries, and besides that, there is a very large group of people who have never been in a position to flee their country but who have been forced to leave their homes: the internally displaced persons (IDPs). As is the case everywhere in the world, the amount of resources that people have determines the distance that they can travel in order to be safe.

Whereas in the 1970s and 1980s, the majority of Somali migrants stayed in the Gulf States and Saudi Arabia, after the war the balance shifted to Western Europe, the U.S.A., Canada and Australia. With these shifts, the source of remittances also changed. In the prewar period, the 'franco valuta' system enabled traders to engage in business between the Gulf States and Somalia, while allowing migrant workers to send remittances to their relatives back home. At that time, migrant workers in the Gulf States and Saudi Arabia were primarily responsible for sending remittances, covering about 60–75 percent of the total amount of money transferred (Gundel 2003: 246; see also Ahmed 2000). According to surveys by the International Labour Organisation (ILO) in 1985, the 165,000–200,000 Somalis living in the Middle East earned 700 million dollars a year, of which approximately 30 percent, 280–370 million dollars, was estimated to be sent back to their native country (Gundel 2003: 247). Outside these areas, a Somali diaspora of any significance in terms of remittances only existed in Italy and the U.K. During and after the war, however, the source as well as the method of remittance-sending changed: Refugees dispersed into a worldwide Somali diaspora, and the transnational *xawilaad* companies, which were set up in the 1980s, established themselves to deal with the growing streams of remittances.

For many decades, the Somali have invested in systems that enabled migrants to keep in touch with those they left behind. This trend greatly intensified when, from early 1991, the largest mass flight took place and one to two million Somalis are estimated to have fled their country. It is commonly acknowledged that the most successful migrant businesses arise in the very interstices created by transnationalism; for example in shipping and cargo companies, import and export firms, labour contractors and money transfer houses (Glick Schiller et al. 1995: 55). This is also true for the establishment of the *xawilaad* companies by Somalis. *Xawil* is a Somali word, derived from Arabic, meaning transfer; usually of money or responsibilities. The *xawilaad* is an informal system of value transfer that operates in almost every part of the world (Horst and Van Hear 2002). It is run by Somalis and mainly used by Somalis; both for remittance sending and business transactions. Most of the Somali money-transfer business used to be handled by three companies: Al Barakaat, Dahabshiil and Al Amal.[5] Since the system overwhelmingly relies on telecommunications, these companies have invested heavily in telephones, mobile radio systems, computer networks and even satellite telecommunication facilities (see e.g. Perouse de Montclos and Kagwanja 2000: 216; Gundel 2003: 246). Whereas transnational links between Somalis have enabled the success of the *xawilaad*, at the same time these businesses facilitate the deepening of transnational relations.

Remittances have, for decades, played a crucial part in the Somali economy, but the sheer size of the current diaspora, combined with recent technological developments in the field of telecommunication and the collapse of the Somali formal economy, have added weight to their importance. Recently, there have been a few studies on the *xawilaad* system and the remittance flows it processes. In light of the fact that there is a war going on in Somalia, and as asylum seekers and refugees, Somalis have an incomparably precarious status, the amounts that they send are astonishingly large and frequent, and the transfers by *xawilaad* are made quickly and with great efficiency (Perouse de Montclos 2000). Estimates of the size of remittance sending amongst the Somali differ significantly from study to study; with a variation as large as from 140 million in one study to 800 million dollars in another (Gundel 2003: 247). Although hard data is difficult to obtain, there is no doubt about the significance of remittances for Somalis. According to the UNDP, migrant remittances exceed the value of exports as well as international humanitarian aid in Somalia, and probably reach more people (UNDP 2001). Perouse de Montclos (2000: 13) calculates a figure of one million beneficiaries, which is one-fifth of the population in Somalia; not including transfers made by petty traders and minor agencies. On the level of individual households, UNDP estimates that most remittances fall in the range of 50–200 dollars per month. These monetary flows do increase in times of economic stress, during droughts or in response to interclan warfare. Data from a UNDP household survey indicate that on average, remittances make up 22 percent of per capita household income in Somalia (UNDP 2001).

The limited studies available create the impression that there is a shift in destination and application of remittances. Whereas in the 1980s, two-thirds of the funds from the Somali communities abroad were used for trade and the other third to assist families, these proportions probably are now inverted. Perouse de Montclos (2000) explains this by the fact that the market in Somalia has gone down since the elite has fled the country, but I believe there is an alternative explanation. Larger and more diverse groups of Somalis have gone overseas after the war, who leave behind their relatives in a country shattered by conflict or in African refugee situations with similarly limited livelihood opportunities. Their primary motive for migration is less likely to be a specific job or educational opportunity, with which trade investments can be realised. Far more often, their main aim is to get a legal status that guarantees them a secure place to stay, which may then also contribute to a better livelihood. In this situation, responsibility for the immediate survival of family members left behind is far more acute than investments in trade. At the same time, a trend that mitigates the consequences of the first was observed. Whereas remittances sent to relatives before the war were used to finance consumption and assumingly 'unproductive' investments such as private housing or marriage, a recent development is that private investments in small businesses or real estate are more common. In Somaliland, for example, a study found that remittances have contributed significantly to the growth of a vibrant private sector (Ahmed 2000). As such, remittances do contribute to reconstruction and development of Somali-inhabited areas.

The Importance of Overseas Remittances for Refugees in Dadaab

The question of whether remittances lead to structural improvements in terms of development is disputed (see e.g. Van Hear 2001), yet it is commonly recognised that remittances do play an important role as a social safety net. They prevent economic collapse in the face of setbacks, such as war or drought at national level and help individual households to deal with these crises. In Dadaab, remittances are essential both in enabling basic survival and in dealing with contingency situations. Quite a large number of refugees receive remittances from Europe, Australia, Canada and especially the U.S.A. Exact figures on how many people receive remittances and how much money flows into the camps were hard to obtain, however. Even getting access to the xawilaad at times was a problem, with some agents denying that they were operating a money transfer business and others refusing to talk to me. Those I did speak to were reluctant when it came to mentioning figures. Some of the *taar* owners were similarly suspicious, depending on the attitude of the government towards them at the time I wanted to talk to them. When I tried to speak to *taar* owners in Garissa, for example, the government was just trying to round up all *taar* and take the owners to court. Thus, I was treated with a lot of distrust and found it difficult to talk to *taar* operators about their business.

I was mainly interested in the viewpoint of the refugees themselves and wanted to understand the importance of overseas remittances in their livelihoods. But the refugees were equally suspicious of questions on whether they received remittances. They feared that admitting to receiving remittances would lead to further cuts in the already meagre resources provided by UNHCR, WFP and NGOs in Dadaab. I tried to avoid their mistrust by working with Somali research assistants, but these young men and women were often facing similar difficulties. On top of that, a number of them were suspected of passing financial information to local *shifta*, who would then come and rob the respondents at night. On one occasion, a group was even chased away from a block because of such suspicions. In another group, I learned that one of the research assistants deliberately downplayed the number of people receiving assistance because he feared budget cuts as a result of my research. Thus, most of the data I obtained on the importance of remittances in the camps did not come from formal interviews. Rather, I collected relevant information during many informal visits and talks with refugees in the camps as well as from those people working closely together with me. Alternative methods, such as participatory group discussions and composition assignments in a primary school, added to my understanding of the importance of remittances in the refugee camps.

Once, I organised a group discussion in the house of Marian Farah, one of the respected women leaders in Ifo. I had asked her to invite some women from her block to come for tea and discuss a number of topics related to refugee life and how they were able to manage their families in Ifo. From the beginning I noticed that the women, and especially the hostess, had their own agenda, just as I had mine. They explained all the difficulties of refugee life to me: how the food was insufficient, how they did not get enough water and firewood, etcetera. And yet, the house in which we were guests was of a clearly higher standard than most of the houses I visited. Marian's family had beds to sleep on, as compared to the mattresses or mats that the majority of refugees owned. The compound consisted of quite a few well built huts, one with a tin door that could be locked, and Marian and a number of other women wore expensive material and golden jewellery. Sahra Yusuf had already informed me that Marian received a monthly allowance from her brother in the U.S.A., which to me would explain her relative wealth. I tried to learn more about the assistance they possibly received and asked how, with all the problems mentioned, they were able to sustain their families. Marian explained that she usually had to beg the neighbours and the women one by one told me stories of how they were struggling on the margins merely to survive. None of them allegedly had relatives overseas, or received any assistance.

Then, Nadjmo Axmed came in late. When I introduced myself, telling her that I was studying at a university in the Netherlands, she told me that her *abti* (mother's brother) lives in the Netherlands: 'My uncle has been very good for our family, because every year he sponsors one or two of his cousins to come to Europe. This year, it is my turn and my sons are now in Nairobi waiting to go to Norway. In fact, I am going to go to Dadaab to talk to my *abti* tomorrow. Sahra here [she pointed out one of the women] has a cousin in Norway from which she receives a monthly allowance and she told me it is a good place to live'. At that point, the women silenced her and I felt very cheated. This was certainly not the first time that people had lied to me about not receiving any assistance, but it had never happened *en masse* and arranged like this. Immediately after Nadjmo had been silenced, the women told me to write down their problems and send a letter to the BBC on their behalf. Afterwards, I realised that the set-up I had arranged was too similar to the one I had seen on a number of occasions. Often, groups of women leaders and 'vulnerable women' were invited to come to a community centre and explain their problems to donors and evaluators. These were occasions during which all the obvious problems in the camps were spelled out and enlarged in order to secure donor funding. The invited women were spokeswomen who fought for the cause of all refugees, and especially women. I guess we somehow had the same goal, but a different approach, dictated by our respective positions. As such, I had to be wary when collecting data, and especially quantitative material, on overseas remittances in Dadaab.

With these reservations in mind, I can give an indication of the importance of remittances from overseas for the refugees in the camps. My impression is based on informal discussions and interviews with refugees and *xawilaad* operators, as well as observations in the camps. Research assistants covered a number of blocks in Ifo to estimate the percentage of refugees receiving remittances. I also asked informants and people who were very involved in my research, like translators and CDWs, for the number of people in their direct surroundings who received assistance. Based on this information, I estimated that on average, at least 10–15 percent of the population in the camps benefited directly from the *xawilaad*. When I used this statement in group discussions, most people found it a fair estimation, although they remarked that it needed some refinement as there was said to be a high variation between the blocks as well as between the camps. In Ifo, the blocks close to the market, the UNHCR offices and the police base have a relatively high number of remittance-receiving refugees, because these blocks are more secure. In Dagahaley, I interviewed a number of refugees in block C3 and was surprised that so many of them received remittances. Later, I learned that those living in C3 were more likely to receive remittances because these were townspeople

who were relocated from Liboya, as opposed to the largely rural population in the camp. Hagadera is supposed to have the highest number of
refugees receiving money through the *xawilaad*, because the majority of
refugees in Hagadera originate from towns.

One group of people receives remittances only occasionally, mostly
when they ask for it in response to a contingency. They receive an amount
of roughly two hundred to five hundred dollars once, twice or maximal-
ly five times a year. The frequency depends on the number of relatives
who stay overseas, their willingness and ability to send money and the
kind of situation for which that money is needed. Yunis Ahmed had
worked for the agencies as teacher and translator on a number of short-
term assignments. He lived in the camp with his aged mother, close to the
house where his brother and wife lived. The brother was having mental
problems that were aggravated to the point where he became a danger to
his wife, threatening to kill her. Yunis tried to do whatever was in his
power, even giving up his teaching position to keep an eye on the family.
He also went to the local hospital for assistance but was told that they
could do nothing for his brother. When matters got out of hand he contacted a cousin in Nairobi who passed the message to their relatives in different places around the world, collecting one hundred dollars from one
family, three thousand shillings from another, and so on. Eventually, he
was able to send a total amount of six hundred dollars, which Yunis used
to take his brother to Nairobi for treatment. Whereas the international
community did not assist Yunis' brother, the Somali diaspora did. As
such, one of the most important benefits of the *xawilaad* system remains
that it provides social security in times of need.

Besides the group of people who receive occasional sums, there is a
group that receives regular (mostly monthly) remittances of about fifty to
two hundred dollars. In Dadaab, these are considerable amounts to spend
and remittances rarely stay within the nuclear family. They are spread and
benefit a much wider group of people, thus enabling the subsistence of
many refugees who could not have survived otherwise in the region, considering current levels of humanitarian aid provision. The largest percentage of remittances received is used for daily necessities, including
food, water, firewood, clothes and shelter. But beyond helping Somalis to
survive, the remittances transferred give people a choice. The money is at
times invested in business, but it is also used to assist others or for educational purposes. Many refugees have decided to use it to move from the
camps: away from insecure and marginal areas, towards economic opportunities, towards a better life or family members. These resources give
refugees in difficult conditions the capacity to assist themselves, and others. They also lead to development initiatives, for example, by improving
training opportunities in the region. In Hagadera, a former incentive
worker set up a computer-training centre in the market after having

received the starting capital for three to four computers from a relative in the U.S.A. This enabled refugees, who, in general, had very limited schooling and training opportunities in the camps, to gain computer skills. Thus, the money that reaches the camps from the West is not only used to improve survival chances or deal with specific occasions or contingencies within a certain family, but it has also led to economic improvement in the camps.

The Transnational Responsibility of Sending Remittances: Kinship and Gender Aspects

Transnational flows of information and particularly remittances are very essential to the livelihoods of refugees in Dadaab. But who exactly is responsible for sending these remittances and what relationship do those people have with the receivers in Dadaab? It is difficult to provide a single answer to this question because social networks operate with a certain degree of flexibility and there are many aspects of social relations, such as descent, kinship, age, gender or residence, on which an individual can rely. In most social organisations, people are involved in a variety of relationships that can cater for their needs. On top of that, kinship, gender or age may not be seen as fixed and clearly demarcated institutions: these aspects of an individual's identity are often used strategically and shaped by circumstances. Social networks consist of complex, multiple human relations in which individuals negotiate and at times switch (power) positions, in order to survive. In general, Somalis in Dadaab receive assistance from a whole range of people, though the large majority of remittance senders are relatives. Sender and receiver can be parents and children, plus all those in similar relationships, including uncles and aunts and nephews and nieces.[6] They are often (ex-)husbands and wives, plus occasionally their in-laws. Or they are brothers and sisters, plus first and more distant cousins.

Not only is the closeness and kind of relationship between provider and receiver a vital determinant of remittance provision, but so too, certainly, are the urgency with which assistance is needed and the ability of the person overseas to send money. I visited Dheka Hassan in Dagahaley, where she lived with her second husband and two young children: a daughter from the first marriage and a son from the second. Her first husband divorced her and now lives in the U.S.A., from where he sends her one hundred dollars a month through the *xawilaad*. Dheka explained:

> My ex-husband was the first to communicate and he gave me his telephone number. Now, I am usually the one calling him: if I have not heard from him for a long time or if I am facing a specific problem. He will then immediately call me back so that I do not have to bear the costs. The money we get from him

only covers our food and most basic needs, and at times it does not last and we have to take credit from the shops. We do not have any other source of income and my present husband does not work. However, my ex-husband cannot send us more money since he is a student in the U.S.A. and he also sends money to his wife in Nairobi. He has no job, but is able to save some money from his government allowance. This is only possible because he is staying with some of his siblings.

It is common for (ex)husbands to send remittances, especially when their (ex)wife is left with the care of smaller children. Similarly, children also often send money to their parents. During my stay in Dagahaley, I was introduced to Hajir Sheikh Ali, who lived in a compound together with his 33-year-old wife, eleven of his thirteen children and six other relatives. He was seventy-one and had seen much of the world throughout his years as a seaman and later through his work for the British in the Yemeni city of Aden. Hajir's son lived in Denmark, his daughter lived in London and one of his nieces lived in the Netherlands. Four other relatives also lived overseas. When I asked him how he was able to sustain the nineteen people in his compound, he told me:

First of all, I get a monthly pension from the British government of about ten thousand shillings or one hundred and sixty dollars. I can collect that money from the British Embassy in Nairobi, or tell them to send it to Barclays in Garissa.[7] Then, my daughter is very good and reliable when it comes to sending us money without me having to ask for it. My son, on the other hand, is stubborn and is causing us problems. He has, in fact, finished his studies at agricultural university, but he spent much too much time chewing qaad. Now, we wonder what he has turned to. Why would he otherwise send us so little money? Last time I asked him to send us something, he only sent two hundred dollars, although he must have a good job there. Nowadays, the Somali have come to realise that their daughters are more valuable than their sons when they go abroad. A daughter will always remember her parents and will send them whatever she can afford. But sons are careless and seem to forget their relatives in the refugee camps.

A considerable number of Somali refugees in Dadaab voiced the complaint that men forgot about their relatives in Dadaab more often than women did, so I decided to examine the gender division of remittance sending in more detail. I added a statement on this topic for discussion in the participatory workshops I held in all the camps with teachers, block leaders and CDWs. During this part of the workshop, I would split up the larger group of between twenty and thirty participants into smaller groups of about five people. These smaller groups were given a large sheet of paper with a very explicit statement, such as: '*Buufis* has done a lot of harm to the Somali community', or 'When going abroad, men forget about their relatives in Dadaab more easily than women'. Every sub-group would discuss the specific statement they were given, writing down arguments for and against it in order to decide whether they agreed with the statement or not. Afterwards, the larger group would listen to the ideas of every subgroup and a discussion would follow. In all work-shops, the 'gender' statement led to very heated debates amongst women and men, but also amongst men themselves.

Those who agreed with the statement claimed that women were more aware of the problems that exist in trying to sustain a family in Dadaab. Since women dealt with the household bills, it was argued that they were better at providing assistance; not only after they had left for resettlement but also while they were still in the camps. Opponents of the statement argued that, according to the Qoran, men carry greater responsibility for taking care of their family's needs and solving problems. In fact, the ques-tion of who was dealing with the household budget and who would feel most responsible for sustaining family members elsewhere was much dis-puted. Participants could, in particular, not agree on the supposed author-ity of men versus women in Western countries. Supporters of the state-ment assumed that Somali women gain a lot of rights when they go over-seas and are expected to manage the family budget there. Opponents, on the other hand, argued that Somali men in resettlement countries usually have far better jobs and thus more money to spend on their relatives. Besides, the money that their wife earns either goes to the husband or will be spent on her own household instead of being sent to Dadaab. Both groups agreed that an important reason for Somalis overseas to assist their relatives in Dadaab was that they wanted to maintain links with their family members. According to some, the underlying reason for wanting to maintain these links varied for women and men: while women needed to keep in touch with their relatives because they had a much weaker position in their new societies, men allegedly needed these links in light of an eventual return to Somalia.

I find these kinds of generalising gender statements very problematic, as gender roles, opportunities and expectations depend on a host of other facts. The same is true for kinship, as well as for other characteristics of social relations possibly influencing remittance sending that were not dis-cussed here. When analysing assistance provision, the particular circum-stances of the family are essential, for example in terms of the needs of family members in Dadaab and the opportunities of those overseas. The question is of how many relatives are living in Western countries and how many dependents they have to take care of; not only in Dadaab, but in any area where an independent livelihood is (temporarily) impossible. Individual characteristics of the men and women involved are also vital, as well as their class, age, educational background, career opportunities, future expectations, family pressures faced etcetera. As such, it becomes impossible, in my view, to talk of gender differences without analysing these other factors, which may or may not be gender-related. Yet, at the same time, I found it vital to problematise the gender division of remittance sending, because transnational activities and movements are too often depicted in an ungendered way, mostly assuming *male* actors (Salih 2001a: 655). My data do not, in any way, support this implicit assumption, as the cases described throughout this chapter, as well as the debates mentioned here, indicate that both Somali women and men play an important role in remittance sending and other transnational activities.

Survival in Dadaab: Handouts or Remittances?

The social networks that contribute to the livelihoods of Somali refugees in Dadaab are made up of flexible, multiple and dispersed relationships between relatives, clan members, neighbours and others. The fact that most Somali refugees in Dadaab assist each other whenever possible, has a cultural as well as a religious base, and many of the aid arrangements in the camps are a continuation of practices that were common in Somalia. In his research amongst the Ogaden refugees in Somalia, Lewis similarly noted that people in the camps were assisting each other, based on previous practices. He states that a 'new society has arisen in the camps based on a combination of the old patterns and the new circumstances' (Lewis 1982). It is essential to look at these assistance networks not just from a local perspective, because livelihood options in the region are scarce and thus opportunities to assist others are limited. Various flows of goods, money and information that stem from far beyond Dadaab determine the livelihoods of the Somali refugees in the camps. Investments in *taar* and *xawilaad* by Somalis around the world have largely enabled these flows, as they are vital for the transmission of valuables and information over large distances and involving remote areas. Due to these technical developments, far-off family members are now able to be involved in each other's livelihood decisions and actions with a much greater speed, frequency and efficiency than in the past.

In my opinion, this change justifies the use of the concept of 'transnational livelihoods' to describe the reality of life in Dadaab: In the first place, transnational assistance networks are essential for the livelihoods of refugees in Dadaab, as they would not be able to survive on the rations alone. And secondly, the transnational family is very involved in the livelihood decisions and actions of its members in various places. The question remains of what the relative importance of migrants' remittances is, as compared to international aid and regional economic opportunities. Refugees would not be able to survive in Dadaab on the rations provided, but would remittances be sufficient to sustain them? And how do both types of assistance interact with or complement each other? In order to answer these questions, it is vital to analyse the possible risks related to remittance sending, and compare them to those created by receiving handouts, as discussed in the previous chapter.

The many examples provided of individual and communal forms of assistance do not imply that all individuals always act according to cultural-religious norms and values. There are also cases of refugees who are in a position to assist but do not help others. In Ifo, Sahra Yusuf stayed with her cousin Abshiro Nasir for some weeks in order to be able to work for me as a translator. She was really disturbed by her cousin's lack of concern for others. Sahra sometimes complained that Abshiro was capable of assisting those in need, but was just too selfish to do so. She told me:

> Abshiro receives a regular amount of one hundred dollars from her ex-husband in Australia, but whenever she gets the notice from the *xawilaad*, she disappears to the other camps. Since I work during the day, I have employed Sagal, who is a close relative of Abshiro, to take care of my daughter. Abshiro treats Sagal very poorly: she does not even want her to take tea, the girl is not allowed to use a mat for resting and she has to work very hard. I sometimes give Sagal some sugar and tea leaves to take home because I know that her family live in very poor conditions. I also decided to give Sagal my *diric* (Somali women's dress), since the girl hardly has any clothes. But Abshiro, who gets a lot of money only to spend on herself and her two children, does nothing to support the girl.

Similar complaints were also made in relation to relatives in resettlement countries. Having relatives overseas is not always a guarantee that these people can or do send a monthly allowance or even an occasional sum.

Stories of refugees able but unwilling to assist others were rare, yet a common remark was that Somalis were no longer in a position to assist each other. Ebla Awas explained this in some detail: 'Assistance is not only a common trait in Somali culture, but it is also an obligation when it comes to our religion. The problem, however, is that here in the camps, nobody has much to assist others with. Only those with jobs at the different agencies or those with a business in the market may be able to help their relatives or neighbours'. During a participatory presentation in which we discussed the Somali culture of assistance, Abdiweli Moxamed made a similar point when he said: 'It is very true that Somalis assist each other and that culture indeed still exists up to this day. Yet we have to realise that as refugees, none of them have anything. What are they going to assist each other with? Even for Somalis who are rich, like those who have gone abroad, it is difficult to decide whom to assist. Who should they give money to, considering the fact that everyone is in need? Even the rich will have to limit themselves to an extremely needy family or someone with a specific crisis situation, as it is impossible to assist everyone'. Thus, an important difference between assistance provided by the international community versus community-based assistance is that handouts are provided to everyone on a regular basis, whereas Somali forms of assistance are constrained and do not provide security for everybody at all times.

The operation of *taar* and *xawilaad* not only bring benefits to the camps but also disadvantages. If the refugees hope or expect to receive remittances from their close or distant relatives overseas, they may spend scarce resources trying to contact them. Halimo Hassan told me that she had travelled outside the camps twice in order to try to communicate to her brothers in the Netherlands and Sweden: 'I was hoping that they could send me a monthly allowance or otherwise a sponsorship for my children. But unfortunately, I never managed to reach them'. Having hopes for a better future is very important in an opportunity-scarce place like Dadaab, but if these hopes lead to risky investments of large sums of money being spent on travel and communication, they may at the same time be quite damaging. Even those refugees without relatives overseas may be affected, because of the improved livelihoods they can observe in others. As Yasiin Hussein pointed out in a workshop in Dagahaley: 'Most people do not benefit from the *xawilaad* because only a small number of the refugees have relatives overseas and receive remittances. In fact, the *xawilaad* is bad because it increases inequality amongst the refugees in the camps. It frustrates those who do not get assistance from outside'. This is an effect of remittance sending that has been observed in other situations as well. Russell (1986), for example, mentions an increase in social and economic tensions and rifts between households receiving and those not receiving remittances.

However, at the same time, these effects are mitigated in Dadaab by the fact that many people beyond the receiver alone benefit from remittance sending. Indirect beneficiaries include, for example, relatives and neighbours of those receiving remittances, who are usually assisted in money or kind, *xawilaad* owners and workers, business people and those employed as maids or labourers by the refugees who receive money. Yunis Axmed told me in this respect: 'The introduction of the *xawilaad* has raised the standard of living in the camps and these remittances help the entire refugee community in one way or the other'. This, to my knowledge, includes both the higher classes, like the wealthier businessmen who see their businesses flourish due to the increasing financial flows in Dadaab, and the lower classes like, for example, the Bantu men hired as labourers by wealthier refugees to construct houses or build pit-latrines.

Indeed, remittances from overseas have generally improved the economy in the refugee camps. Livelihood opportunities in the region are scarce, yet the refugees have the cash to buy their daily necessities and at times more than that. The markets of especially Hagadera, but also Ifo and Dagahaley, are thriving, although this improved economy simultaneously led to price inflation, again not affecting everybody equally. Thus, it is not unlikely that, although in absolute terms the 'transnationalisation' of refugee livelihoods in Dadaab has benefited all refugees, it has benefited some relatively more than others. For the group of refugees not profiting in any way, which could be 10 to 15 percent of the population, handouts are vital to their survival.[8] These people have to survive under highly insufficient conditions, and malnutrition is common. The large majority of refugees, say 70 percent, benefits from remittances indirectly or has other vital sources of income, thus being able to supplement the insufficient rations. These people use additional funds to buy sugar, tea, milk, firewood, vegetables and occasionally meat; or use saved up funds to start a small business. Finally, the 10 to 15 percent of refugees directly benefiting from remittances are able to substantially improve their livelihoods and, at times, use larger amounts of remittances for investment in business, education or migration. For this group, remittances are at least as important as the rations provided.

Another vital benefit that the *xawilaad* system has brought to the refugee camps is that it has improved social security. In times of contingency, at least a section of the camp population has relatives in the West to call upon, whereas the international refugee regime usually does not provide any assistance. Those who receive regular remittances are also more easily given credit by businesspeople when necessary. On the other hand, according to some, this can lead to an attitude of dependency. Since it is easy to take things on credit, patterns of expenditure are said to change. Whereas in general, a 'dependency syndrome' created through remittance sending is as unlikely as one created through handouts, some individual cases do occur. Nuradin Yusuf, for example, had not received any assistance from his daughter in the U.S.A. for four months when he called one of his relatives who lived close to her. He asked the man what had happened to his daughter and whether she was still alive. Nuradin was told that his daughter's husband was in hospital because he had been involved in an accident. Besides, the couple had moved. When Nuradin received the new telephone number, he immediately called her. She apologised to her father for not having contacted him for a long time and sent him three hundred dollars. She also included fifty dollars for his sister Fartun and promised that from now on she would send him money every month. Nuradin was very annoyed with his daughter because she knew that he did not have a job. He had to pay off 13,000 shillings at the shops for credits for expenditure on milk and clothes. Whereas in this case, the relationship between father and daughter was re-established, there are also cases of Somalis in the West who choose to 'disappear' in order to escape the mounting pressure of family obligations (see Rousseau et al. 1998: 403).

A related problem is that those receiving remittances are even said to stop working for their daily bread (Russell 1986), or use the money unwisely. In Dadaab, a common complaint is that too much remittance money is spent on chewing *qaad*. This unproductive attitude may be caused by the fact that they know their relatives in the West will continue to provide for them, but the reason may also be that they start 'suffering' from *buufis*. Some of the refugees who see the flows of money coming into the camps want to go to the source of that money in order to live an independent life in freedom. Dahabo told me how Nuradin was affected:

> He used to work for the UNHCR and for CARE in these refugee camps. He got a job very easily because he came with his recommendation letters from the UNHCR in Somalia. But for the last three years he has not worked and neither have I. I would like to start a business in the market, but since there are no people from my clan in the camps, nobody would buy from me. As for my husband, he has got a disease called *buufis*. Every day, he goes to UNHCR to follow up on his case, though I do not see a clear line in his actions. His mind has gone abroad already and he only follows what has happened in relation to resettlement issues, what is being planned for the future and which agency or embassy is coming to Dadaab. That is his only work. He has *buufis* and is not ready to do any other work any more. Luckily, his daughter boosts our morale by regularly sending us some dollars.

In Dahabo and Nuradin's case, one may wonder whether it really is lucky that Nuradin's daughter sends them remittances, as it has focused Nuradin's attention away from his life in Dadaab, towards the dream of going elsewhere.

Notes

1. You own a small part of your brother's property.
2. For an interesting analysis of the interplay between religion, clan and '*Somalinimo*' see Al-Sharmani (1999).
3. Inside and outside the camps. The difference between clan members and relatives is of course not absolute, as clan members are always related and all relatives on the father's side are also clan members. The distinction is based on the closeness of the kinship and whether or not it is still traceable.
4. Whereas transnational care activities are mainly carried out by women, this should not lead to the conclusion, proposed by Salih and others, that transnational remittance sending is mainly the responsibility of men, as examples from this chapter clearly illustrate.
5. Al Barakaat was closed down in November 2001, being on the list of organisations suspected to have links with Al Qa'ida (see Horst and Van Hear 2002).
6. Amongst the Somali, relationships between uncles/aunts and nephews/nieces are counted through various genealogical links. Not only are 'ego's' [an anthropo-

logical term to denote the 'I' from whose point of view kinship relations are being reckoned] parents' siblings his/her uncles/aunts, but so are ego's grandparents' grandchildren, and so on. The number of genealogical links that separate relatives determines the level of closeness. Furthermore, a distinction is made between links through the mother and the father. For an excellent overview of Somali kinship reckoning, see Lewis (1994).

7.   During my stay in Dadaab, Barclays Bank in Garissa closed down because the Kenyan Somali inhabitants of the region were no longer borrowing, saving or sending money through the bank. I was informed that this was caused by the competition from the *xawilaad* offices, which were trusted and used far more than formal banks.

8.   Christensen (1987) distinguishes three similar economic categories amongst (Ogaden) Somalis in refugee camps in Somalia.

5

Buufis: Imagining or Realising Migration to the West

Bashir Mahat and Abdulahi Noor collected information on *buufis* in Hagadera after participating in a course I organised on 'Data collection and report writing'. They experimented with a number of the methods of data collection that I had discussed and submitted reports to me of several structured and unstructured interviews as well as unobtrusive observations that they had carried out in the camp. One of their reports describes how they visited a Somali man in their block with the intention of interviewing him, using a list of questions they had prepared on *buufis*. The man told them that he had dreamt of going overseas before, but was cured of *buufis* after seeing its dramatic consequences on a teenage boy to whom he was related. Bashir and Abdulahi asked the man whether he could tell them about that boy, and their report provides the story that the man told them:

> Nasir was living with me here in Hagadera and he was satisfied with his life. It was not a good day for him when one of his brothers decided to sponsor his resettlement. Nasir went to Nairobi to wait for his sponsorship. He spent over one year there, while *buufis* was growing in his mind. He learned English and developed his skills. He was sure that he would soon be in America, or that he was in America already; he was thinking about that during the day and dreaming about it at night. Whenever he and his friends were together, all they used to talk about was America and the way the Americans live.
>
> One day he was called for his interview and he fortunately passed. He invited all his friends, relatives and companions in *buufis* to celebrate with him. During his *buufis* period, he had also met a girl whom he loved very much. They had promised each other that their wedding ceremony would take place in the U.S.A. As soon as Nasir reached there, he was going to send her a visa and ticket so that they could reunite in the U.S.A. After a while, the Immigration and

Naturalisation Service (INS) called Nasir for screening. Early that morning, he went to his girlfriend's house. She walked with him to see him off, hoping for success, and they agreed to meet in the lodge where he lived. When he came back to the lodge where his girlfriend was waiting for him, he told her that he would receive the decision in a month's time. He was sure of success. They waited for the outcome happily and eagerly. Then he was called for the result and was given the white envelope. He opened it on the spot. Unfortunately, the title of the letter was VERY SORRY. He glanced away, not trusting that this was his own letter. But when he glanced back, he read his name on the letter. He then put it in his pocket but his feelings had been hurt and his mind was sending wrong impulses. He went away.

On his way, he came to the site for Garissa busses and he boarded one of them until he reached Garissa itself. Then, he took another bus which brought him to Hagadera. As he came out of the bus, he reached a small tree between the butcher and the bus station. First, he put off his shirt and hung it on one of the branches of the tree, and after that, he took off his trousers and hung it on another branch. Then, he took off his t-shirt and pants and hung them on another branch, after which he started walking. Although people were occupied with their business in the market, some were close to him and saw what he was doing. That is when they realised that the boy was simply mad and they forcibly reclothed him.[1] He is now in Kismaayo where traditional healers are trying to cure his illness.

In this chapter, my main aim is to shed light on the different aspects of *buufis*, which at times leads to resettlement in the West and sometimes has extreme consequences like in the case of Nasir. After providing a description of the word *buufis* as used in the Dadaab camps, I will discuss various factors that are important in interpreting the migration dream as well as the realisation of that dream. Then I will describe the possible routes that Somali refugees can take in order to leave the camps for the West.

Defining *Buufis*

Coming back from my first fieldwork in Dadaab and mentioning the word *buufis* to Somali refugees in the Netherlands and elsewhere in the diaspora, I was surprised to find out that most of them had never heard of it. Some, who had, informed me that it was an expression only known and used in Kenya. Others used the word differently, to indicate mental health problems of any kind. Thus, during my second fieldwork I no longer assumed that *buufis* was a common Somali word, but instead I asked more questions concerning its origin and exact meaning. *Buufi* means 'to blow into or to inflate' (Zorc and Osman 1993). This literally refers to air, *hawo*, which also stands for a longing or desire for something specific, an ambition or even daydream. Thus, by inference, *buufis* could indicate a longing or desire blown into someone's mind. In Dadaab, whereas *buufis* is mostly used to refer to someone's hope, longing, desire or dream to go for resettlement, it is also applied in a number of other, closely related ways. The Somali refugees in the camps use it in three other contexts: resettlement itself, the people who long to go overseas and the madness that at times occurs when the dream to go overseas is shattered. When I asked Somalis in Dadaab and Nairobi about the origins of the word, I was mostly told that it was first used like this in 1991, after the outbreak of the civil war. A number of Somalis told me the word originated in Kenya, and some specifically mentioned the former refugee camp Utange as the place where the word *buufis* originated.

During an interview with Arte Awas in Eastleigh, I mentioned my surprise at the fact that *buufis* was not a common Somali word. I told him that I had had to explain to Somali refugees in the Netherlands how the word was used in Dadaab and asked Arte whether he could tell me where and when the word originated. He gave me a fascinating genealogy, answering:

> The word originated in 1901 and was first used by Sayyed Moxamed Abdulle Hassan.[2] Sayyed Moxamed used the word for those who tell lies. At that time, the English and the Italians had colonised Somalia and some Somalis were collaborating with them. He called the people who cooperated with the colonisers *buufis*. The term was later revived in 1991 in Ras Garad, a place in Somaliland where Sayyed Moxamed used to be a lot. From there, it moved to Utange with some of the refugees who went there. There were many businesspeople and government officials who were staying in Utange and they travelled a lot. Thus, by that time, the word *buufis* spread all over Kenya.

Unfortunately, I only heard this account once and it was definitely not common knowledge: no one has acknowledged or denied it. If it is a true story, it would link the word to a historical scepticism and resistance towards the West and a feeling of betrayal by those who want to be associated with it.

Various recent studies on Somalis make note of a migration dream existing amongst those who have not yet fled their country and those who have found asylum in the region. Research that specifically focuses on 'the pre-migration dream of leaving' amongst young Somalis in Ethiopia and Somaliland (Rousseau et al. 1998) describes patterns remarkably similar to those in Dadaab. The authors link what they call the 'myth of departure' to the traditional role that travel has played in Somali society. 'Travelling, whether for the purpose of scouting for water and green pastures or finding out about foreign countries most likely to offer a good education and favourable socio-economic conditions, is a way to gain information and perspectives that promote the economic development of the community' (Rousseau et al. 1998: 390). Although the authors mainly refer to the traditionally economic role of travelling for Somalis, the element of exploring new grounds certainly also has sociocultural and religious importance both for individual and communal growth.[3] Travelling is a common activity amongst Somalis and investments have been made for many decades in order to send community members elsewhere. The first waves of these kinds of sponsorships were mainly in search of pastures and education and were restricted to Somalia, Kenya, Ethiopia and Yemen. With the oil boom in the Gulf States, people were increasingly sent to countries at a greater distance from Somalia for the purpose of finding employment. At the time, only intellectuals and seamen went to Western countries but after the war, large-scale immigration to the West became commonplace.

Before reaching the 'final' destination, Somali refugees often have to stay in an intermediate country where their life revolves around visiting embassies and airports, obtaining papers and being interviewed. It is common for refugees in these countries of first asylum not to be interested in staying there (Kusow 1998: 120). Mostly, it concerns neighbouring countries that are themselves economically depressed and cannot provide any livelihood opportunities for the refugees. During their stay, they are dependent on international aid and the aim of many is to move on to a more permanent destination. In Egypt, for example, Somalis are offered only temporary refuge. Hence, most Somalis in Cairo strive for asylum in Western countries where there are possibilities of permanent residence and employment (Al-Sharmani 1998: 2). In the words of Al-Sharmani, '[t]he West is physically far but very much present in the lives of the refugees'. They exchange stories of families and friends who live in the West and constantly try to attain the ultimate goal of gaining asylum in one of the countries in Europe or North America (Al-Sharmani 1998: 57).

In their research in Somaliland and Ethiopia, Rousseau et al. (1998: 394) describe this period of waiting in an intermediate country as 'a crucial time, in which the *young man* must count not only on his own resourcefulness, but also on his family ties at home and abroad, and his peer relationships' (emphasis mine). Collective and individual dreams of the successes of others and their own anticipated departures turn the difficult transition period into a highly meaningful time and space. The partial substitution of dream travel for real travel enables them to survive the wait and escape despair, but also puts them at risk of losing contact with reality and sliding into madness (Rousseau et al. 1998: 388). This detailed description is very similar to what I encountered in Dadaab, although the phenomenon is not called *buufis*. One point of difference, which may be caused both by the different locality as well as by the focus of the researchers, is that only the migration dream of young Somali men is described. This would be inaccurate in the case of Dadaab, where resettlement is evenly divided between men and women. As Abukar Hassan pointed out during a workshop: 'The agencies are more on the side of women with, for example, special resettlement programmes for vulnerable women. This stimulates *buufis* and enhances the chances of women to go overseas'.

A second point of difference is that the account presented by Rousseau et al. only gives a pathological perspective. For example, they describe how it is commonly assumed by older Somalis that those who 'suffer' from the dream of leaving are possessed by the *saar* (spirit) of travel (Rousseau et al. 1998: 386). Curing such a person is done in ways similar to cases of *saar* possession, where the healers question the possessing spirit, the *saar*, about the causes of the misfortune. The *saar* then expresses its wishes through the person and promises to leave once the wishes have been fulfilled (see also Lewis 1971). Helping the person leave a state of being possessed by migration dreams is the responsibility of the community, which must mobilise to send him or her on a trip in order to satisfy the *saar's* desires. Whereas this is a fascinating and very useful approach to analysing *buufis* in the extreme case of Nasir, something that would merit further study by medical anthropologists and others, I find it far too restrictive for a sound analysis of the existence of *buufis* in Dadaab in general. I object to this narrow focus since it rules out the potential of imagination as a social practice that can fuel action and is central to all forms of agency (see Appadurai 1996). Instead, I prefer to see *buufis* as entailing both risk and potential, an ambiguity that the following oral and written texts produced by refugees also voice.

Buufis *as Described in the Camps*

Idris Hussein was one of the participants in the training on data collection and report writing that I organised in Dagahaley at the end of 1999. He volunteered to assist me in my subsequent research but had too many obligations to attend group meetings. He was a twenty-year-old standard seven pupil who was looking for an incentive job in order to pay for his mother's medical expenses. Since his mother had lost a leg during the war and Idris was her only son she really needed his assistance. Idris attended primary school and participated in as many workshops and training sessions as possible, while doing voluntary work in the school library as well as an occasional short-term job. Although he was not in a position to attend the follow-up meetings, he still collected data for me. He gave me three written interview reports and also asked me whether I could give him an empty tape. I did and some time later I received the tape and was told that it contained a number of interviews. Idris had recorded these interviews as if they were being broadcast on the radio and I was really impressed by his creativity as well as by the fruits of a participatory approach. In the training sessions I had repeatedly stressed the importance of 'active learning' and I had tried to stimulate participants to be responsible for their own progress. Active learning to me entailed asking as well as answering questions, experimenting with the theory and practical exercises worked on in class and developing a (self)critical attitude in the training sessions. I was amazed by the creative way a number of people picked this up (Fig. 5.1).

The tape first contains three interviews that Idris conducted about the possibilities for communication that refugees have in Dadaab. After these interviews, he welcomes 'somebody suffering from *buufis*'. The man starts a monologue, occasionally supported by Idris' hums and words of approval.

> My name is Zigzag. The word *buufis* stems from the Somali language and involves a person who has sent his or her application letter to outside countries. When the first rejection letter arrives, stating that he has to go back to the motherland and find peace there, the person may nearly go mad. He starts running to the UNHCR offices every day, looking for a chance to go. At night, when other people worry about their safety, that person thinks about what to do when going to the UNHCR the next day. Before sending the application letter, the person might have heard rumours or might have known refugees with relatives in the West in the camps. He then wants to know how people live there, whether they are wealthy or not. If he learns that they are prosperous, he starts wondering why he does not go there. 'If Abdi goes, then why not me?' This is how people adapt to outside countries while they are physically in the camps. In fact, *buufis* is a kind of disease that is spread through verbal expressions. It can have an advantage, because when someone goes to the UNHCR every day consecutively, he may be given resettlement. But it can also be life threatening, because if the person recognises that he cannot go overseas, he may kill himself, starve himself or simply go mad. Hey, take my advice and do not fall into the trap of *buufis* programmes!

Figure 5.1 *Young man in Hagadera.*

Idris then asks Zigzag: 'Why do you use a pseudonym, when you are only suffering from *buufis*, which is very common in Dadaab? If you are ashamed of your disease why did you not try to save yourself from it at an early stage?' Although Zigzag unfortunately avoids answering this question, it clearly sums up the ambiguity of buufis. On the one hand, it is very risky to fall into 'the *buufis* trap', which causes the refugee's mind to be focused on resettlement and what it takes to achieve that. As a consequence, time and energy are invested in a possible future elsewhere, instead of in local opportunities, and if this future elsewhere cannot be reached this may lead to madness or even death. But, on the other hand, when it pays off and leads to resettlement the gains may be very considerable. According to Zigzag, this knowledge actually causes people to apply for resettlement: they start suffering from *buufis* when they learn about the prosperity of life in the West, seeing others pick the fruits from it and wondering why they should not. Thus, imagining life elsewhere and believing that it is possible to live such a life is an essential factor in the creation of *buufis*.

During the two months that I taught English composition to standard seven pupils in Midnimo, one of the primary schools in Ifo, I gave them a number of homework assignments. One of those assignments was to write a composition about *buufis*. Most of the pupils started their text with an introduction to *buufis*; what does the word mean? The translations of *buufis* varied from 'going abroad' or 'resettlement' to 'hopes for abroad' and 'everyone who is interested to go abroad'. Xared Cali wrote:

> *Buufis* is a Somali word, and the meaning of the word is 'resettlement'. People changed its meaning and said that it is a disease that attacks people who are mentally in America and physically in Ifo. While I was in the refugee camps in the Dadaab division, I recognised that the issue that everybody is most looking forward to is acquiring resettlement to a Western country and especially to the U.S.A. or Canada. Many refugees get a chance to go there, either through a sponsorship or an opportunity given by the Protection Officer in the area. The most likely cases are those of people who lack security and rape cases. Others are those who claim to be from a minority tribe.

Fatuma Moxamed also concentrated on the criteria of eligibility for resettlement: 'The requirements for granting a refugee visa or a special humanitarian visa are that the applicant must be subject to persecution or substantial discrimination, as a consequence of gross violations of human rights in the home country. If these conditions are met, the decision-makers will then assess the person's need for resettlement and his or her interest in entry in the First World. During the early days of the camps, people were not interested in resettlement because they believed that overseas countries were the lands of the Christians, where no Islamic life could exist'. The main text then mostly concentrated on the causes and consequences or the positive and negative sides of *buufis*. Here, the pupils talked about issues that I will discuss in more detail shortly, such as the fact that *buufis* is caused by the insufficient livelihood conditions in the camp combined with hopes for better circumstances overseas; the risk of focusing only on a place far away, potentially leading to madness; the positive effects of resettlement in terms of education and remittances; the negative effects in terms of the risk of failing; and the influence that life abroad may have on the culture and religion of Somalis living there.

From this main argument, the conclusion then focused on whether *buufis* was a helpful or damaging phenomenon for refugees in Dadaab. Most of the compositions expressed a true ambiguity towards *buufis*, in both translations – the hope to go for resettlement and resettlement itself. Cali Axmed expressed the complexity well: 'It is good, but still it is bad. If someone fails the interview, he may tell you that it is better to die than to live in Africa. Many people have failed in *buufis* and became mad, or committed suicide. Others, however, pass the interview and go abroad. They send money to their relatives, and some are successful in their new countries; there are even a few who are now among the ruling parties'. Abdulahi Bashir is more pessimistic about the effects of resettlement: '*Buufis* affected the people of Africa seriously because every day, people are standing in front of the UNHCR compound in order to be accepted. When they leave Africa to go abroad, they will no longer contribute to Africa's economic development, and they will also take their property. It is foolish of people to have more interest in staying in a foreign country than in their home country, since in your home country you can cultivate your own land and live more freely than in any other place'.

Forced or Voluntary? Migration and Choice

Migration theories explain in various ways the drive to migrate, though few of them shed light on the intensity of migration dreams as in the case of Nasir mentioned earlier. While his is indeed an extreme case, at the same time *buufis* is widespread in Dadaab and needs to be explained in all its variations. When analysing motivations to migrate, many theories implicitly assume a 'rational choice', following a considered evaluation of the options available to the migrant (Richmond 1988: 13). A distinction is generally made between 'push' and 'pull' factors in the countries of origin and destination. Human needs and aspirations are often represented in terms of economic benefits, social mobility or family reunion. In the case of refugees, however, the concept of 'rational choice' is seen to be less appropriate. In refugee theory, the common denominator is rather a sense of loss of control over one's own fate, migration being 'forced' upon the individual by mainly political factors. But according to Richmond (1988: 17), migratory decisions, even those taken under conditions of extreme stress, do not differ from other kinds of decisions in that structural constraints and facilitators influence social action and human agency.[4] Thus, the distinction between voluntary and involuntary migration is misleading, since all behaviour is seen to be determined to some extent by choice; it is only the degree of freedom that varies.

Richmond alternatively suggests a continuum from proactive to reactive migration: under certain conditions, the decision to move may be made after due consideration of all relevant information, whereas at the other extreme the decision may be made in a state of panic facing a crisis situation which leaves few alternatives but escape from intolerable threats (Richmond 1988: 17; 1993). In other words, migration is always a decision made, but the opportunity and time available to weigh one's options and thus the level of feeling in control over one's own fate varies. As Dahabo's story in chapter 2 makes clear, even in times of war individuals may still weigh their options when deciding whether to move or not. Dahabo looked for safety by moving between places within Somalia that she was linked to, through birth, marriage or property and anticipated residence. Only when her husband traced her and asked her to join him, and after thorough consideration, did she decide to move to the refugee camps in Kenya. And Dadaab, again, is not likely to be the final destination of Dahabo and Nuradin, nor of most of the refugees who live there, which makes the distinction between forced and voluntary migrants even more problematic. Their migration dream is closely related to the transitory nature of the camp set-up, combined with slim chances of stability in Somalia or permanent residence in Kenya. Their experience is less accurately phrased in the dual terms of forced versus voluntary or political versus economic migration, but may be more usefully described in terms of their ability to weigh options and make choices; taking into account the reality of life in Dadaab and expectations of life elsewhere, as well as opportunities and constraints experienced while trying to achieve decided-upon goals.

Explaining the Migration Dream in Dadaab

One of the reasons why many Somali refugees are suffering from *buufis* is simply the poor quality of their life in the camps. In a participatory meeting that I organised in June 2000 in Dagahaley, to share my preliminary results with the elders in the camp, I asked them whether they could explain to me the existence of *buufis* in the camps. A woman stood up and said: 'When the refugees came to Dadaab, they soon realised that life in this area is very problematic. Basic necessities like food, water, education and healthcare were missing and the refugees faced insecurity and found

their movements restricted. That is when they started to look for alternatives, and *buufis* developed. At every distribution, I cry when I wait for
my ration and see how the respected elders and religious leaders of
Somalia are standing in line. I weep when I witness how a man cannot
even respect a pregnant woman, but pushes her aside to be first in line'. I
was told how, over the years, *buufis* has increased, since the situation in
the camps has got worse and a solution to the war in Somalia seems far
off. Abukar Warsame, a poet and artist from Hagadera, expressed his
views as follows: 'In Somalia, no freedom, no human rights and no security for people and property exist. On top of that, at the moment I do not
have any finances to start a new life. *Maxay ku nuugtaa maxayse ka nuugtaa?* If a baby has no lips and the mother has no breasts, what will he suck
with and where will he suck from?'

Another factor that makes the Somali refugees dream of resettlement is
their need for peace and security. There is no real hope for a speedy solution to their plight as the refugees have no prospect of being allowed to
remain and settle in Kenya, whereas lasting peace in Somalia seems
unlikely in the near future (Crisp 1999b: 22). According to some, the level
of *buufis* was directly related to the state of security in the camps and in
Somalia. During the peace negotiations in Djibouti I was told how *buufis*
was reducing in the camps since the Somali refugees were hoping for
peace in Somalia. At the same time, feelings of insecurity in Dadaab may
grow as a consequence of clan fighting or *shifta* activities, increasing the
wish to go elsewhere. Bashir and Abdulahi interviewed Abukar Warsame
almost one year after I did. When they asked him about the first time he
thought of resettlement, he replied: 'I though of it first here in Hagadera,
when bandits came to the blocks at night; killing an old man and raping
and torturing a virgin young woman. Some days later, five of them came
to my own block and went out with a heavy load on their backs having
robbed my neighbours. Since I have recently married, fear and worry
have multiplied in me because if bandits attempt to rape my wife in my
presence, I will definitely defend her, which may be my death. On top of
that, I do not want to lose my children's future, though mine has already
been lost'.

I got a similar picture from a participatory matrix exercise I used during my trainings in the camps. In a group discussion, I asked the participants to answer two questions, which I then organised in matrix form.
The first was 'What are the future options open to the refugees in
Dadaab?' and the second was 'What are the criteria on which to judge
these options?'. The criteria that refugees mentioned in order to judge
where best to live were related to whether it would provide a durable
solution, a livelihood as well as security, freedom and safety. Then, I asked
them to award scores from one to five according to how well they expected a certain place to fulfil a certain criterion, of which table 5.1 provides
one example, taken from a training session in Hagadera, early 2000. As is

clear from table 5.1, Dadaab scored low in all aspects and local options in general were not very popular as durable solutions; in the first place, because of an experienced lack of security and freedom. In the case of repatriation, participants said that they could only return if there was maximum peace and security in Somalia. Thus, they opted to give five points for peace/security, freedom and human rights in order to stress that these were necessary conditions for their return. Resettlement in this matrix exercise was seen to be the best durable solution, scoring high in all aspects that the refugees found relevant for the options open to them in the future.

Table 5.1 *Future Options for Refugees in Dadaab Participatory Matrix, Workshop Hagadera, May 2000.*

Options / Criteria	Repatriation	Resettlement	Stay in Dadaab	Local Integration	Go to Nairobi	Relocation to Other Camp
Durable Solution	3	4	1	1	1	2
Education	1	5	1	2	4	2
Self-reliance	1	5	1	3	4	1
Food/ Economic Stability	2	5	1	3	3	2
Security/ Peace	5	5	2	2	2	3
Freedom	5	2	1	2	1	1
Human Rights	5	3	1	1	1	1
Total	22	29	8	14	16	12

Besides the fact that the refugees are not satisfied with their life in Dadaab, another reason for their wish to migrate is that they imagine a better life elsewhere.[5] As Collinson (1999: 5) states, the global communications revolution and the expansion of global electronic mass media and global mass marketing might encourage more people to move from the South to the North. The media produce and disseminate information and images about the world, providing large and complex repertoires of representation and narrative. According to some authors, this has led to a fundamental change in the nature of imaginations over the past decades. Images of the lives of others are presented, in which the lines between the realistic and the fictional are blurred; especially for those far from the realities described. Besides the media, other important sources of imagination are 'contacts with, news of and rumours about others in one's social neighbourhood who have become inhabitants of these faraway worlds'

(Appadurai 1991: 197–98). Being exposed to these two sources of information, more people in more parts of the world see their lives through the
prisms of the lives of others. This is not necessarily a positive observation,
implying more happiness or more choices to more people around the
world. Rather, inequality has become more obvious and ordinary lives are
tied up with images, ideas and opportunities from elsewhere. This may
stimulate agency, by allowing people to consider migration; but it may
also lead to all manner of frustrations if dreams cannot be realised or their
accomplishment does not bring the solution hoped for.

Refugees in Dadaab do not only want to migrate in order to leave their
harsh living conditions behind, but also because they anticipate certain
opportunities and conditions elsewhere. In the first place, the prospect of
getting a good education is highly valued, as it was before the war. Bashir
Mahat and Abdulahi Noor interviewed a young man who 'had chosen
Australia for his resettlement' because of its educational opportunities.
They asked Hassan Moxamed about the first time he thought of resettlement and Hassan answered:

'As soon as I completed my secondary education in Somalia, in late
1988, I tried my best to go to the U.S.A. to pursue a higher level of education. Unfortunately, I failed because of budget problems. At that time
another misfortune befell me, since the civil war erupted'. When Hassan
was asked to elaborate on his choice of country, he explained:

> There are two wonderful universities in Australia which I greatly admire and I
> would like to spend years studying there. They are the Bond University on the
> Gold Coast, Queensland, and the Southern Cross University. I studied books
> from both universities which were sent to some of my fellow refugees, adver-
> tising the subjects one can study there and showing photographs of the facili-
> ties that are offered to students. That was when I started hating being in the
> refugee camp.

Secondly, a number of refugees say that they want to go to resettlement
countries for economic reasons. Life abroad is often seen as prosperous
and is appreciated for giving those resettled the ability to assist themselves and their relatives. At the same time, remittances sent to the camps
lead to envy and heightened migration dreams.

Who Dreams of Going Overseas and Who Does Not?

While *buufis* is widespread in the camps, this certainly does not mean that
everyone wants to go for resettlement. There are various reasons why
Somali refugees and locals do or do not long to go abroad.[6] Some see it as
the only way out of their difficult circumstances; especially when they are
treated as outcasts within their own community. I met Zeinab Yasiin, a
young Kenyan Somali woman living in Dagahaley, through one of the

CDWs. Her family came from Wajir, but had expelled her after she became pregnant out of wedlock. She told me that she had fallen in love with a young man from another clan, whom her parents did not accept. After her families' refusal to their marriage, she nevertheless continued seeing her boyfriend, and became pregnant. When her family members found out, they threw her out of the house. She lived in a small room in town for some time, but the tension increased between Zeinab and her relatives and she became ashamed to walk around the town, where she knew most people. That is when some of her friends who were working in the camps decided to take her to Dagahaley for fear that she might hurt herself or her baby. This was not an imaginary fear, considering the fact that suicides by young Somali women in Garissa and Wajir who became pregnant out of wedlock were not uncommon, as I learned during my fieldwork. Often, these were cases where the father of the expected child disappeared as soon as he learned of the pregnancy. The relationship that Zeinab had with the father of her child may have been similar, since her stories about him changed constantly. Initially she told me he was in Nairobi, but later she said that he had moved to South Africa and they were waiting to reunite. I suspected that the truth embarrassed her too much.

Zeinab often talked about going for resettlement and told me that it was the only option remaining for her.

> This is not the right place to raise my daughter, and I also have nothing to feed her with. The rations are insufficient and I cannot continue disturbing my friends. I cannot go back to Wajir where my relatives are waiting to kill me. [She showed me a letter.] I received this letter from my cousin and it is full of threats. He tells me that if I ever set one foot in town, he will personally kill me. Where can I be safe now? The only solution for me is to go overseas with my husband and daughter. Then I will send my family money every month so that they will realise their mistake.

Thus, Zeinab's dream of a possible future overseas is created by her feeling of currently having no place to live, belonging nowhere; but at the same time she imagines that once overseas, she will be able to reclaim her position in the community by sending remittances to the same family members who exiled her. This seems to be in contrast with the idea that those who dream about leaving are the ones who can best afford it because they have the support of a family network that can assist them (Rousseau et al. 1998: 400). I agree with Rousseau et al. that there is no point in dreaming for nothing, but I also assume that almost every refugee in Dadaab could have at least one reason to believe in his or her chances to migrate. As for Zeinab, she had gone to school with one of the clerks at UNHCR. Furthermore, she lived next to a Bantu family willing to sell her their ration card at a time when the Bantu were being processed in a group resettlement case.

Others start longing to go for resettlement because their relatives, friends or neighbours have managed to go. According to Choldin (1973), the decision to migrate is often made after a relative has moved. This not only increases the opportunities of those left behind due to access to the necessary funds and contacts, it also stimulates the wish to go through images that reach them. Reports from the early migrants on the situation in the new community, as well as their encouragement and help, often influence the decision (Choldin 1973: 166). At the same time, the fact that relatives, neighbours or peers have already left may cause those remaining behind to feel envious and wish for the same. In an interview report by Bashir Mahat and Abdulahi Noor, a young man answered their question as to when he first thought of going overseas as follows: 'It was in 1997; when the Somali Sudanese resettlement process began. At that time, I saw a large number of my friends going to the U.S.A. and later they sent sweet stories about their lifestyle there[7]. They were living a new life while I was still struggling with this harsh life on the Hagadera soil, even though they were the same age as I am'. One of the people Kusow interviewed in Canada offered a similar explanation: 'I kept hearing that so and so went to Germany, and so and so went to Holland, you know, so I asked myself why don't you go to one of these places?' (Kusow 1998: 117).

And yet, there are those who do not wish to go overseas. Farah Abdinoor told me:

> I do not want to move any further. My family has no problems in the camps and our life is okay. Here we are close to Somalia so when peace is reached we can return to our homes quickly. On top of that, the proximity is convenient because since we came to Dadaab I have frequently moved back and forth between Kenya and Somalia. The last time I came from Kismaayo was only six months ago and I stayed there for five months in order to work on my farm, but I was back in Hagadera before the most recent fighting erupted. When the war started and we left Somalia, we just locked the doors to our houses. Now, even the roof and the bricks from the walls have been taken. But the fields are ours and we can still profit from them. Only in 1997, because of the heavy floods, I lost almost the whole harvest. And now that the fighting has started again, I will most likely not be able to profit once more.

Throughout his years in Dadaab, Farah has kept the link with Somalia alive, still hoping to go back one day. There are others like him, who have no interest in moving beyond Kenya, because they dream of going home instead. Ayaan Moxamed explained: 'I am not interested in going overseas, even though many of my relatives are there. I just do not want to live in another country. Even here, in Kenya, I live in a foreign state. Eventually, I just want to return to my own country'.

Those who refuse resettlement as a durable solution are mainly of the older generation, and at times may be left behind in the region while their younger family members leave. Abbas Warsame, another young man who actively participated in the training and follow-ups I organised in Dagahaley, told me that his family was planning to go for resettlement without his father. His eldest sister went to Ottawa, Canada for studies in 1988. She recently moved to Ohio, U.S.A., stating that she was a new arrival from Dagahaley and her family was still there. She had told her family members, who were staying in Mogadishu, to shift to the camps. In May 1999, Abbas and two of his siblings, his stepbrother and his *eedo* (paternal aunt) came from Mogadishu by plane. Their father did not want to come while an aunt did want to join them, so Abbas' sister had said that her father died during the war and her mother was still alive, while in reality the opposite was true. When I asked Abbas why his father was not ready to join them, he told me: 'My father is too old and wants to stay in his own country. He told us that we are still young and can build our future by getting a good education, but for him there is no use in going'. In the camps, a number of elderly people mentioned a similar reason for their lack of interest in moving to the West, maintaining that this was something for the younger generation.

The issue of going to Western countries or not at times causes disputes within families and amongst the refugee community. In one of the reports by Bashir Mahat and Abdulahi Noor, they describe how they started up a group discussion on *buufis* and then observed the results without further intervention. A heated debate arose on the topic, with those who were in favour of going overseas arguing with those who were against. The report provides a wonderful example of a rather unobtrusive way of collecting information that I personally could never engage in, simply because I am not Somali. Bashir and Abdulahi describe their observations as follows:

> Yesterday afternoon, we sat down with a group of people discussing the Djibouti conference. After some time, we asked a question about *buufis* because it was rumoured in the camps that some people were supposed to meet JVA soon. Most of the people under the tree started talking about it, enjoying the topic. Someone said that he must be a wizard because he has failed to get an opportunity for resettlement. An old man engaged in the discussion, and the field became divided into those in favour and those against. We enjoyed listening to what happened between them.

> The old man placed his seat carefully, while beating his stick on the earth to keep the situation calm. He said: 'Listen to me, listen to me. I want to bring to your attention that we are Somalis, not Americans. We have a deep-rooted culture and although we have fled from our country we must not lose the principles of that culture. This resettlement issue that rests in your minds is meant to defile our culture and our young generation. The young are not wise enough to know what is good and what is bad; they will adapt to the new lifestyle that they find in the West. Besides, resettlement is a modern way of colonising Somalis: no matter how highly a Somali is educated, when he is resettled he is

considered ignorant. On top of that, the Somalis are discriminated against because of their colour and restricted in practising their religion or culture'. Someone else interrupted him saying that whatever problems there are in the West, the Somalis are between two fires. At least life is more stable there than it is in the camps, and it is just temporary: you can go back whenever you want.

Then, the old man spoke again, exclaiming: 'I wonder at how silly you are! There are long-term objectives behind resettlement in Western countries. This is obvious from the fact that even American citizens are dying of hunger and spend their nights on the streets. They want to secure certain interests'. When the man was asked what those interests were, he answered: 'a first objective is to have Somalia ruled by people who are physically Somalis and mentally Westerners. Secondly, since development is influenced by a country's man-power, resettlement is designed to take useful people in large numbers. The youth are the only people interested, and they have not yet reached the mental stage where they can compare different cultures in order to keep their dignity, culture and religion'. A young boy then criticised the old man, saying that he was now abusing the youth but if he would be given a chance he would soon go for resettlement. The old man replied with a Somali saying: '*Gaalo caad foola sheeda joogto, gowsse heelama aado*. If you stay in a white man's fore teeth, do not pass to his molars. They will grind you'. With those words, he stood up to go.

Resettlement Opportunities: Official Policies

In order to study the migration process of Somali refugees from Kenya to the West, it is not sufficient to analyse people's dreams of migrating. Actual migration only follows when facilitating factors outweigh migration restrictions. As Klaver (1997: 41) notes, policies regarding immigration and emigration are very essential in determining international migration, though they are hardly addressed in migration theories. Yet, for those who dream of leaving their life in the refugee camps behind to move towards a Western country, a resettlement chance is a rare opportunity. Only a very small percentage of the total refugee population in Kenya is granted resettlement through the UNHCR, in cooperation with countries like the U.S.A., Canada and Australia. In earlier research in Dadaab it has been observed that the proportion of resettlement cases processed through UNHCR is less than 5 percent of the total population (Crisp 1999b: 23). Besides these individual and group-based resettlement cases, another official option for leaving is through family reunion procedures. Considering the restrictive measures that Western countries continue to develop, the social and financial investments needed and risks taken to obtain resettlement are ever growing. In this section, I will discuss the increasingly restrictive international migration laws and the limited official options that remain open for refugees. Then, in the next section, I will look at the resulting growing use of human smugglers and the increasing social and financial investments needed and risks taken to obtain resettlement.

Closed Borders

Different ways of achieving resettlement involve different kinds of investments and also different risks. The current restrictive trends in international migration negatively affect people's ability to obtain resettlement through legal means. Thus, it becomes increasingly common amongst refugees to resort to clandestine practices and trafficking networks. It is important to note, however, that the international legal regulation of migration is a relatively recent development (Farer 1995: 258). Its foundation was based on the principle of the sovereign state, in combination with the idea of citizenship rights for individuals that developed as a consequence of the French Revolution. As such, there has always been a fundamental tension between the interests of individuals and the interests of nation-states. The migration of individuals is one of the important ways in which the borders that shape nation-states are being contested. Up to this day, control over national borders continues to be the essence of national sovereignty and national sovereignty remains the linchpin of the international political system (Ferris 1993: xx). Although in recent years, within regional arrangements like for example the European Union, nation-states are seemingly willing to lessen their control on migrants, this is only possible due to agreements on restrictive migration policies and strong outer borders. On the other hand, individuals do not want to be, and cannot be, restricted to a confined geographical area. They need or wish to move across borders for a wide range of economic, environmental, sociocultural and political reasons.

National borders have been imposed on the Somali as on many others and have been rather meaningless, especially for the nomadic section of the population. Rousseau et al. (1998: 406) even claim that 'travelling is so deeply ingrained in the Somali social fabric that geographical space is a continuum and it becomes difficult to integrate the idea of boundaries'. Yet, at the same time, borders are real, since they often impose restrictions on free movement. In the international tug-of-war between the rights of states and those of individuals, migration has ended up in an ambiguous position. Whereas the UN Convention on Human Rights (Article 14) provides the right to leave a country as well as the right to 'seek and enjoy' asylum, it does not provide any complementary right of admission elsewhere, as this remains the prerogative of the receiving state. Thus, international migration has largely been treated as a deviance from the prevailing norm of social organisation at the world level (Zolberg 1983: 6). In the same vein, nomads are treated with a lot of suspicion and are often 'encouraged' to settle by their national governments. A major advantage of theories on transnational processes is that they challenge the common assumption that sedentary life is the natural state of society, while at the same time recognising the real-life quality of borders.

In recent decades, technological developments in transport and communication have increased the number of migrants and the distances they travel, while reducing the time that they take in the process. Still, this has not led to a diminished importance of boundaries. Even as the world is becoming globalised, there are more national borders and within those borders there is a greater emphasis on ethnic, regional and national values (Ferris 1993: xvi; Kibreab 1999: 385). The situation is even more complex considering the fact that the movement of people across boundaries simultaneously benefits global capital. Many of the Western economies depend on (illegal) migrant labour for profit. Thus, industrial societies are struggling with their conflicting interests of on the one hand maximising cheap labour supply, while on the other hand protecting the 'cultural integrity' on which their nation-state is supposedly built (Zolberg 1983: 15). In the end, it adds up to a rather hypocritical development of increased restrictive immigration policies combined with a laissez-faire attitude towards illegal migrants. Thus, the migrant's position is worsening, to the benefit of many national economies.

These general migration restrictions in many ways determine the position of asylum seekers and refugees. In the last two decades, the issue of refugees has become very topical in various Western countries. This is not only caused by the fact that their numbers have increased but also because of the way that media and governments have brought these numbers to the fore (Cohen and Joly 1989: 8). They are repeatedly expressing their concern and quote 'alarming' statistics, but this semi-hysteria seems disproportionate to the actual numbers. Set against figures in Africa and Asia, the numbers of asylum seekers in the West appear very small. Besides, there is a very high overall rate of rejection, with, for example, an average of only 9 percent of applications being accepted in Europe in the early 1990s (Farer 1995: 281). One of the developments that has worsened the situation is that the real or perceived costs associated with refugee protection are no longer offset by the powerful political imperative that existed during the time of the Cold War (Collinson 1993: 70). Refugees from, for example, Cuba entered the U.S.A. and Hungarians entered Europe because they were 'fleeing communism' and thus were deserving of protection. After the end of the Cold War, asylum opportunities in the West have reduced even more.

In Western Europe, a regional harmonisation of migration controls has led to increasingly severe asylum controls at the outer borders of the European Union through a number of measures. One of them is the carrier liability, a uniform system of fines for carriers that bring persons without entry visas to European points of entry. Another restriction is the requirement of a visa itself, which seems to be the main obstacle to entering Europe. Thus, the non-refoulement obligation is evaded through a refusal to grant, or a readiness to cancel, visas for people who are assumed to be seeking asylum (Farer 1995: 277). Other measures are the development of a list of safe countries to which asylum seekers can be sent back and the introduction of the common practice of returning asylum seekers to a country of first asylum. Similar restrictive measures have been introduced in other Western countries. In Canada, for example, a new immigration law was implemented in February 1993. This Bill C86 required that claimants, even after being found to be Convention refugees by the International Refugee Board, possess documents proving their identity (Affi 1997: 444). In the case of Somalia, these types of documents were not widely used and, besides, they often got lost during flight. Similarly, family reunion has been made more difficult for refugees since the restricted immigration law only allows sponsorship of spouses and children below nineteen years of age (Affi 1997: 445). This is in accordance with the Western idea of the nuclear family as an interdependent unit, but it does not fit Somali practices of social responsibility.

Individual Case Resettlement Through the UNHCR and Governments

One of the options to go for resettlement is through individual case determination, possibly resulting in family reunification.[8] The UNHCR decides whether certain individual cases in Dadaab are particularly deserving of a durable solution because of the severity of their fear of persecution while in Somalia, or because they are still insufficiently protected in Dadaab. Accepted cases are then referred to governments since, as Hathaway (1995: 291) notes, 'the UNHCR has no shelter of its own in which to provide protection to refugees'. After receiving the case from the UNHCR, the Immigration Board of that specific country will interview the refugee in order to decide whether resettlement can be granted according to national asylum regulations. Governments can also influence the decision as to who should be granted resettlement directly, by reserving positions for refugees with particular characteristics; for example a certain nationality or vulnerability, as in the case of Sudanese unaccompanied minors or Somali rape victims. In the case of family reunification, the initiative also stems from the government, dealing with requests from accepted refugees in that country to allow certain family members to join them. It is a matter of national law as to if and when resettlement of these family members is granted.

Even when the UNHCR has referred a case to a certain state, it remains up to the government whether or not, and if so when, to allow an individual entry within its borders. Arte Awas had been accepted by the UNHCR in December 1998 and in January 1999 the Canadian government had already agreed to give him resettlement. Yet, from there, the process went so slowly that he even had to repeat his medical examination in Nairobi. When he went for a second medical test in June 2000, he decided to stay in the hotel that the UNHCR uses to house refugees going for resettlement. Arte still has high hopes of leaving, but tells me the story of a woman in the same hotel, whom people call Rukia *Buufis*:

> Rukia first became a refugee in 1977, during the Somali-Ethiopia conflict, and has lived in Nairobi for many years. For two or three years, she slept in front of the UNHCR gate in Nairobi with her children, in order for her case to be heard. Finally, the UNHCR listened to her and accepted her case. She was referred to the Canadian Embassy, but received a rejection letter from them. Then she had an interview at the Australian Embassy, but again her case was rejected. Now, the UNHCR is looking for yet another country that might be willing to take her.

Those who are given priority for resettlement are the 'most deserving' 1951 Convention refugees as well as protection cases. The 'most deserving' Convention refugees are offered a durable solution outside the camps due to the severity of the experiences that caused them to flee their country. One of the field officers I spoke to was extremely sceptical about applying this option to the Somalis in Dadaab.

> I have rarely seen a true case for resettlement. None of the refugees ever told me a story of having faced specific individual fear of persecution; everybody has a story of escaping a general war situation. And when it comes to those who belong to minority groups, they only claim to have been discriminated against and that is not a reason for being accepted for resettlement. They never say that they have been persecuted specifically because of belonging to that minority tribe. The task of a field officer is to find those refugees who fulfil the terms of the 1951 Convention and offer them a durable solution. Instead, I hear the same story ten times; so then how do I decide who should be allowed to go? It seems like a lottery to me. That could be the reason why all the field officers in Dadaab have been a bit reluctant to select Somali refugees for resettlement, even though they would be in a position to send thirty to forty cases each month. It is only that they do not want to do so, because the Somali are too cunning and they are no true Convention refugees.

Despite the scepticism of this field officer, amongst the Somali refugees in Dadaab there were certainly those who described their experiences in terms that matched the 1951 Convention. Awas Moxamuud asked me to type and print a letter and then post it to the UNHCR office in Nairobi, because he did not have much faith in the above field officer.[9] He had entitled it 'application for a durable solution on humanitarian grounds', and described in great detail the reasons for flight into Kenya and the continued insecurity that the family faced. He concluded the letter with a summary of his most important arguments.

Back in Somalia, one of the four brothers who were killed in Mogadishu was a military advisor to the late Siyad Barre's regime. The others were civil servants for the same regime. We were recently informed through secret informants in Somalia that the family of the military advisor is thought to be targeted by organised militiamen. In Ifo, my sisters have repeatedly been beaten and harassed and armed men came to our house twice, asking for my brother and me. We belong to the Marehan tribe and were very close kin to Barre's subclan, Koshin. Our main problem is based on the previous political activities of some of our family members and as a result, we face harassment and mistreatment. Therefore, I present my plea to you to extend a helping hand. Any extension of our stay here may result in prolonged suffering and death.

Awas provides a story that not only may fit the 1951 Convention but could also be treated as a protection case. Some refugees have fled from Somalia to Kenya but are still not safe from the persecution they faced in their home country. When I visited an NGO assisting Somali refugees in Nairobi, I was told about the case of a Somali young man in Kakuma who was a Christian. His religious conviction caused him problems there, so UNHCR offered to relocate the young man and his sister to the Dadaab camps. The day that they arrived in Dadaab, the young man was beaten up. He brought the case forward to UNHCR and the field officer promised that he would look at it after his leave. During this period, the sister was killed and the young man received further threats. When the field officer came back, the case was dealt with very fast and within three weeks the young man was resettled to Canada. Only a small minority of Somalis are Christians, many secretly, but they face severe threats. Through e-mail, I established contact with someone who used the name Brother Rashid. He told me that he had converted to Christianity in 1986, and had become an active member of a 'house church'. Between 1994 and 1996, his 'fellow Somali believers' were hunted down and killed one by one, until only himself and another man survived out of an initial group of fourteen people. These are the cases that may be offered a durable solution outside Dadaab because their security is not guaranteed there.

The U.S.A. is one of the favourite resettlement countries for Somali refugees and might also be responsible for the largest number of departures from Dadaab, followed by Canada and Australia. There are a number of grounds on which a refugee can apply for resettlement to the U.S.A., but the procedure always involves the UNHCR, JVA and the INS of the U.S. government. In Nairobi, I talked to a staff member of JVA who mentioned three categories of resettlement cases: 'In all instances, the government cannot accept people who have violated human rights themselves and, in general, individuals are only eligible for resettlement to the U.S.A. if they fulfil the criteria of the 1951 Convention and the 1967 Protocol. First priority goes to the most urgent protection cases and those who most profoundly fear persecution, according to the Convention.

Second priority goes to cases of group determination, where individual refugees are shortlisted for an interview because of belonging to a certain ethnic group. Third priority is given to family reunion cases and most Somalis fall into this category'.

On the subject of family reunion, another JVA employee told me: 'There are very many Somalis in the U.S.A. filling in those forms which only apply to closest family members like husband, wife, children and under-age siblings. The problem is that often the exact addresses of the relatives are not provided and refugees tend to move around a lot. This is a particular problem when dealing with the Somali community, since they are highly mobile even within the U.S.A.'. I met a number of refugees in Dadaab and Nairobi who were about to travel to the U.S.A. on a family reunification case, and asked them about the details of the procedure. Just a few weeks before their departure, Roble Abdiraxman explained to me how his daughter Aman, in the U.S.A., had arranged a family reunion case: 'Aman is not paying for our ticket, but it is to be subtracted from her social welfare allowance over a period of three years. Once we are in the U.S.A., she does not have to pay anything. The government will provide us with a house and a monthly allowance. The sponsorship is only for my wife, my seven youngest children and me because Aman cannot apply for a sponsorship for her siblings above the age of twenty. But once I am in the U.S.A., I will be able to arrange a sponsorship for them as well because I am their father'.

Before Roble and his family had reached the point of near-departure, many steps had taken place. The procedures for screening refugees for resettlement to the U.S.A. are rather complex in Dadaab: The UNHCR first selects the refugees in the camp, after which JVA does the 'pre-screening'. This entails interviewing people as well as assisting them with filling in the forms and presenting their case in the best possible way. They prepare the background information used by INS when the refugees come for the actual interview. Then, once the case has been accepted, JVA assists them to fulfil all the bureaucratic requirements associated with being accepted for resettlement in the U.S.A., including medical examinations. Moreover, they organise a five-day orientation course in Nairobi for refugees to become acquainted with life in the U.S.A. Thereafter, the IOM (International Organisation for Migration) is responsible for arranging the flight. This procedure seems standard and unbiased, decided solely on an individual's refugee experience, but according to a staff member of JVA, macropolitical reasons have always been of major importance in the history of U.S. immigration policy: 'The Cold War has played an essential role in accepting or refusing refugees in the U.S.A., and this factor was very important for refugees from Vietnam, various South American countries and Ethiopia. With the end of the Cold War, attention has shifted to Islam as the new 'cause of concern' for the U.S. The Sudanese, many of whom are Christians fleeing an Islamic regime, are being assisted on that basis, whereas the JVA program for Somalis in Dadaab has only been introduced quite recently'.

A Relationship of Mutual Distrust

There are many other factors that play a role in determining who, in the end, is granted resettlement and who is not. Resettlement may be the most desired 'handout' that refugees in Dadaab can acquire from the agencies assisting them. The demand for resettlement is far greater than the number of available positions and it is difficult to decide who is 'most needy'. Every day, a large group of refugees waits in front of the UNHCR gate in each camp, hoping to be able to present their case or follow up on an existing case. There are many similarities with the provision of food aid that I described in chapter 3. One of the parallels is the level of distrust that exists between refugees and organisations as a consequence of this distribution of 'scarce resources'. The UNHCR, NGOs and governments are often very suspicious about the truth of a refugee story and, indeed, experiences are sometimes 'adapted' to the criteria used to judge whether someone deserves resettlement or not. On the other hand, the refugees do not trust the UNHCR to decide on resettlement cases fairly, as they believe that those with money can buy approval of their case. Again, these assumptions are at least true in some cases, and in the last few years, a number of UNHCR employees have already been sacked because of corruption.

For those who manage to speak to a UNHCR officer or hand in a written application, how they present their resettlement case is very important. I spoke to Hassan Ali in a lodge in Eastleigh and he told me that he had been translating for various embassies as well as for JVA. What he recalled from the work was the fact that people invented a lot of stories: 'If you want your case to be accepted for resettlement, you need to have at least some of your close relatives killed. A number of applicants managed to tell those stories with tears in their eyes.[10] The officer interviewing would judge on the spot whether the story was true or not, using his or her best judgement only. Many people got away with cheating and were rewarded with resettlement'. Hassan's account did not seem unlikely to me, considering the fact that I had personally witnessed a most remarkable case of inventiveness that permitted hundreds of Somalis to move to the U.S.A. In Hagadera, I once visited K3, a block that hosted 'Somali Sudanese' before their resettlement to the U.S.A. Although the larger part of the group had already been resettled, the block was still densely populated with people claiming to be Somali Sudanese. I slowly learned that the block was thriving on the power of imagination.

When I first met her, I thought Fatuma Arte was immune to the language and politics of the Somali Sudanese case, despite living in K3. She was a neighbour to Mama Halima, one of the people who said that she was a spokesperson for the Somali Sudanese. During my visit to Mama Halima, Fatuma came in and seemed very critical and open. In an attempt to get behind the layers of stories that were told to support the Somali Sudanese case, I remarked that refugees are actually forced to lie because of the restrictive policies they face. Fatuma agreed and took her own case as an example. She told me that she had fled with her husband from Mogadishu to Nairobi, where they stayed for one month before being referred to Dadaab. Fatuma confessed that during her interview in Nairobi she had said that she was of the Eyle minority, though both she and her husband were Hawiye. She told me that, as someone from a minority group, she would at least have a chance of being accepted for resettlement, but as Hawiye her chances were very small. Considering the problematic reputation of the Hawiye, seen to be the aggressors in the Somali war, especially in the U.S.A., I understood why Fatuma had tried to heighten her chances.

I was happy to have another opportunity to talk to her when she invited me for lunch at her house. Yet, much to my amazement, this time she presented the story that she earlier told me they had invented to claim resettlement, as if it were a true story. Fatuma now said that they were Eili, and her husband showed me their application letters while elaborating: 'We both belong to the Eyle, a hunter and gatherer group of people that is not related to any of the Somali clans. We practised shifting cultivation in the region around Buur Hakaba, but during the war bandits took our lands near the river. We had always faced severe discrimination in Somalia, but when we also lost our livelihood, we were forced to flee'. I was really disappointed with this unexpected change in Fatuma's representation of her past experiences since I had hoped to receive some insights from her about the Somali Sudanese case. In an attempt to understand what had happened, I assumed her husband had wanted to use the opportunity of my visit to bring forward their resettlement case. The incident made me realise that, no matter how much I tried to be explicit about who I was and what I was doing in Dadaab, even after many months a number of refugees still told me certain things because of what they thought they could gain from me; for example in the shape of financial assistance, recommendations to donors and agencies, or resettlement. Whether I wanted it or not, I was part of the power play between refugees, practitioners and 'analysers' that leads to the creation of stories of who was a 'true' refugee and thus entitled to assistance and protection.

This process has also been illustrated by Kusow (1998), who describes the position of Somali asylum seekers arriving at Canadian airports and borders. He explains how individual Somali applicants learned that the Immigration Board mainly uses their clan membership to determine whether someone has a profound fear of persecution. Thus, irrespective of their actual clan, these asylum seekers started to identify themselves with clans more likely to be granted a residence permit for Canada. Between 1988 and 1990, there were two opportunities available. It was possible to claim that one was against the Siyad Barre regime or one could claim to be from the northern region (Kusow 1998: 127). In later years, it was an advantage to claim to be from the less powerful clans. As one of Kusow's informants explained: 'I can claim any clan I desire if I know the chain of that clan. If I say my clan is so and so from the South, and I know what the clan goes by, they will never know who I am' (Kusow 1998: 129). I agree with Kusow that the fact that someone claims a clan membership that is not his or hers does not necessarily suggest that he or she is not a refugee. Rather, Somalis who seek entrance to a Western country want to heighten their chances and know that they are likely to be judged on their clan membership. Mulki Al-Sharmani, a researcher amongst Somalis in Cairo, informed me that she attended gatherings of Somalis exchanging their views on what they think the UNHCR wants to hear from them in order to be given asylum. According to her, the problem is that the UNHCR reifies clan identities and perpetuates a vicious circle in which the asylum seekers are forced to present their plights and circumstances only in one language: that of the clan.

In this interaction, not only the level of trust that exists on the side of the UNHCR and governments towards the refugees is of importance. Refugees and a number of NGO employees complained about corruption within the UNHCR, saying that only those with money could secure a resettlement case. Accusations of corruption ranged from the level of the clerks in the camps to the level of officers at the Nairobi office. On a few occasions, I managed to talk about the subject with UNHCR staff willing to discuss such a sensitive issue. A field officer in Dadaab mentioned the shock of discovering corruption amongst the clerks:

> I once spoke to a girl in Hagadera, who at that time did not know I was a field officer. The girl was about eighteen and translated for me. She spoke good English and I asked her about her background. The girl said that her family were all safe and well in Somalia. That is when I asked her why she herself was in the camps. The girl answered that she wanted to go to the U.S.A. I thought it was a joke, but then I found out she was serious. The girl explained to me that she was closely related to one of the UNHCR clerks, and that he would assist her. I checked her story, and got very annoyed when I found out that she indeed had a resettlement case.

For those with connections or money, these kinds of practices may be beneficial. Yet, for others they are not. A number of young women complained to me that UNHCR clerks had asked them for 'favours' if they wanted their case to proceed. They were convinced that their case was subsequently frustrated because they had refused sexual requests or marriage proposals.

On the issue of corruption, Ibrahim Yasiin told me: 'The UNHCR is very corrupt when it comes to resettlement. It started with one of the field officers in the camps who was willing to sell resettlement cases for 100,000 Kenyan shillings per person. Thus, I never managed to go through the procedure in Dadaab. Now that I am in Nairobi for studies, I want to put my application forward directly to the Nairobi office'. Yet, from what I experienced with the UNHCR office in Nairobi, I doubted whether Ibrahim would be more successful there. In August 2001, I went there with Sahra Yusuf and found many refugees waiting in front of the gate. I was told that they spent the night or came very early in the morning in order to be able to enter or be given an appointment. Some were standing in front of the main office, some had entered, and others were waiting behind fences inside the compound. Besides the hordes of people waiting for an appointment, to the side of the building a group of women had built their residence. These refugee women were sleeping on the streets in makeshift tents made up of plastic sheets and pieces of cloth, at night protected by an iron gate that was closed and guarded by security personnel. Their situation was pathetic, and I found it extremely difficult to go into the compound without feeling that I should not be there, as if I was a disaster tourist. The fact that I only had a couple of days left before leaving Kenya added to my reluctance.

Yet before I could make up my mind, one of the women, who looked particularly feeble and raggedly dressed, came to us and started talking to Sahra. She introduced herself as Fario and told us that she had come from Hagadera eight months ago. When I replied to her in Somali, she was encouraged to tell us about her problems. Alhough I did not understand everything she was saying, I wanted her to keep talking and told Sahra to fill me in on the details later. We made an appointment to come back a few days later and at that time, I was invited into the compound where the women lived. Fario told us that she had been selected by the U.S. Embassy in 1998 as one of the vulnerable cases to go for resettlement and continued: 'I later found out that my case had been sold, since I was never invited for an interview and learned that others had gone in my place. When we complained, my husband and I were threatened and abused. On top of that, because our resettlement case had been processed, even though we never went anywhere, our ration card number was cancelled. I ran away to Nairobi because refugees cannot complain in Dadaab'. She left her family in Dadaab and started living next to the UNHCR office so that her case would be heard. There were at least a dozen women with problems similar to hers. They all had complaints about corruption and sold cases, often carrying many cancelled appointment letters with them. At that time, almost all those dealing with resettlement at the Nairobi office had been sacked, and all cases had been put on hold, pending investigations.

The Politics of Group Resettlement

Group determination for Somalis in Kenya first occurred in Marafa and Utange, from where approximately three thousand Somalis of Banaadiri and Baraawan origin were resettled to the U.S.A. Resettlement programmes that have an ethnic slant entail a number of difficulties. First of all, they set in motion complex processes of reassertion and modification of collective identities that before exile were highly problematic. The Somali Bantu, for example, have been heavily discriminated against and had a lower-caste or even slave-like status in Somali history. During the war, they were again a common and easy victim because they were less inclined to move from their property and land (Menkhaus 1991; Lehman 1993). They have been selected in the latest group resettlement case, which has caused a redefinition of what it means to be Somali Bantu, even leading to marriages between Somalis and Bantu. Whereas being Bantu in Somalia in general had very negative connotations, in Dadaab it is now associated with the positive fact of eligibility for resettlement. Yet, this change is based on the same ethnic differentiation that has been the cause of discrimination and abuse in Somali history.

Secondly, and worse still, resettlement of refugees as groups rather than as individuals has led to increased conflict in the camps through identity reconstruction among refugees in a 'cutthroat scramble for communalised resettlement' (Kagwanja 2002: 10). Whereas these group determination processes are intended to protect the rights of ethnic minorities and vulnerable groups, these people are not necessarily the ones who benefit. The reason for this is precisely the fact that they belong to a minority or vulnerable group and thus lack the political and economic strength to present their case more convincingly than others. Many people claim to be a member of an ethnic group that is in the process of resettlement or want their ethnic group to be recognised for group resettlement. According to a UNHCR report quoted in Crisp (1999b: 23), 'We have started receiving a lot of letters from different communities in the refugee camp, including some groups of whom nobody has ever heard, claiming persecution and hoping for consideration for group resettlement. As the chances for individual resettlement remain slim, the Dadaab refugee community is now betting on the vulnerable group element'. A very clear example of this is provided by the earlier-mentioned case of the Somali Sudanese.

I first learned about the Somali Sudanese in Hagadera in July 1999, by which time the majority of them had been resettled to the U.S.A. Never before had I heard of the Somali Sudanese, nor had I ever read about them, so I was rather curious to hear the story. Moxamed Farah was the first to mention the group to me when he told me that he had expected to go to the U.S.A. with the Somali Sudanese. He had received a rejection letter to his individual application and was now waiting for the decision on his appeal. He asked me to type a list of twenty-five cases, individuals and families, who had been included in their application as a group but received a negative answer. Some of the Somali Sudanese had gone to the U.S.A., including Moxamed's cousin, whereas others had received a rejection letter as well as a negative decision on their appeal. Moxamed was still hoping for a chance to go, since he had not received any response to his appeal yet. I knew he was not a Somali Sudanese, but I also wondered who was. When I visited block K3 with Sahra Yusuf, my aim was to find an answer to that question. I was brought to the house of Mama Halima, who appeared to be the spokeswoman of the remaining group. She was used to speaking on behalf of 'the Somali Sudanese' and told me her story mixed with the history of the group.

> I am from Afgooye, where all the Somali Sudanese are from. During the First World War, Sudanese from the north of Sudan fought as soldiers in the British army that went to Somalia. When their job was finished, some of them decided to remain. My grandfather, who was one of them, settled in Afgooye where he married a Somali woman. Those people and their descendents had a very rough time in Somalia since they were constantly discriminated against. When the war began, we came to live together in Utange near Mombasa with approximately one hundred families from Afgooye and lived as one community. When that camp was closed in 1993, we moved to the Dadaab camps. Again, we are all living together in K3 of Hagadera. This is the only block where Somali Sudanese can be found in Dadaab. We are still experiencing the same discrimination as before. I would not be able to do business in the Hagadera market, for example, because people would chase me away or else no-one would buy anything from me. In 1998, our case was first considered by the UNHCR. We were given the opportunity to go to the U.S.A. and Australia but we decided that we would all go to the same place and chose the U.S.A. By now, sixty families have been resettled through JVA and only forty remain. Of these forty, twenty-five received an answer to their request that urged them to strengthen their case.

During my fieldwork, a number of Somalis told me that the Somali Sudanese case had been invented. Ismail Gedi, a Kenyan Somali working for CARE, explained how he had once challenged a UNHCR field officer by saying that there had never in the history of Somalia been a group who identified itself as Somali Sudanese. How, then, could he buy a story like that? The officer just replied that these were orders from Nairobi and the only thing that they were supposed to do was follow those orders, whether the Somali Sudanese existed or not. A UNHCR report quoted in Crisp (1999b: 23) wrote that the resettlement process for Somali Sudanese had created a lot of bad blood, misunderstanding and false expectations amongst the refugee population. The report stated that the Sudanese communities in the three camps came to the UN residential compound in Dadaab to protest, believing that this group had the least right for consideration as they had only been in Dadaab for a short period. However, Ibrahim Yasiin told me that the main reason for the protests was that the whole case had been invented. The Sudanese launched a complaint explaining everything that was going on in the blocks and how people were cheating. Unfortunately, according to Ibrahim, those dealing with the case within UNHCR did not seem to care about the truth of the matter, as long as the claimants were resettled.

These comments from Somalis who were not involved in the case further confirmed the statements and behaviour of those who were. When I discussed the Somali Sudanese resettlement case with Moxamed Farah, he explained how he became involved: 'The head of our subgroup of twenty-five families is a distant relative and since nobody could read and write English and Somali, I was included. We invented a story, and everybody studied his or her role. But we were rejected because of "inconsistencies" in our stories, so we wrote a new letter asking to be forgiven for our mistakes'. When I asked Moxamed why he did not apply using his own experiences, he said that he feared he would not fulfil the criteria necessary to be considered for resettlement. Moxamed was the only person to tell me that he had invented a 'Somali Sudanese' story, but others who claimed to be Somali Sudanese accused fellow applicants of having invented stories. I found it difficult not to get drawn into this highly politicised case, as a number of people appealed for my assistance. However, since they were mainly refugees in relatively powerful positions, who were clearly trying to manipulate me and the translator or CDWs who accompanied me, I decided not to get involved.

Liban Suleiman, a senior member of the Security Committee in Hagadera, once approached me to ask for my maximum support for the Somali Sudanese case, claiming that he had no further interest in the case than seeing justice done. I later learned that a number of Liban's children were on the list of pending Somali Sudanese cases, making Liban far less 'neutral' than he claimed; particularly in light of the fact that he was of the same Darod clan as my translator. Mama Halima, who was also of that clan, asked me to support their case and I told her that I first wanted to see who the people were on behalf of whom she was talking. She explained to me that the original list of the forty remaining cases in Dadaab that was kept at the UNHCR office, had been replaced by a fake one. Although she was one of the leaders of the case, she could oddly enough not present me with the original list and kept on giving me all kinds of lists with different names. At the same time, she told me that they could not protest because the new list contained the names of many Dadaab residents including a *shifta* who had threatened to kill them if they would speak up. Meanwhile, Mama Halima had already managed to send three of her children to the U.S.A. through the programme. Through these and other attempts to gain my support for the Somali Sudanese case, I was able to understand the high level of manipulation involved in group resettlement. These manipulations brought considerable gains as Somalis had been willing to pay thousands of dollars for a position on the list of Somali Sudanese. As Adoy Moxamed explained, 'once it became known that the Somali Sudanese case had been accepted, people came from Garissa, Nairobi and places in Somalia carrying a lot of money to buy a position'.

Resettlement Opportunities: Alternative Routes

A UNHCR resettlement case that goes through one of the embassies is not the only way to enter a Western country. There are numerous other opportunities, although these usually involve higher costs and greater risks. The dividing line between official policies and alternative routes is only tenuous, since official options are often used in a number of 'alternative' ways. Ibrahim Yasiin assisted an old man in Eastleigh with memorising the details of a UNHCR resettlement case that he had bought, originally belonging to a man who had already moved to the U.S.A. He told me:

> For the last few months, this man has started memorising straight after morning prayers and then continues for several hours in the evening. I help him by asking questions, since the story is very complex. According to the case, the man was married to a first wife, who died and left him four children. Then, he married a second wife, whom he divorced and had three children with. Again, there is a third wife, etcetera…. Of course, he needs to know the names and ages of all 'his' wives and children, the places they lived and the story of their lives together. He is waiting for the interview almost as if it were an exam. The outcome is of great importance to him since it will determine whether he can go to the U.S.A. and join his daughter there.

These kinds of existing cases can be bought or invented individually or through a middleman and new opportunities can also be created through the 'employment' of a *mukhalis* (human smuggler or carrier). In all these cases, the costs and risks involved are high and mostly require financial and nonmaterial support from a social network of relatives, who often are already in the West.

Mukhalis: *Finding Other Ways to Reach One's Destination*

Increasingly restrictive immigration policies have affected all types of migrants moving from the 'developing' to the 'developed' world, but Somalis may be treated with extra suspicion. According to one of Farah's (2000: 78) informants, Somalis travelling to the West embark on their trip in full awareness of the fact that anyone travelling on a Somali passport is suspect, even if he or she has all the necessary papers in immaculate order, and has proper documentation to enter the country of destination. Commercial airlines do not sell air tickets to Somali travellers without first putting them and the documents they bear through a most rigorous scrutiny. More spot-checks await them at every step of the way, hurdles put in their way at every curve. Once aboard an aircraft, they might be asked to hand over their passports to a stewardess, who would hand them to an immigration official of their country of destination, an officer waiting to receive them at the steps of the plane. Somali travellers are treated like unaccompanied children, only no-one is kind to them.

Because of these difficulties, most Somalis prefer to hire a *mukhalis* to take away the hurdles for them. This is in line with the general trend from the later 1980s, in which various forms of 'people movers' became increasingly important as entry regulations were tightened, particularly in the West (Van Hear 2001: 206). While restrictive immigration laws may affect the decision to migrate, these barriers to movement have been far from successful in actually controlling migration.

One of the ways in which Somalis can try to go for resettlement is to buy a position within an official case or buy a complete case; depending on the amount of money spent and the level at which the case is sold. Ibrahim Yasiin gave me an example of the first situation: 'Someone in the U.S.A. may have applied for family reunion for ten relatives, but a number of those people cannot be found. Some are in Somalia, some have died and others will have already resettled. When the case has been accepted for interviewing, the remaining places can be sold. The person abroad will be informed that he should not be surprised to find strangers at the airport and he should just play along'. Instead of selling these positions, they can also be given away to other close relatives, or good friends. One of the teachers of Midnimo Primary School remembered how a standard six girl was taken to Canada by the family of a classmate, simply because the two girls were very close friends. Buying a complete case mostly occurs through corruption within the organisations, as I learned from Fario and the other women outside the UNHCR office who had become victims of such practices.

A second way of leaving Kenya for the West is by travelling on a Kenyan passport. This option is open both for Kenyan Somalis and Somali refugees, who can, for example, buy a KLM or British Airways ticket to go to Costa Rica or another South American state. Having a stopover in Amsterdam or London, for example, they make a 'technical disappearance', although these days this is increasingly difficult. They hide or destroy their Kenyan passport, for example by flushing it down the toilet, and then use another passport with a Schengen visa[11] to get through customs and enter into Europe. There, they can apply for refugee status or remain illegal. Somali refugees may buy Kenyan passports or hire them from local residents. Kagwanja (2002: 11) describes a case of three Somali women who travelled via Amsterdam to London on passports that were not theirs. They were accompanied by a Kenyan official of Somali descent, claiming that the three were his wives. Similarly, Kenyan passports can be used to get a visa to study in a European country. Then, after one or two months of studies, the holder can decide to disappear from the university and try his or her luck in other ways.

Besides using Kenyan passports, there are other documents that may be used to enable travel. A Somali woman who wants to go to the U.S.A. may, for example, use her sister's U.S. passport to get there. As Kusow (1998) describes, there are many ways of entering the West. His informants travelled via various routes, one of which was to take a Romanian visa and travel with Aeroflot to ensure a stopover in Moscow. From Moscow, it used to be relatively easy to disembark and take a train to Finland. The Aeroflot ticket at that time became subject to an underground market. Another route went through Italy, from where passports of U.S. residents could be used. From the U.S.A., it was not hard to travel to Canada overland. Routes become popular as soon as someone has managed to use them successfully. After a time, they then become unpopular because they have been discovered and thus the risk of being caught increases. That is why I feel I am in a position to mention some of these ways of entering the West, since they are old and the authorities are mostly familiar with them. But whatever the routes chosen, the reasons for using them are the same. One of Kusow's informants states it very simply: 'I came to Canada illegally because no one would give me a visa' (Kusow 1998: 114). No matter how great the risks and high the costs, these routes are more likely to be successful than trying to enter a Western state through official policies. That is the only reason why people use them.

Because of the high risks involved in these kinds of undertakings, many refugees prefer to use the services of 'migration experts' whose job it is to help people pass all the hurdles of border restrictions. There are gaps in the institutional structures of international cooperation and in the fragmentation of domestic government law-enforcement efforts that human smugglers can easily exploit (Martin 2001: 14). These human smugglers are far more experienced and skilled in border crossings than the average refugee would be, which greatly reduces their chance of getting caught. Somali asylum seekers and their carriers seem to be engaged in some kind of battle of wits with the immigration authorities; as if they are saying to the authorities who think up all manner of legal constraints that they, as refugees, are equal to the dare (Farah 2000: 78). Whereas government authorities want to control their borders, asylum seekers want to be allowed to enter and in the process of trying to reach their goal, both parties constantly raise the stakes involved. A carrier interviewed by

Farah (2000: 79) said that European immigration officers are well aware that the higher the bar to be scaled, the more fatal the fall. He described his task as making sure that the falls, if they occur, are not as dangerous as the authorities predict.

In representing their profession, the *mukhalis* to whom Farah spoke all had their own motivations and viewpoints, but the picture they painted was mostly an unrealistically positive one: they allegedly were not out to make money, but rather wanted to assist Somali asylum seekers in reaching their destination safely. Although they were willing to talk to Farah, at the same time the *mukhalis* answered only a few of his questions and kept on referring him to others. In the end, Farah found it very difficult to write much about the topic, except for the few pieces of a much larger puzzle that he was handed by different individuals. After a few referrals that hardly brought him any information, having been warned about the risk of being too nosy, he gave up. Considering the criminal nature of human smuggling, it is not surprising that question-askers are treated with due suspicion. Personally, I found it extremely difficult to get information from *mukhalis*, because they were behaving very guardedly towards me. Once, Sahra Yusuf introduced me to a carrier in Nairobi, but she had not dared to tell him why I was interested in talking to him. She told me to approach the topic very carefully, but as soon as I asked a couple of questions on *buufis* and resettlement, he became reluctant to talk and made it clear our discussion was over.

In hindsight, I did get a lot of information from someone I now strongly suspect to be a *mukhalis*, although I did not realise it at the time. When I went to Kenya in February 1998 in order to prepare my fieldwork, an Italian missionary who had worked in Somalia introduced me to 'Koofi Cad'. Before I had started collecting data and before I had heard of *buufis* or developed an interest in resettlement issues, he drove me around Nairobi. At that time, I thought he just wanted to show me some of the places in town that were important for Somali refugees, but now I assume he was simultaneously doing business. We first went to the JVA office, where Koofi Cad checked the list of those who were supposed to go to the U.S.A. He then showed me a letter from someone who had been invited for resettlement and was included in the JVA list, but had already returned to Somalia. He told me that this letter would be worth a lot of money, easily 4,000 dollars. We then drove to Eastleigh, where many people approached Koofi Cad, who exchanged information with them and handed out money.

At last, we went to the lounge of one of the international hotels for a coffee and talked about Somali refugees migrating to the West. I told him that I was worried about the ethics of what to write, and how to do so, since there is always the risk that information will be misused. An important question that remains, I said, is what refugees themselves are gaining from the kind of knowledge we are trying to contribute (see also Horst 2002: 87–88) and the last thing I would want is to contribute to detrimental policies. Koofi Cad gave me an example: once, a journalist from a European newspaper had interviewed him on remittance sending by Somalis. When he found his words in the newspaper, he realised that they had been used to question the fact that refugees received social benefits in that country. He told me that one's words and intentions could always be misread or misused, but that this should not stop someone from voicing his or her opinion. The only caution one can take is to be very specific about the message that one tries to put across, which might, at times, mean leaving out information that could be misinterpreted. Koofi Cad told me that he trusted me in my decisions, but I have always found them very difficult to make. My (partial) solution has been to give Somali refugees in Dadaab and the wider diaspora ample chance to comment on earlier versions of this book.

Based on this rather anecdotal information, combined with data from earlier studies, a number of characteristics can be assumed. There are various types of *mukhalis*, offering various services. The smaller ones are often mere middlemen, for example mediating between those who have an extra position within their resettlement case and those who want to buy such a position. It is important to find a case that matches the characteristics of an individual and *mukhalis* are in a better position to know what cases are available. In Nairobi there are 'market places' where different *mukhalis* offer the available cases to interested buyers. It is common to pay a few hundred dollars commission before the interview, and when the case has been accepted the rest of a few thousand dollars is paid. The larger part of this sum goes to the seller, a percentage goes to the *mukhalis*. Ismail Gedi told me how a Somali once approached him in Eastleigh and asked him whether he knew anybody with 3,000 dollars. That person would be resettled within a week, through a UN case. Ismail told me that these were the middlemen for UN officers in Nairobi and he had heard that one of them even wanted to open an office in Eastleigh.

Professional *mukhalis* offer a far wider range of services, assisting refugees in the different phases of the migration process. Several types of services may be offered, such as assistance in crossing without inspection, houses in which the migrants can hide from the authorities, transport to interior locations, and links to employers (Martin 2001: 14). It depends on the individual smuggler as to what he or she can or will provide and what the procedures are. One of the *mukhalis* Farah spoke to told him: 'Each carrier has his own style. I prefer carrying two refugee travel documents, one to be used, another to fall back on in the event of unprepared-for bottlenecks. We meet at an appointed place and time to rehearse possible scenarios: problems and what to do about them; no-problems and how to proceed so as not to create problems. Once aboard the aircraft, I sit furthest from them' (Farah 2000: 79). Another person told him that he preferred recruiting young women: 'Put simply, I paid for a woman's travel and relevant expenses, claiming she was my wife, which relationship granted her entry into Italy, once I organised my own papers on the basis of a forged document. The woman entered into a deal with me by signing an affidavit. On arrival here, I put her in a *pensione* and found her a job through an employment agency, which was in on the deal, their cut guaranteed. They deducted their commission at source and ensured that the woman reimbursed my money with interest' (Farah 2000: 84). *Mukhalis* and migrants may enter into a number of different agreements, mostly travelling together, but once something goes wrong in the deal, the migrant is almost always on his or her own.

Professional smuggling and trafficking operations have emerged as facilitators of migration as a consequence of increasingly restrictive immigration controls. Although human smuggling has existed from the time national borders existed, what is new is the scale of smuggling, measured in numbers and profits, as well as its increasing professionalisation (Martin 2001: 13). Accordingly, the prices that migrants pay to be ferried across borders have also increased. The Somalis I spoke to in Dadaab and Nairobi mentioned prices, paid to individuals or *mukhalis*, of between 2,000 and 6,000 dollars per person. Most of the times, it is not possible for an individual or household to pay the thousands of dollars needed to migrate. Earlier studies have shown some of the strategies that refugees use to collect such money (see e.g. Koser 1997; Van Hear 2001). Substantial numbers of Sri Lankan households, for example, resort to moneylenders, which might entail borrowing money at interest rates of 15 percent a month. Alternatively they might sell, mortgage or pawn assets like land, equipment, houses, shops or jewellery (Van Hear 2001: 207). The Somali refugees in Dadaab and Nairobi never mentioned moneylenders and only a small minority had sufficient assets to sell, mortgage or pawn. In most cases, people had to resort to their relatives already overseas.

Some smugglers may act like legitimate business people, guaranteeing their services and agreeing to receive final payment when the migrant reaches the destination, but other trafficking operations are far less benevolent. Smugglers pack large numbers of migrants into small, unventilated spaces to cross borders or reach ports (Martin 2001: 14). In recent years, there have been media reports of smugglers who have left migrants without oxygen, water or protection from the hot sun, at times causing death. Many Somalis are known to have died, for example, while trying to move from Libya to Italy by boat (Al-Sharmani 2004: 29). Others take the migrant to the West, but not to the agreed country. There are cases of Somali refugees who, for example, end up in the Netherlands although they had paid to be taken to the U.S.A. Besides these situations of abuse by human traffickers, success is never guaranteed. The *mukhalis* interviewed by Farah mentioned a rate of failure of 15–33 percent (Farah 2000: 78, 80). In case of problems, the migrant is likely to be left to his or her own destiny, unless it happens in a country where dollars are accepted by authorities. Within Western countries, the carrier will not risk being caught and will almost certainly walk out. Their advantage over migrants is the migrants' dependence, ignorance and lack of recourse when agreements are not fulfilled (Martin 2001: 14). In most of the cases of failure, money is not refunded, and thus a large and valuable investment is lost.

Who Goes? The Central Role of Relatives

In view of the above, it is clear that resettlement does not just benefit those who most need it because of fear or vulnerability. Not everybody is in a position to go overseas, since the resettlement applicant not only needs a convincing story, but also a certain amount of luck and dedication. Often, it may be more helpful to have sufficient finances or useful contacts, either with people in influential positions or with relatives abroad who can send a 'sponsorship' in the form of funds or a family reunion case. The refugees in Dadaab are not necessarily in the best situation to possess these resources and have to compete with Kenyan Somalis and Somalis living outside the camps in Kenya and Somalia. When refugees are selected for resettlement in Dadaab, more affluent Kenyan Somalis and Somalis from Somalia move into the camps with enough money to buy a case. Thus, those trying to secure resettlement in the West are not only refugees. Once, I went to the Dadaab post office to buy stamps and entered into a conversation with Abdi Omar, a Somali Kenyan working there. When I said that I was from the Netherlands, Abdi smiled and said his brother was in the Netherlands. I asked what he was doing there and Abdi told me: 'My brother is in your country as a refugee. He recently called, saying that it is no good to live in the Netherlands as a refugee, and he informed me that he is now trying to go to the U.S.A.'. Indeed, when a case can be bought, the well-off stand a better chance. In other cases, it may be an advantage to know the system and have the right contacts.

At family level, due to the criteria used in certain resettlement programmes and the expense of buying a position, it often happens that not all members can go overseas simultaneously. It is more likely that one or a few members of a family unit go, while the others remain behind in the hope that they will be given a chance in the future. The decision as to who goes and who stays is a very difficult one, at times leading to mothers leaving young children behind, hoping to sponsor them once they become permanent residents (Affi 1997: 443). Rashid Ibrahim told me the story of a family that has split up due to a combination of resettlement policies and the choices they made. They had decided that the wife would claim her husband had died in Somalia, in order to increase her chances. The case was accepted and the wife was going to join her brother in the U.S.A. In August 1999, the husband waved goodbye to his wife and their five children, as well as three children that had been added to the case though they were not theirs. He hoped to find an opportunity to follow his family later. Rashid told me that many families are torn apart because resettlement policies do not favour families: 'All categories of vulnerable women are supported for resettlement, which leads many families to claim that they are not complete. It is also common that children are added to a family; whether they are related or not. But afterwards, problems arise because these children do not necessarily recognise the authority of their new parent or parents'. Thus, the choices that people make, as based on existing resettlement policies, may seriously affect family relations.

Another effect of existing resettlement policies is that they influence people's movements. In order to secure resettlement, many refugees' movements were shaped by their ideas on what would enhance or reduce their chances. Since interviews and other activities related to the processing of asylum requests and family-sponsored immigration applications were conducted in the camps, many Somalis commuted to the camps in order to establish a camp residence, although they were resident elsewhere. Some even came from Somalia in order to be able to apply for resettlement, as in the case of Abbas Warsame and his family, who moved from Mogadishu to Dagahaley. Others move within Dadaab, from one camp to the other, if they believe it may benefit their case. Abukar Hassan had been worried about his family's resettlement case for a long time since it was a complex case that involved his parents and siblings as well as some of his uncles. His family stayed in Dagahaley, his uncles lived in Hagadera and he himself originally worked for an NGO in Dagahaley but was then transferred to Hagadera. On top of that, the UNHCR field officer who was dealing with the case had also been transferred from Dagahaley to Hagadera. Whereas Abukar was satisfied with the way this field officer had dealt with their case, he was not pleased with the officer who took over. Thus, he spoke with the transferred officer in Hagadera, who agreed that he would look at the case if the family moved to his new camp. Because he worked for an NGO, Abukar managed to get his ration card transferred and moved his family to Hagadera.

Besides movement, another strategy to increase resettlement chances is related to marriage. Those with good chances to go overseas, because they have relatives in Western countries or because they have an accepted resettlement case, are very popular marriage partners. Once, I was invited to visit a newly married couple in Hagadera. One of the CDWs who accompanied me told me that the young woman had received a large number of marriage proposals before her present husband eloped with her to Garissa. A number of her close relatives were already in the U.S.A.

and her father had recently passed the interview with the INS. Thus, according to the CDW, all the young men in Hagadera had dreamt of marrying her. This influence on marriage patterns at times caused great frustration amongst young people. I spoke to young women who said they would not marry in the camps but wait for their opportunity to go for resettlement. Young men on the other hand, feared that the girl they loved would not want to marry them unless they went overseas. As a young man interviewed by Bashir Mahat and Abdulahi Noor put it: 'Real men are those who go to the U.S.A.; others are only so-called men'.

Many studies have stressed the importance of kinship in enabling migration, suggesting that social networks greatly influence who does and who does not migrate.[12] Yet, within the field of refugee studies, little attention has been paid to the role played by social networks in prompting, facilitating, sustaining and directing the movement of asylum seekers and other migrants into Western Europe (Crisp 1999a: 5). In studies on transnational communities, there has been some increased interest in the importance of social networks for refugees recently (see e.g. Koser and Al-Ali 2001). If these studies are analysed, it becomes clear that transnational social networks perform a number of important functions in the process of asylum migration. They provide an important source of information, link the migrant to the organisational infrastructure that enables migration and often provide the financial resources necessary for movement. In studies amongst Somalis, this fact has certainly been recognised. Many of the refugees who went to Cairo, for example, were able to leave their homeland for Egypt through the assistance of a family member (Al-Sharmani 1998: 26). Hopes of moving further, to the West, were again linked to the assistance that relatives could provide. Similarly, Rousseau et al. (1998: 394) describe the process of migration to the West as 'at first haphazard, but soon reorganising according to traditional patterns of sponsorship. Kinship and a whole array of agnatic ties, contractual in nature, guarantee both financial and logistic support: papers, passports, visas and the means to obtain them, as well as room and board during the intermediate stages of the journey'.

Conversely, migration often forms an important part of family livelihood strategies. Thus, when and how to move, who should go, how to raise the resources to travel and how to use any proceeds from migration are commonly matters for the whole household rather than the individual migrant (Van Hear 2001: 206; Salih 2001a: 660). In the case of the Somali, it is a matter even beyond the household, dealt with at the level of the extended family. Those who do not have any members of their extended family abroad, or otherwise in a well-off position, find it difficult to go abroad. When I interviewed Dek Osman in Eastleigh, I asked him where his family members were staying. He answered: 'Many of my relatives are still in Somalia. I do not have any relatives abroad, which makes it very difficult for me to find an opportunity to resettle. If one has relatives abroad, they might send some money, like one hundred or two hundred dollars on a monthly basis. Then, if they get tired of that after one or two years, they may decide to send a large sum of money in order for you to buy a resettlement case'. Farah (2000: 80) similarly notes: 'The better-off relations in the West, tired of coughing up enough funds to maintain their relatives in camps in Yemen, Kenya and Ethiopia, pay the expenses need-ed for their migration to the West'. This is an investment to them not only in the sense that they no longer have to send remittances to that person, but also in the sense that the new migrant soon will share the responsi-bility of sending remittances to relatives in the region and ultimately may provide another person with the opportunity to migrate. In this way, sponsorship creates a kind of chain migration: Expansion of the network leads to more migration, which, in turn, leads to a further expansion of the network (Shah and Menon 1999: 364).

Migration from Dadaab involves considerable investments, taken care of mainly by Somali kinship networks, but there is also an expectation that there will ultimately be some return on these investments. Reciprocity may be expected in the form of monthly remittances or of a contact person in the West who can enable others to migrate. A relative in a Western country can facilitate new migration by providing information, a family reunion case or the finances to buy a resettlement position. Van Hear (2001) notes that perceiving migration in this way suggests that remittances are not a simple one-way transfer from those abroad to those at home, but rather that the process should instead be viewed as a kind of exchange. Amongst the Somalis there are definite pressures and responsibilities as regards assisting those left behind. Before departure, peer groups, lineage mem-bers and the community as a whole are all mobilised by the desires of the individual who is leaving to execute his plan and keep the dream alive (Rousseau et al. 1998: 402). After the person leaves, the pressures are reversed, with the traveller now indebted and expected to give back what has been received. Those who go carry the responsibility of supporting rel-atives left behind and possibly facilitating their resettlement in the West. This may be a heavy burden on the shoulder of the migrant, as research amongst Somalis in Minneapolis has indicated (Horst 2004).

In conclusion, there are many ambiguities associated with *buufis*. It is a dream that brings hope in the camps, but it is also often characterised as a disease that the refugees are suffering from. Resettlement may be a solu-tion for the most vulnerable in the community, such as those without social networks, but at the same time, refugees with money or connections stand a far better chance of actually achieving it. *Buufis* is something that, once realised, may lead to increased socio-economic security both for the migrants and for those remaining behind. Yet in order to obtain resettle-ment, high risks are taken and often many losses are suffered, both in terms of financial 'investments' and in terms of human lives. And finally, one of the main attractions of resettlement for Somali refugees is that it allows them to move away from an area where they are dependent on the assistance of others, to a place where they can sustain themselves. Simultaneously, this move confronts them with the responsibility of taking care of others, who become dependent on their financial assistance. In the end, the main reason why *buufis* exists in Dadaab is because to many, having no regional alternative, it is the 'best available' option. Refugees who live in camps like Dadaab need to sustain a dream for a better future. As long as it is not realistic to dream of a peaceful, safe and stable life in their home or host country, they will continue dreaming of a future in the West.

Notes

1. In Somali, madness is described as *maraduu turay*, 'he has thrown away his clothes' (Rousseau et al. 1998: 403).
2. For a detailed account on Sayyed Moxamed's role in Somalia's history and anticolonial struggles, see Brons (2001: 137–44).
3. In this respect, literature on migration and Islam (see e.g. Eickelman and Piscatori 1990) and anthropological work on travelling as rite of passage (see e.g. Chatwin 1988) is of relevance.
4. These points are strongly influenced by developments in structuration theory, largely informed by the work of Anthony Giddens (1984; 1990).
5. Similar processes have been described in studies on migrant workers (see e.g. Gardner 1995; McMurray 2001: 152).
6. As Kagwanja (2002: 11) notes: 'the craze for resettlement has also caught up with Kenya's ethnic Somalis in the Dadaab camps'. A number of them even register as refugees because of the prospects of resettlement.
7. 'Sweet stories' refers to very positive, tempting, seducing stories about a life others would yearn for.
8. An 'individual case' may comprise a number of family members. 'Individual' refers to the fact that resettlement is granted on a case-by-case basis and not as part of a much larger group determination process.
9. We discussed the letter's contents and Awas agreed that I could quote it in my book as long as his real name was not mentioned.
10. This remark certainly does not do away with the fact that many, if not most, of the Somali refugees did lose relatives during the war and experienced dreadful things and may simply recount what happened to them.
11. A person travelling with a Schengen visa may enter one Schengen country and travel freely through the Schengen zone; as agreed on in June 1985 when a treaty was signed to end internal border controls within Europe. At present, there are fifteen Schengen countries: Austria, Belgium, Denmark, Finland, France, Germany, Iceland, Italy, Greece, Luxembourg, Netherlands, Norway, Portugal, Spain and Sweden.
12. A number of these studies are mentioned in Choldin (1973) and Shah (1999).

6

Historical and Transnational Approaches to Refugee Studies

By studying the transnational assistance networks of Somalis in Dadaab, thus linking the livelihoods of refugees in camps to those of their relatives elsewhere, I have attempted to move away from compartmentalised studies on IDPs, returnees, refugees in regional camps, urban refugees and resettled refugees. In my view, refugee studies should develop a more integrated, transnational approach that analyses the connections between these different groups. Furthermore, I have stressed the need for a historical analysis of the situation of those who live in protracted refugee situations.[1] Like many others in refugee camps, Somalis in Dadaab were familiar with insecurity before their flight to Kenya. In order to understand their responses to camp life, it is of great importance to examine their ways of coping with various insecurities in Somalia before the war. Having said that, it is also important to realise that the actual experiences that refugees have gone through – violence, persecution, hunger, general warfare or torture – whether experienced, witnessed or inflicted, are unique to them. As Hassan Jamaac claims when we meet in Eastleigh, a refugee is 'like the *sufriye* that people make use of to cook on the fire. When you use it the first time, it gets burned badly. But later, it develops a thick layer of charcoal and cooks only slowly. Our hearts are like that. We have experienced so many things that we are now very strong. We have hardened with life'.

The Somalis in Dadaab are not just refugees in a camp: they are people with a past, hoping to move towards a future beyond the camps. Their life histories are as essential to their present situation as are their links with and dreams of a future elsewhere. The question now is of whether the historical and transnational approach, which I have used to analyse the ways that Somalis in Dadaab cope with refugee life, can contribute something to theoretical debates within refugee studies; and if so, what? How can refugee studies theorise both the agency and vulnerabilities of refugees (see also Essed et al. 2004) without contributing to the common labelling of refugees as 'cunning crooks' or 'vulnerable victims'? In my opinion, at least part of the answer to these questions lies in finding a balance between the individual narratives of refugees and the political economy that determines their position. By analysing the life histories of individual refugees in the context of the larger history of their country and the refugee regime, the opportunities open to them and the restraints they face become clear. Similarly, by placing the lives and livelihoods of refugees in a particular location within a global context, through studying transnational networks and the various flows they bring about, the opportunities and constraints that refugees face locally are analytically expanded to a global level.

Historical Approaches to the Study of Refugees

In an article for the Journal of Refugee Studies, Davis (1993) argues against the divide between two kinds of anthropology. The one, according to Davis, is prestigiously 'academic', producing monographs concerned with social groups that are represented as working more or less normally, with occasional spasms of adjustment. The other, of which refugee studies could be an example, is concerned with breakdown and repair as a consequence of natural and manmade disasters and in his description is marginal, soft-funded and mainly produces advocacy and policy reports. Many authors would agree with the critique that refugee studies is still very much policy-oriented work of a reactive nature, with only a small number of publications making an effort to discuss conceptual or theoretical questions (Crisp 1999a; Wahlbeck 2002). Besides, the studies that do address such questions often do so on a macropolitical or highly abstract theoretical level, without making much effort to link this level to the actual experiences of refugees.[2] As such, my ethnographic descriptions of livelihoods in Dadaab have been an attempt both to integrate the two kinds of anthropology, as Davis suggests, and to tackle these general criticisms towards refugee studies by addressing conceptual and theoretical issues without losing sight of the everyday life experiences of refugees.

Davis' proposal on the action that should be taken in order to integrate the two kinds of anthropology, bringing the study of crises to the centre of the discipline, is to present the suffering caused by war and famine as a normal state of affairs. He shows how the experience, causes and ways of dealing with extreme kinds of suffering are, in many cases, continuous with ordinary social experience: 'famine that kills'[3] is an extreme form of regular scarcity; it has a history (Davis 1993: 151). The same is true for war, which in most societies has a place in social memory and is incorporated into accumulated culture (Davis 1993: 152). In order not to describe various types of insecurities and the ways that people have found to deal with them as occasional spasms of adjustment within an otherwise stable society, historical approaches are essential. Studying the life histories of refugees within the context of their society's past will allow scholars in the field of refugee studies to move beyond processes of refugee labelling. Studying the history of assistance provision and mutual obligation or reciprocity between the refugees and their host community and country, as well as between the refugees and the international aid regime, will enable these scholars to shed new light on questions of agency and vulnerability.

Refugees are People with a Past: Studying Life Histories Within Their Regional Context

Collecting refugees' life histories and placing these narratives within the history of their community of origin enables the researcher to analyse the responses of refugees to their current conditions to a far better extent. Refugees are people with a past and very often this past includes insecurities. People in protracted refugee situations, the majority of whom are to be found in extremely poor states (Crisp 2003), have often experienced insecurities such as hunger, violence and conflict during their lives. It is essential to understand this, in order to understand their responses to current crises, since the social security mechanisms that refugees employ are largely based on precedents (Kibreab 1993). In the case of Somali refugees in Dadaab, it is clear that past experiences and livelihood strategies in many ways enable them to deal with the harsh conditions and limited opportunities available locally. Because the ecological and political environment in which Somalis lived before their flight was highly variable and mostly unreliable, they had developed a number of social security mechanisms that largely functioned to minimise risks in the event of contingencies; based on what I have called a 'nomadic heritage'. My use of this term goes far beyond the actual activity of moving around with animals by an individual or his/her parents. It refers instead to a mental attitude, as well as an actual strategy of coping with life by looking for greener pastures elsewhere and investing in different activities and people in different places. A very essential feature of Somali culture in this respect is the existence of strong transnational assistance networks, based on both a cultural and a religious responsibility to assist those who have less.

This responsibility to meet the needs of people who are (temporarily) not able to provide for themselves is common in most sociocultural and religious systems across the world. Thus, it remains to be seen to what extent a nomadic heritage is the sole rationalisation behind the patterns that I discerned amongst the Somalis. In my view, remittance sending and migration patterns can be observed in many other refugee groups, whether they have a nomadic background or not. Yet, the intensity and frequency of assistance responsibilities and mobility across borders amongst Somalis are unique, and can be explained by their nomadic background. The economic strategies of the Somali people take place within an integrated economy that has never respected state borders (Brons 2001: 72). This makes their current transnational livelihood strategies a mere expansion of historical patterns, as can be seen from the great ease with which Somalis move, while still feeling responsible for their relatives elsewhere. Somalis move, for example, from the Netherlands and Denmark to the U.K. in very large numbers, because of their inability to send remittances from the former countries (see Reek and Hussein 2003; Bang Nielsen 2004). It is important to compare the exact ways in which various groups of refugees deal with the insecurities they face, using a historical perspective in order to analyse possible differences.

A further question to ask is what effects the experiences of flight and the (institutionalised) circumstances of life in refugee camps have on existing social security mechanisms. Although some studies have claimed that the strength of assistance networks weakens in times of scarcity and crisis, others state the opposite. During a severe famine in Sudan, De Waal (1989) noticed that people's principle aim was to preserve the basis of an acceptable future way of living, which to them involved not only material well-being but also social cohesion. In research amongst 'internal refugees' in Sri Lanka, Schrijvers (1997) also stresses the importance of restoring social relations to restore a sense of humanity and human dignity. During my research in Dadaab, I found many examples of the ways that the refugees were assisting each other. At camp level, various clans held collections of food rations, which would be redistributed to the most needy families; incentive workers living in certain blocks pooled together their resources to assist vulnerable block members; and neighbours or clan members contributed to daily survival and during specific contingency situations, such as illness, robbery or death. These and other practices were mainly based on customs that existed in Somalia before the war, though people's ability to assist was limited now that they were living in a refugee camp. An analysis of community-based forms of assistance and to what extent these have been affected by flight and exile would be vital amongst other refugee communities as well. Such an approach would focus on how refugees themselves were dealing with their day-to-day survival instead of focusing on how they were dependent on international aid. Assisting others involves a level of agency, of transformative power and choice, that is not easily associated with refugees, although it is an important aspect of their lives and livelihoods. As such, it deserves a far more central position within refugee studies than is currently the case.

The Relationship Between Refugees and Their 'Caretakers': Agency Versus Vulnerability?

Whereas the UNHCR was initially intended as a temporary body with a three-year life span, it celebrated its fiftieth birthday in 2001. In those fifty years, the UNHCR has seen the conditions under which it operates deteriorate further. The relationships between the actors of the refugee regime, including the UNHCR, governments, implementing agencies and donors, have become increasingly strained and the willingness to provide growing numbers of refugees with assistance seems only to be declining. Since the 1980s, Western governments have developed increasingly restrictive policies as they have been faced with more and more refugees from non-Western countries. A fear of a large influx of refugees, stimulated by stereotypical media coverage, has led to attempts to close borders in Europe, Australia, the U.S.A. and Canada. In reality, the vast majority of refugees remain in the developing world and the refugee regime is now being utilised to contain refugees there. At the same time, restrictive policies in the West are combined with relief-aid budget cuts, leading to a situation where developing countries have also become reluctant hosts. Because of the strict divide between relief and development aid, the UNHCR lacks initiatives to improve refugee livelihoods in the region and NGOs have also done little more than initiate microscale income-generating activities which do not address structural causes of regional poverty but just provide a limited income to those participating.

Many of the present complexities surrounding refugee assistance can be explained by the existing conceptualisation of refugees and the common motives for this type of aid, which are often related to providing relief to human suffering. The humanitarian aid that is provided to refugees in camps like Dadaab is insistently formulated as part of a benign and universal human project of 'technical fixes', focusing on the provision of food aid, nonfood items and protection. The idea that refugees are vulnerable due to the experiences that caused their flight and exile easily leads to the conclusion that they need assistance from outside their own community. This may certainly be the case for most refugees at the initial postflight stage, when many resources have been lost and people have just experienced violence, upheaval and other traumatic events and losses at community level. Yet, at the same time, they have managed to survive by choosing flight and depending on other social security strategies. Moreover, the vulnerability that leads to the initial dependency on 'external' aid is not a static or permanent reality. Refugees move on and many overcome the insecurities faced, often relying on familiar strategies, such as those that involve relatives and friends. Even in situations in which the community as a whole has been affected by some kind of natural or manmade disaster, people often do share the little they have in order to regain a sense of humanity. Being able to assist others may be one of the most important ways of regaining a sense of dignity and agency. Thus, vulnerability and agency are multidimensional, relative and fluid concepts which capture the realities of different refugees at different stages of their lives.

The most problematic aspect of the institutional labelling and confinement of refugees is that it is a circular process in two ways. In the first place, refugees themselves have an interest in being labelled as such because this entitles them to material assistance and legal protection. Yet, inclusion requires conformity, which means that in order to be entitled to humanitarian aid the refugee must prove his or her vulnerability. NGO programmes in Dadaab involve the group-based allocation of resources for specific groups of refugees, identified as particularly vulnerable. Such programmes lead to a rather problematic commoditisation of NGO-defined labels, with refugees at times even simulating vulnerability in order to qualify for specific benefits. If, for example, divorcees are entitled to certain benefits, Somali women who are divorced may claim that they are 'vulnerable' so as to guarantee extra resources. Besides, women who are not divorced may say they are for the same reason. If this entitles a woman to benefit from a resettlement opportunity for 'vulnerable women', she will end up in a Western country without her husband, with varying effects on her level of choice and power. This, in a way, 'creates' additional numbers of vulnerable refugees, as defined by the NGOs, thus legitimising and reproducing existing policies. At the same time, a group-based strategy leaves out individuals who may need assistance in order to survive in Dadaab, but do not fall into any of the NGO-determined categories.

Secondly, a circular process exists that causes the actual increase of the numbers of 'vulnerables' or refugees who need assistance in order to survive. Those involved in humanitarian aid provision often assume that refugees are not just temporarily vulnerable because of having lost most of their material resources, but permanently so because they have lost their sociocultural resources as well. Only when they stop being refugees, for example by repatriating to their home country, do they stop being perceived as vulnerable. Based on these assumptions, aid programmes for refugees are likely to supply handouts continuously without providing the refugees with the responsibility and chance to establish their own livelihoods. Officially, the ultimate aim of the refugee regime is to assist refugees to move from dependency on external protection and assistance toward a situation in which they can take care of their own lives and livelihoods self-sufficiently; replacing emergency aid with providing 'durable solutions'. But when refugee assistance projects confine people in marginal areas with limited economic opportunities, without in any way enabling their local self-sufficiency, it is not surprising that these refugees will indeed require continued handouts in order to survive. Besides, some refugees develop depression or lose hope after many years of living in a hopeless situation, and this may affect their actions and self-motivation. The label of vulnerability informs 'handout policies', which consequently create refugees who increasingly fit the original label. At the same time, whereas one may interpret this as a failure of the refugee regime to achieve official aims, it may also be seen to produce effects that are part of a process of increased control over refugees, combined with a depoliticisation of this process (see also Ferguson 1990). In order to provide food aid, the refugee regime requires refugees to remain in camps and be registered, but the bureaucratisation this involves ultimately also enables the containment of refugees.

Transnational Approaches to the Study of Refugees

A transnational approach focuses on how the political, economic and socio-cultural connections that exist between migrants, their homelands and the wider diaspora affect lives and livelihoods in a certain place. These connections and their impacts are not new and thus need to be understood from a historical perspective. Rather, the research focus within a transnational approach is new, enabling researchers to ask different questions. The implications of such a perspective for the study of refugees are essential in two ways. First, the concept stresses that mobility, including mobility that crosses borders, has always been an essential part of many people's livelihoods and identities. Besides, new forms of mobility have emerged due to technological developments, enabling transnational flows that have affected a much wider group of people, including refugees in relatively remote camps like Dadaab. Secondly, transnationalism shifts the focus of studying migration from the reasons why migrants leave and their level of participation in the host society, to the connections they entertain with their relatives and community members in the homeland and across the diaspora. These connections are not merely analysed in respect to their value or cost in relation to integration or potential return to the home country. Rather, they are analysed in their own right, enabling a new perspective to inform current migration debates. Within EU countries like the Netherlands, unfortunately this seems not to be happening yet, as integration and return are currently still presented as the two sole options within the national debate.

Whereas refugees have largely been excluded from research on transnationalism, in the last couple of years, interest in the transnational connections that refugees maintain is slowly increasing. Such interest includes not only their political but also their economic, social and cultural activities. This is related to the realisation that the conceptual distinction between refugees and other migrants is at best blurred, with political, ethnic, economic, environmental and human rights factors combining to cause people to move. It is also related to a better understanding of the complex relationship that exists between refugees and their homeland(s), with transnational sociocultural, economic and political ties between the two determining much of people's lives on both sides. Refugees do not merely wait for a political change in their country so that they can return, or if this is not forthcoming, put their efforts into integration in their new society. Often, they continuously engage with their home country through remittance sending, sociocultural exchanges or 'long distance nationalism' (Anderson 1983). On top of that, refugees do not live in isolation from other migrants, but are often part of a network of a larger diaspora. Somalis have lived in Europe and the U.S.A. not only as refugees and asylum seekers but also under a variety of other legal statuses (Crisp 1999a). Thus, it is more useful to focus on such communities as a whole, instead of trying to create an artificial distinction between 'economic migrants' on the one hand, and refugees on the other.

Refugee Transnationalism: Comparative Cases

The transnational networks and dreams of Somali refugees in Dadaab are certainly not unique to them, but apply to a wide range of other groups of refugees. Transnational networks, and the flows of resources, people and information that they enable, are crucial to an understanding of any refugee situation, touching on various aspects of migration, refugee livelihoods and identity formation, as well as a whole range of other areas. There is still hardly any specific literature on the transnational activities of refugees, but the few studies that have become available over the last decade do enable an interesting comparison to be made with the Somali case and confirm the importance of transnational approaches to the study of refugees. The first article to make the argument for the use of this analytic concept within refugee studies appeared in 1996 in the Journal of Refugee Studies (Shami 1996), taking examples from the Arab Middle East and Islam. Remarkably, it has remained the only article on the topic in this leading journal on refugee issues for many years.

Another author commonly associated with the transnationalism debate is Malkki (1992), who contests the 'national order of things' by asserting that people are chronically mobile and routinely displaced, thus creating deterritorialised nations. Her work on Burundian refugees in Tanzania demonstrates a postmodern concern for issues of space and national identity and, as such, cannot easily be linked to the transnational networks and flows that practically influence or even enable the day-to-day survival of refugees. Wahlbeck (2002), on the other hand, does combine both aspects in his study amongst Kurdish refugee communities in Europe. He analyses the process of ethnic or national deterritorialisation as well as the flows of information, ideas, capital and people between the countries of origin and settlement. He particularly stresses the political commitment that exists amongst Kurds in Europe towards Kurdistan, showing how this national consciousness simultaneously serves to reinforce identity and a sense of order and purpose in the fragmented lives of the refugees. Similar processes have been observed amongst Bosnian women, who compensate their feelings of isolation in the host society by regular contact with relatives and family in Bosnia (Al-Ali 2001: 107).

In my opinion, transnational research on refugees is highly relevant in the first place if it combines the study of different types of flows, for example in the shape of migration, remittance sending, 'long distance nationalism', media images etcetera and looks at how these flows interrelate to influence locally based lives. Such an approach is particularly interesting if it analyses the different directions these flows can take: whether from host to home country and vice versa, or from the host country to elsewhere in the diaspora. As such, a holistic picture can be developed that reflects the effects of all sorts of global transformations on the daily lives of refugees anywhere in the world. In the last few years, efforts have been made to develop such a perspective in academic writing; especially in studies by Al-Ali and Koser (Al-Ali et al. 2001; Koser and Al-Ali 2001). Through their work on the mobilisation and participation of transnational exile communities in postconflict reconstruction, these authors have called for the incorporation of refugees in transnational studies. This call conversely starts from the argument that the distinction between labour migrants and refugees is unclear, and thus typologies of labour migration should also be applicable to situations of forced migration (Koser 1997). In my opinion however, the argument should be reversed. The main advantage of transnational studies is that there is no longer an exclusive focus on the motivations for migration, which are often blurred and impossible to categorise in dualistic terms like forced versus voluntary or political versus economic.

Irrespective of this different entry point, Al-Ali and Koser's work analyses a number of interesting aspects of the level of transnationalism of Eritrean and Bosnian refugees in Europe. First, they document and categorise a wide variety of political, economic, social and cultural activities that can be described as transnational. These activities take place at individual and communal levels, initiated from the side of both the home country and the host country, by citizens as well as governments. As the authors point out, nation-states increasingly view their communities in exile as legitimate constituencies. In the Eritrean case, for example, the government has continuously, though in changing ways, engaged with its diaspora both economically and politically. It has collected tax and expected regular contributions from Eritreans in exile both for military and reconstruction purposes. And it has also developed efforts to engage

Eritreans in the diaspora politically, such as through their close involvement in the Referendum for Independence as well as in the drafting of its constitution (Koser 2001a: 144-145). A similar process occurred in both Somaliland and Puntland (a region in the northeast of Somalia), where members of the diaspora were actively involved in drafting a new constitution, using the Internet as a forum for discussion. Many other well known examples of such 'long-distance nationalism' can be given, for example, amongst the Palestinians, Israelis, Kurds and Sri Lankans (see also Van Hear 1998b).

Governments are usually not the only parties interested in transnational activities, and both Bosnian and Eritrean refugees relate to their respective countries in many economic, sociocultural and political ways. These refugees send remittances to help relatives and friends to survive and to assist in reconstructing the home country through communal projects and individual activities. At the same time, they engage in transnational sociocultural and political activities in order to maintain a sense of identity in the host country. Most Bosnian and Eritrean refugees in Western Europe do not intend to return to their home country, so these activities are not just attempts to enable a future return (Al-Ali et al. 2001). I would rather suggest that they, just like in the Somali case, are motivated by a combination of two factors. First, the will that people have to survive, both in physical or economic terms and in terms of maintaining a 'national identity', and secondly the responsibility they feel to guarantee the survival, in similar terms, of relatives, community members and close friends elsewhere. By maintaining links with relatives and friends, despite physical distance, (forced) migrants and 'stayees' create a level of agency and choice that their politico-economic position might otherwise not have allowed.

The Pitfalls of a Transnational Approach

One of the main strengths of transnational theories, and a major reason why they appeal to me so strongly, may indeed be that they emphasise human agency in an age of globalisation and other processes that are easily interpreted as reducing the power of individual decision-making (Al-Ali 2001: 100). Yet, simultaneously, this characteristic can lead to one of the major pitfalls of a transnational approach. Focusing attention on the transnational can easily lead to the homogenisation of refugees by disregarding the structural inequalities of class, ethnicity, gender, age and caste within national borders that refugees and other migrants have to face. When looking at the position of refugees in the diaspora, for example, issues like economic exploitation and racism are disregarded (Clifford 1994: 313). These concrete, cross-cutting structures, racialised, classed and gendered, need to be taken into account to underscore differences not only between migrants and their hosts, but also amongst the migrants themselves. There is a danger of essentialising transnational communities that in actual fact are comprised of very heterogeneous groups of people. Furthermore, other negative aspects of focusing on transnational networks and activities need to be taken into account in order to avoid an overcelebratory stance.

In the first place, there is a risk of ignoring the majority of migrants and nonmigrants who cannot be described as transnational because they do not have the means or wish to engage in transnational activities. By stressing that Somali refugees in Dadaab are part of a network of 'transnational nomads', I do not want to deny the fact that many of the poorer refugees have to depend solely on the refugee camps for their livelihoods. Many refugees do not have an alternative, neither in the form of a remittance-sending relative nor in the shape of a migration dream. Instead, they survive through marginal income-generating activities and strategies of gaining additional rations, or through the help of those refugees who do have relatives outside the camps. This raises questions on whether transnational networks, in the end, do not contribute to increasing inequality, as members of a certain community do not all have the same opportunities to profit from transnationalism. Although this may be the case in Dadaab, at the same time the effects of such inequality are mitigated by a redistribution of transnationally obtained resources. Many refugees are able to profit indirectly from remittances sent to others because the cultural and religious obligation to assist those who have less is very strong amongst Somali refugees in Dadaab. Besides, the increased economic power of a section of the community benefits the various classes of the population trying to sell their products or labour. Nevertheless, when studying the transnational activities of refugees it remains important not to assume that all refugees benefit equally.

A second point that should be addressed with caution is that, despite the fact that strong social networks exist, the relationships between those who stay in their country, those who live in refugee camps and those who go for resettlement, are not necessarily good. There are many suspicions and prejudices between them, related to the fact that those who remained in their country feel betrayed by those who left, and those who left feel that the 'stayees' are guilty of the partiality required in wartime. There are numerous examples of the problematic relationship between refugees and stayees, which in many ways resembles the relationship between migrants and nonmigrants in general. A study amongst Bosnians (Stefansson 2001; 2002) clearly describes the many prejudices that exist amongst the stayees towards the refugees. A third factor to take into account is that the reasons for engaging in transnational activities are not only positive but are often also related to the moral pressures of feelings of guilt; a phenomenon that Al-Ali (2001: 115) terms 'forced transnationalism'. These pressures may be so great that migrants cannot fulfil them, and indeed, not all Somalis who have left the camps send back money to their relatives left behind. Finally, it is important to stress that trans-national flows also have negative outcomes, since remittances not only alleviate the consequences of violence and war but are also utilised to sustain conflict. In many regions, including Somalia, Eritrea, Sri Lanka and others, financial flows are used for obtaining arms and other material to support warring factions (see e.g. Koser 2001b; Van Hear 2002). Although I have mainly focused on the role of transnational remittances and other flows in giving refugees a level of agency and choice in determining their livelihoods, it is important to bear in mind that these flows have a wide range of other effects as well.

Suggestions for Further Research

Whereas I have tried to be as all-inclusive as possible in carrying out this research, there are a number of areas I did not have the opportunity to go into despite their relevance for transnational studies on refugees. In the first place, when looking at the importance of transnational networks and flows of remittances, goods and information for the livelihoods of refugees in the region, it is also vital to investigate these networks from the point of view of those providing assistance in resettlement countries. During a few interviews with Somalis in the Netherlands as well as during e-mail 'conversations' with Somalis in the U.K., U.S.A., Canada and other Western countries, I got the impression that providing assistance to relatives in the Horn was a very complex issue with many sides to it. Questions arose on the ability of Somalis in the West to send remittances and the constraints they are facing when trying to do so, but also their will to send. A number of remarks made by Somalis in the diaspora gave me the impression that, at times, there was a clash between their individual hopes and dreams and the communal obligations they faced and that it was not always easy to deal with that clash. Indeed, preliminary work amongst Somalis in Minneapolis MN (Horst 2004) does indicate the ambiguity created by transnational responsibilities. While resettled Somalis are aware of the vital role they play in the survival of their relatives in the region and thus send whatever they can, at the same time, the obligation to assist is often a real burden to their own livelihoods. Recent work amongst Sudanese refugees suggest similar difficulties (Riak Akuei 2005). As such, Al-Ali's concept of 'forced transnationalism' would, according to me, be a very interesting entry-point when further studying transnational networks from the perspectives of refugees in the West.

Related to this, it would be interesting to look at the potentials of transnational communities as 'durable solutions' to protracted refugee situations, as Van Hear (2002) suggests. This is highly relevant both as a research topic and as a policy issue. In order to answer the question of whether transnational networks would provide durable solutions, it is important to study the level of endurance of these networks, particularly as they last or do not last across generations. Another issue to take into account is the fact that these networks also produce a range of negative effects. How can these be checked and countered in order to stimulate efforts of structural development and peace building? Do all refugees benefit from these networks, or do they increase inequality and create a new underclass of those without relatives elsewhere? Furthermore, it may be relevant to study some of the possible types of collaboration that the UNHCR, NGOs, governments and members of a particular refugee diaspora could engage in. This would require active involvement and the will to experiment with such forms of cooperation from all those involved.

A final area that needs further exploring is of a methodological nature. In my attempts to include the views of Somalis in the diaspora, I have experimented with the use of the Internet and e-mail in doing transnational research. I became convinced that, in order to fully grasp 'transnational linkages', it would not be sufficient to study transnational communities or networks in multiple localities. I believe that, in addition, it is essential to develop new research methods *between* sites. There are quite a number of Somali Internet sites very active in providing written and oral information on the latest developments in Somalia, missing people, business, world news etcetera to the Somali diaspora. These sites offer a space for Somalis all over the world to discuss issues related to, for example, culture, religion, the war and being refugees and immigrants, and they also enable people to share their knowledge and experiences of life in a certain place with others who are often in similar positions. The Internet, thus, first provides a large source of information about specific refugee communities, and the effect of electronic media on refugee diasporas would be a very interesting field of research. Secondly, the Internet can assist in data collection, as it is ideal for gathering information from a widely spread and highly mobile community, or for stimulating group discussions within a refugee diaspora. Finally, electronic media like the Internet and e-mail are very easy and fast ways of disseminating and discussing findings amongst refugees, policy makers and implementers as well as academics. Such virtual dialogues provide a very important addition to more common, (multi)sited forms of research, though this would require further exploration. In all this, 'the key to doing research in complex transnational spaces devolves less from methods, multidisciplinary teams or theoretical frameworks - although these are, of course, important – than from the suppleness of imagination' (Stoller 1997: 91).

New Directions in Aid Provision?

While stressing the importance of transnational networks for the survival of Somali refugees in Dadaab, I do not want to deny the fact that they are dependent on the food rations provided, since most of the refugees would not be able to survive in the camps without these handouts. At the same time, it is highly unlikely that the refugees would be able to survive in Dadaab *only* on the food rations allocated to them, as the decidedly insufficient caloric and micronutrient content of the handouts illustrates. It is the combination of international humanitarian aid and transnational assistance networks that makes it possible for the Somalis to build up a livelihood in Dadaab, giving them a certain level of choice and transformative power towards their lives and the lives of others. Yet, their options are still limited and do not lead to sustainable livelihoods or durable solutions for a large majority of the refugees. I want to conclude my argument with suggesting new directions in aid provision that do allow refugees to develop sustainable livelihoods.

My recommendations start from the premise that a symbiosis between international assistance and assistance amongst community members is necessary. Both types of aid do not operate unproblematically. Assistance by relatives and friends is mainly used for subsistence by refugees in the region, with only limited potential to invest money and goods for structural development. Research has shown that the majority of remittance monies from migrants are being used for household expenditure and the remainder is saved or spent on microenterprise (Wimaladharma et al. 2004: 3), and refugees in Dadaab are no exception to these general trends. Many of those who receive regular remittances cannot do anything but consume them, as a monthly allowance of fifty to one hundred dollars per month is essential for enabling a family's daily survival but cannot facilitate much more than that. Larger lump sums do allow for greater economic independence and are used to start up businesses in Dadaab, for example allowing the purchase of electrical equipment to provide services, tools to begin a certain craft, or goods to sell in the market. Though these initiatives are very vital for the welfare of many refugees, they do remain small in scale. Furthermore, transnational responsibilities may create high pressure on those providing assistance, possibly threatening the continuation of transnational networks (Horst 2004).

Then, international assistance is problematic first of all because of the increased reluctance to provide appropriate aid to refugees in the North as well as in the South and secondly, because of the relief-development divide. Currently, both the UNHCR and EU governments look at opportunities to link humanitarian aid with developmental processes. Within UNHCR's Convention Plus initiative, development assistance has once more taken up an important place[4]. This type of assistance focuses on repatriation, reintegration, rehabilitation and reconstruction in countries of origin; as well as on host countries of first asylum. EU states have simultaneously worked on this idea, linking it to their asylum policies from the assumption that if the general situation in the region improves, refugees are best cared for in the region[5]. Improving refugee livelihoods is central to this debate, as is acknowledged, for example, by UNHCR's initiative to set up the Refugee Livelihoods Project.[6] Yet these 'new' developments do not lead to structurally different approaches as the underlying image of refugees and the related motives for the provision of aid change very little. Refugees remain seen as vulnerables or crooks and these initiatives are developed for them; not with them. The important role of refugee diasporas in enabling refugee livelihoods in the region similarly is not acknowledged.

The symbiosis I am referring to first of all requires a thorough knowledge of refugee livelihood strategies from a historical and transnational perspective, as argued in this book. Livelihood strategies employed by forced migrants derive from existing socio-economic structures and concepts of identity. Furthermore, self-reliance includes the responsibility to take care of others, which is not only a local responsibility but also a transnational one. By ignoring this or not having sufficient knowledge about it, current policies effectively frustrate refugee livelihood strategies. Sustainable livelihoods are difficult to pursue when 'transnational nomads' like the Somali are expected to live in camps in marginal areas with limited rights. Projects in resettlement countries that do not acknowledge the transnational family responsibilities of Somalis and other forced migrants are similarly doomed to fail.

When knowledge is gained on historical and transnational strategies, existing skills and capacities can be acknowledged and further improved, whereas constraints can be reduced. Refugee diasporas are agents of post-conflict reconstruction and development, and can be assisted in their efforts, for example, by increased political support, dual citizenship rights, inviting them to participate in forums for dialogue on development, and cooperating with diaspora communities in regional sustainable livelihood-creating schemes (Nyberg Sorensen 2004: 25). Other practical ways of improving existing strengths are enabling refugees' access to micro-credit and banking opportunities; and improving their educational qualifications by accrediting home-country certificates and providing vocational and language courses. Furthermore, their rights need to be improved in various areas, including, for example, freedom of movement; property rights; right to work and conduct trade; and legal status (see also Smith 2005). It is important not to deny the constraints that refugees in general face, nor should we ignore the most marginal groups within refugee populations. As this book has illustrated, targeting the most vulnerable is a very difficult task, since one may wonder by what criteria vulnerability is defined. A common approach is to focus on specific categories of people, like vulnerable women or children. Yet, in my view, vulnerabilities differ according to the specific situation and individual characteristics of these 'vulnerable groups'. A refugee's social network, personal assets, level of mobility, education, and language skills are some of the important factors to take into account when addressing vulnerability; which requires a far less group-based approach than is currently the case.

Besides gathering knowledge on refugee livelihood strategies and supporting strengths while reducing constraints, a radical shift in thinking on forced migration and refugees is required for a successful symbiosis of international and community-based assistance. The focus is still largely on the economic, and other, costs of refugees, leading to a 'migration management' approach; whereas both local and donor governments could benefit greatly from viewing refugees as a resource for regional reconstruction and development. In order to tap this resource, it is imperative to realise that refugees are those with best knowledge and understanding about their livelihood practices and the constraints they face. Throughout this book, I have attempted to illustrate how vital and fruitful it is to involve refugees in analysis and problem solving, through describing research tools that involved active dialogue between refugees, agencies and academics. Refugees are agents not only in their actions but also in their reflections, and thus, new directions in aid provision need to allow them a much stronger voice in policy developments that affect their lives and livelihoods.

Notes

1. 'Protracted refugee situation' is a concept first launched at the UNHCR's Evaluation and Policy Analysis Unit (EPAU) and has been defined as a situation in which refugees 'have lived in exile for more than five years, particularly in camps and otherwise designated geographical zones, without the immediate prospect of finding a durable solution for their plight by means of voluntary repatriation, local integration or resettlement. As such, these refugees find themselves trapped in a state of limbo' (Crisp 2003).

2. I am referring, for example, to work by Malkki (see e.g. 1995a) and Hyndman (2000).

3. Davis here refers to a study on famine in Darfur, Sudan, in the mid-1980s (De Waal 1989).

4. Betts (2005) argues that there are strong parallels between current debates on Targeting Development Assistance for refugee solutions (TDA) and the refugee aid and development debates of the 1980s. As such, it is important to learn from those past debates and their practical implications.

5. A good overview and critical analysis of these developments is provided by Amnesty International (2003).

6. See http://www.unhcr.ch/cgi-bin/texis/vtx/research?id=3f7152407.

Glossary

Abti	Mother's brother, maternal uncle
Adeer	Father's brother, paternal uncle
Af-soomaali	Somali language
Al Amal (Arabic)	Trust, expectation, high hopes
Al Barakaat (Arabic)	Blessings
Asanteni (Swahili)	Thank you (plur.)
Askari (Somali and Swahili)	Soldier; guard; policeman
Ayuuto (Italian)	Lit: Help
	In Somalia: Money-go-round savings and loan system
Baafin	Lit: Inquiry, search
	Also: Missing people
Baahanay	Needy, destitute
Bhang (Swahili)	Marihuana
Buufi	Blow into, inflate; spray
Buufis	A hope, longing, desire or dream to go for resettlement
Ciid	Holy day, religious holiday. Arabic: iid
Dabadheer	Lit: Having a long tail; prolonged; lasting a long time
	Also: Drought from 1970-1975 in Somalia
Dahabshiil	Lit: Melted gold
	Also: Name of one of the *xawilaad* companies
Dariiqo	Sect, religious group (e.g. Sufi Derwish)
Diric	Somali women's dress
Diya (Arabic)	Compensational payment
Dugsi	Koran school
Eedo	Father's sister, paternal aunt
Gaadiid	Lit: Beast of burden; transport, vehicle
	Also: Practice of borrowing a beast of burden for movement
Gaal cadeen	White non-Muslim
Garoob	Widow, divorcee
Gharaama (Arabic)	Shared expenses
Habar yar	Mother's sister, maternal aunt

Hajj (Arabic)	Pilgrimage to Mecca
Hawo	Air
Hijra (Arabic)	The flight of the prophet Mohamed from Mecca to Medina, the base year for the Muslim calendar (A.D. 622)
	Also: The obligation to migrate from lands where the practice of Islam is constrained
Ilmo	Children
Kitu Kidogo (Swahili)	Lit: Something small [bribe]
Macallin	Teacher, educator, male instructor, professor [a respectful term]
Mahadsanid	Thank you
Maslaxad	Community-based arbitration between two parties
Matatu (Swahili)	Minibus
Mimi (Swahili)	I, me
Miraa (Swahili)	Qat; Narcotic plant (see *qaad*) [Throughout Kenya known as miraa after the Meru district where it is cultivated (Cassanelli 1986: 256)]
Mukhalis	Human smuggler or carrier
Nasiib	Luck, fate, destiny, fortune, chance
Qaad	Qat: a small tree or shrub whose young leaves, stem tips and tender bark are chewed for their stimulating effect (Cassanelli 1986: 236)
Qaaraan	Collection of money or livestock for the needy
Qabiil	Clan
Reer	Family, lineage
Rihla (Arabic)	Travel in search of knowledge
Sambuusi	Samosa: three-cornered flour rolls filled with meat, onion, pepper etc.
Shaloongo (Bantu)	Money-go-round savings and loan system
Shifta / Shufto	Robber, bandit
Simsim	Sesame seed
Somali sijui	Kenyan Somalis ['sijui' literally means 'I don't know']
Soor	Porridge of maize, sorghum or other grain
Sufriye	Cooking pot
Taar	Radio communication transmitters
Tol	Clan, tribe, descent group
Wayo' arag (Waaya-arag)	Experience; expert, experienced person
Xaaraam	Prohibited in Muslim law
Xawil	Transfer, usually of money / responsibilities
Xawilaad	Informal value-transfer system
Xeer	Temporary cooperation contract
Xiirso	System of contributions for the needy
Zakat (Arabic)	Islamic system of redistribution, requiring Muslims to give a certain percentage of their income or wealth to the needy

Bibliography

Abu-Lughod, L. 1991. 'Writing Against Culture'. In R. Fox (ed.), *Recapturing Anthropology: Working in the Present*, pp. 137–62. Santa Fe, New Mexico: School of American Research Press.

———— 1993. *Writing Women's Worlds: Bedouin Stories*. Berkeley: University of California Press.

Adamson, F. 2001. 'Mobilizing for the Transformation of Home: Politicized Identities and Transnational Practices'. In K. Koser and N. Al-Ali (eds), *New Approaches to Migration? Transnational Communities and the Transformation of Home*, pp. 155–68. London: Routledge.

Affi, L. 1997. 'The Somali Crisis in Canada: The Single Mother Phenomenon'. In H. Adam and R. Ford (eds), *Mending Rips in the Sky. Options for Somali Communities in the 21st Century*, pp. 441–48. Lawrenceville NJ: The Red Sea Press.

African Rights 1993. *The Nightmare Continues... Abuses Against Somali Refugees in Kenya*. London: African Rights.

Ager, A., W. Ager and L. Long 1995. 'The Differential Experience of Mozambican Refugee Women and Men', *Journal of Refugee Studies* 8(3): 248–67.

Ahmed, A. 1994. 'The Relevance of Indigenous Systems of Production to Food Policies: A Horn of Africa Perspective'. In M. Salih (ed.), *Inducing Food Insecurity: Perspectives on Food Policies in Eastern and Southern Africa*, pp. 204–16. Uppsala: The Scandinavian Institute of African Studies.

Ahmed, I. 2000. 'Remittances and Their Impact in Postwar Somaliland', *Disasters* 24(4): 380–89.

Al-Ali, N. 2001. 'Trans- or A-national? Bosnian Refugees in the UK and the Netherlands'. In K. Koser and N. Al-Ali (eds), *New Approaches to Migration? Transnational Communities and the Transformation of Home*, pp. 96–117. London: Routledge.

Al-Ali, N., R. Black and K. Koser 2001. 'Refugees and Transnationalism: The Experience of Bosnians and Eritreans in Europe', *Journal of Ethnic and Migration Studies* 27(4): 615–34.

Al-Sharmani, M. 1998. 'The Somali Refugees in Cairo: Issues of Survival, Culture and Identity'. MA Thesis. Cairo: The American University in Cairo.

———— 1999. 'The Somali Diaspora in Canada: Issues of Identity'. *Paper presented at the AAA Annual Meeting*, Chicago IL.

———— 2004. 'Refugee Livelihoods: Livelihood and Diasporic Identity Constructions of Somali Refugees in Cairo'. Working Paper No. 104, *New Issues in Refugee Research*. Geneva: UNHCR.

Amnesty International 2003. *Niemandsland. Opvang van Vluchtelingen in de Regio.* Amsterdam: Amnesty International.

Anderson, B. 1983. *Imagined Communities.* London: Verso.

Appadurai, A. 1991. 'Global Ethnoscapes: Notes and Queries for a Transnational Anthropology'. In R. Fox, (ed.), *Recapturing Anthropology,* pp. 191–210. Santa Fe NM: School of American Research Press.

_____ 1996. *Modernity at Large: Cultural Dimensions of Globalization.* Minneapolis: University of Minnesota Press.

_____ 2000. 'Grassroots Globalization and the Research Imagination', *Public Culture* 12(1): 1–19.

Ardener, S. and S. Burman 1995. *Money-go-rounds: The Importance of Rotating Savings and Credit Associations for Women.* Oxford: Berg Publishers.

Aronson, D. 1980. 'Must Nomads Settle? Some Notes Toward Policy on the Future of Pastoralism'. In P. Salzman and E. Edward (eds), *When Nomads Settle: Processes of Sedentarization as Adaptation and Response,* pp. 173–84. New York: Praeger.

Bang Nielsen, K. 2004. 'Next Stop Britain: The Influence of Transnational Networks on the Secondary Movement of Danish Somalis'. Working Paper No. 22. Sussex : Centre for Migration Research.

Basch, L., N. Glick Schiller and C. Szanton Blanc 1994. *Nations Unbound: Transnational Projects, Postcolonial Predicaments, and Deterritorialized Nation-states.* Langhorn: Gordon and Breach.

Bastlund, C. 1994. *Rethinking Refugee Policies: Issues of Humanitarian Intervention, Relief, Development and the United Nations Refugee Definition.* Roskilde: Roskilde University, International Development Studies.

Baxter, P. 1994. 'From Telling People to Listening to Them: Changes in Approaches to the Development and Welfare of Pastoral Peoples'. In M. Salih (ed.), *Inducing Food Insecurity: Perspectives on Food Policies in Eastern and Southern Africa,* pp. 217–31. Uppsala: The Scandinavian Institute of African Studies.

Benda-Beckmann, F. v. and K. v. Benda-Beckmann. 1994. 'Coping with Insecurity', *Focaal* 22/23: 7–31.

Besteman, C. 1996. 'Representing Violence and "Othering" Somalia', *Cultural Anthropology* 11(1): 120–33.

Betts, A. 2005. 'International Cooperation and the Targeting of Development Assistance for Durable Solutions: Lessons From the 1980s'. Working Paper No. 107, *New Issues in Refugee Research.* Geneva: UNHCR.

Black, R. 1995. 'Political Refugees or Economic Migrants? Kurdish and Assyrian Refugees in Greece', *Migration* 25: 79–109.

Braun, G. 1992. 'Survival Strategies and the State in Somalia: Dependence, Independence or Patronage?'. In K. Raffer and M. Salih (eds), *The Least Developed and the Oil-rich Arab Countries: Dependence, Independence or Patronage?* pp. 111–27. London: Macmillan.

Brons, M. 2001. *Society, Security, Sovereignty and the State in Somalia: From Statelessness to Statelessness?* Utrecht: International Books.

Bruijn, M.d. and H.v. Dijk 1995. *Arid Ways: Cultural Understandings of Insecurity in Fulbe Society, Central Mali.* Amsterdam: Thela Publishers.

Buchwald, U.v. 1991. 'The Refugee Dependency Syndrome: Origins and Consequences'. Paper presented at the International Conference on the Mental Health and Well-being of Refugees and Displaced Persons. Stockholm.

Buzan, B. 1988. 'People, States and Fear: The National Security Problem in the Third World'. In E. Azar and C. Moon (eds), *National Security in the Third World: The Management of Internal and External Threats*, pp. 14–43. Aldershot: Edgar Elgar.

Callamard, A. 1994. 'Refugees and Local Hosts: A Study of the Trading Interactions Between Mozambican Refugees and Malawian Villagers in the District of Mwanza', *Journal of Refugee Studies* 7(1): 39–62.

CARE 1995. 'The Refugee Assistance Project of CARE Kenya'. *Annual Report 1994*. Nairobi: CARE.

CASA Consulting 2001. *Evaluation of the Dadaab Firewood Project*. Geneva: Evaluation and Policy Analysis Unit (EPAU), UNHCR.

Cassanelli, L. 1986. 'Qat: changes in the Production and Consumption of a Quasilegal Commodity in Northeast Africa'. In A. Appadurai (ed.), *The Social Life of Things: Commodities in Cultural Perspective*, pp. 236–57. Cambridge: Cambridge University Press.

Castles, S. 2001. 'Studying Social Transformation', *International Political Science Review* 22(1): 13–32.

Central Bureau of Statistics 1994. *Kenyan Population Census 1989*. Nairobi: Office of the Vice President, Ministry of Planning and National Development.

Chatwin, B. 1988. *The Songlines*. New York: Penguin Books.

Chimni, B. 2000. 'Globalization, Humanitarianism and the Erosion of Refugee Protection', *Journal of Refugee Studies* 13(3): 243–63.

Choldin, H. 1973. 'Kinship Networks in the Migration Process', *International Migration Review* 7(2): 163–75.

Christensen, H. 1987. 'Spontaneous Development Efforts by Rural Refugees in Somalia and Pakistan'. In J. Rogge (ed.), *Refugees: A Third World Dilemma*. Totowa NJ: Rowman and Littlefield.

Christie, D. 1990. '*We Are All Neighbours*'. Documentary. BRT 2.

Clifford, J. 1994. 'Diasporas', *Cultural Anthropology* 9(3): 302–38.

Cohen, R. and D. Joly 1989. 'Introduction: The 'New Refugees' of Europe'. In D. Joly and R. Cohen (eds), *Reluctant Hosts: Europe and its Refugees*, pp. 5–18. London: Aldershot.

Collins, G. 1999. *Garissa District Livelihood Security Assessment*. Garissa: CARE.

Collinson, S. 1993. 'The Asylum Dilemma'. In S. Collinson (ed.), *Beyond Borders: West European Migration Policy Towards the 21st Century*, pp. 59–87. London: RIIA.

———— 1999. 'Globalisation and the Dynamics of International Migration: Implications for the Refugee Regime'. Working Paper No. 1, *New Issues in Refugee Research*. Geneva: UNHCR.

Crisp, J. 1999a. 'Policy Challenges of the New Diasporas: Migrant Networks and Their Impact on Asylum Flows and Regimes'. Working Paper No. 7, *New Issues in Refugee Research*. Geneva: UNHCR.

———— 1999b. 'A State of Insecurity: The Political Economy of Violence in Refugee-populated Areas of Kenya'. Working Paper No. 16, *New Issues in Refugee Research*. Geneva: UNHCR.

———— 2001. 'Mind the Gap! UNHCR, Humanitarian Assistance and the Development Process'. Working Paper No. 43, *New Issues in Refugee Research*. Geneva: UNHCR.

_____ 2003. 'No Solutions in Sight: The Problem of Protracted Refugee Situations in Africa'. Working Paper No. 75, *New Issues in Refugee Research*. Geneva: UNHCR.

Davis, J. 1993. 'The Anthropology of Suffering', *Journal of Refugee Studies* 5(2): 149–61.

De Waal, A. 1989. *Famine That Kills: Darfur, Sudan, 1984–1985*. Oxford: Clarendon Press.

Diaz-Briquets, S. and J. Perez-Lopez 1997. 'Refugee Remittances: Conceptual Issues and the Cuban and Nicaraguan Experiences', *International Migration Review* 31(2): 411–37.

Diaz-Briquets, S. and S. Weintraub 1991. *Migration, Remittances and Small Business Development*. Boulder CO: Westview Press.

Dietz, A. 1996. *Entitlements to Natural Resources. Contours of Political Environmental Geography*. Inaugural speech, University of Amsterdam. Utrecht: International Books.

Dietz, A., A. Verhagen and R. Ruben 2001. 'The Impact of Climate Change on Drylands with a Focus on West Africa'. Final Report for NOP. Wageningen: ICCD.

Doornbos, M., L. Cliffe, M. Ahmed Abdel Ghaffar, and J. Markakis 1992. *Beyond Conflict in the Horn: Prospects for Peace, Recovery and Development in Ethiopia, Somalia and Sudan*. London: Currey.

Dreze, J. and A. Sen 1989. *Hunger and Public Action*. Oxford: Clarendon Press.

Eickelman D. and J. Piscatori 1990. *Muslim Travellers: Pilgrimage, Migration and the Religious Imagination*. London: Routledge.

El Hadi El Nagar, S. 2001. 'Changing Gender Roles and Pastoral Adaptations to Market Opportunity in Omdurman, Sudan'. In M. Salih, A. Dietz and A. Ahmed (eds), *African Pastoralism: Conflict, Institutions and Government*, pp. 247–77. London: Pluto Press.

Essed, P., G. Frerks and J. Schrijvers 2004. *Refugees and the Transformation of Societies: Agency, Policies, Ethics and Politics*. Oxford and New York: Berghahn Books.

Farah, M. 1993. *From Ethnic Response to Clan Identity: A Study of State Penetration Among the Somali Nomadic Pastoral Society of Northeastern Kenya*. Stockholm: Almqvist and Wiksell.

Farah, N. 2000. *Yesterday, Tomorrow. Voices From the Somali Diaspora*. London and New York: Cassell.

Farer, T. 1995. 'How the International System Copes with Involuntary Migration: Norms, Institutions, and State Practice'. In M. Teitelbaum and M. Weiner (eds), *Threatened Peoples, Threatened Borders: World Migration and U.S. Policy*, pp. 257–92. New York and London: Norton Publishers.

Ferguson, J. 1990. *The Anti-politics Machine: 'Development', Depolitization and Democratic Power in Lesotho*. Cambridge: Cambridge University Press.

Ferris, E. 1993. *Beyond Borders: Refugees, Migrants and Human Rights in the Post-Cold War Era*. Geneva: WCC Publications.

Fog Olwig, K. and K. Hastrup 1997. *Siting Culture. The Shifting Anthropological Object*. London and New York: Routledge.

Gardner, J. and J. El Bushra 2004. *Somalia: The Untold Story: The War Through the Eyes of Somali Women*. London and Sterling, Virginia: Pluto Press.

Gardner, K. 1995. *Global Migrants, Local Lives: Travel and Transformation in Rural Bangladesh*. Oxford: Claredon Press.

Gersony, R. 1990. 'Why Somalis Flee: A Synthesis of Conflict Experience in Northern Somalia by Somali Refugees, Displaced Persons and Others', *International Journal of Refugee Law* 2(1): 4–55.

Giddens, A. 1984. *The Constitution of Society*. Cambridge: Polity Press.

――― 1990. *The Consequences of Modernity*. Cambridge: Polity Press.

Glick Schiller, N., L. Basch and C. Szanton-Blanc 1995. 'From Immigrant to Transmigrant: Theorizing Transnational Migration', *Anthropological Quarterly* 68: 48–63.

Göbel, B. 1998. 'Risk, Uncertainty and Economic Exchange in a Pastoral Community of the Andean Highlands'. In T. Schweizer and D. White (eds), *Kinship, Networks and Exchange*, pp. 158–77. Cambridge: Cambridge University Press.

Gorman, R. 1985. 'Private Voluntary Organizations in Refugee Relief'. In E. Ferris (ed.), *Refugees and World Politics*. New York: Praeger.

Gundel, J. 2003. 'The Migration–Development Nexus: Somalia Case Study'. In N. Van Hear and N. Nyberg Sorensen (eds), *The Migration-Development Nexus*. Geneva: IOM.

Haas, H. d. 2003. 'Migration and Development in Morocco. The Impact of Out-migration on Social and Economic Development in the Todgha Oasis Aalley'. Ph.D. Dissertation. Nijmegen: Katholieke Universiteit Nijmegen.

Habib, N. 1996. 'The Search for Home', *Journal of Refugee Studies* 9(1): 96–101.

Hansen, A. 1991. 'Dependency and the Dependency Syndrome'. Oxford: RSP International Research and Advisory Panel.

Haraway, D. 1991. 'Situated Knowledges: The Science Question in Feminism and the Privilege of Partial Perspective'. In *Simians, Cyborgs and Women: The Reinvention of Nature*, pp. 183–201. New York: Routledge.

Harrell-Bond, B. 1986. *Imposing Aid: Emergency Assistance to Refugees*. Oxford/New York/Nairobi: Oxford University Press.

――― 1996. 'The Protection of Refugees in the "Least Developed States"'. In A. Alfredsson and B. Macalister (eds), *The Living Law of Nations*, pp. 47–60. Kehl: NP Engel.

Harrell-Bond, B. and E. Voutira 1994. 'In Search of the Locus of Trust: The Social World of the Refugee Camp'. In E. Daniel and J. Knudsen (eds), *Mistrusting Refugees*, pp. 207–24. California: University of California Press.

Harrell-Bond, B. and N. Mahmud 1996. 'Refugees and Other Forcibly Displaced People in Africa: A Background Paper for the IFRC's Pan-African Conference'. Oxford: Refugee Studies Centre.

Harrell-Bond, B., E. Voutira and M. Leopold 1992. 'Counting the Refugees: Gifts, Givers, Patrons and Clients', *Journal of Refugee Studies* 5(3/4): 206–25.

Hathaway, J. 1991. 'The Development of the Refugee Definition in International Law'. In J. Hathaway (ed.), *The Law of Refugee Status*, pp. 1–27. Toronto and Vancouver: Butterworths.

――― 1995. 'New Directions to Avoid Hard Problems: The Distortion of the Palliative Role of Refugee Protection', *Journal of Refugee Studies* 8(3): 288–94.

Helland, J. 2001. 'Participation and Governance in the Development of Borana: Southern Ethiopia'. In M. Salih, A. Dietz and A. Ahmed (eds), *African*

Pastoralism: Conflict, Institutions and Government, pp. 56–80. London: Pluto Press.

Hjort af Ornäs, A. 1990. 'Town-based Pastoralism in Eastern Africa'. In J. Baker (ed.), *Small Town Africa: Studies in Rural–Urban Interaction*, pp. 143–59. Uppsala: The Scandinavian Institute of African Studies.

Horst, C. 1997. 'Theories on Ethnicity and Nationalism. Contributions to an Understanding of Kurdish Identity'. Oxford: Refugee Studies Centre.

———— 2001. 'Vital Links in Social Security: Somali Refugees in the Dadaab Camps, Kenya'. Working Paper No. 38, *New Issues in Refugee Research*. Geneva: UNHCR.

———— 2002. 'Inspiration in Transformation: Beyond "A Better World"'. In E. Lammers (ed.), *Making Waves: Inspiring Critical and Feminist Research, A Tribute to Joke Schrijvers*, pp. 86–90. Amsterdam: Aksant.

———— 2004. 'Money and Mobility: Transnational Livelihood Strategies of the Somali Diaspora'. Working Paper No. 9, *Global Migration Perspectives*. Geneva: GCIM.

Horst, C. and N. Van Hear 2002. 'Counting the Cost: Refugees, Remittances and the "War Against Terrorism"', *Forced Migration Review* 14: 32–34.

Human Rights Watch 1993. *Seeking Refuge, Finding Terror: The Widespread Rape of Somali Women Refugees in North-eastern Kenya*. New York: Human Rights Watch.

Hyndman, J. 2000. *Managing Displacement: Refugees and the Politics of Humanitarianism*. Minneapolis: University of Minneapolis Press.

———— 2001. 'The Field as Here and Now, Not There and Then', *The Geographical Review* 91(1–2): 262–72.

Hyndman, J. and V. Nylund 1998. 'UNHCR and the Status of Prima Facie Refugees in Kenya', *International Journal of Refugee Law* 10(1/2): 21–48.

Jackson, M. 1987. 'On Ethnographic Truth', *Canberra Anthropology* 10(2): 1–31.

———— 1995. *At Home in the World*. Durham: Duke University Press.

Kagwanja, P. 2002. 'Subjects of the Good Samaritan: "Traditional" Culture and Refugee Protection in the Kenyan Camps', *Politique Africaine* 85: 45–55.

Kaiser, T. 2002. 'Participatory and Beneficiary-based Approaches to the Evaluation of Humanitarian Programmes'. Working Paper No. 51, *New Issues in Refugee Research*. Geneva: UNHCR.

Kaye, R. 1998. 'Redefining the Refugee: The UK Media Portrayal of Asylum Seekers'. In K. Koser and H. Lutz (eds), *The New Migration in Europe: Social Constructions and Social Realities*, pp. 163–83. London: MacMillan Press Ltd.

Kearney, M. 1995. 'The Local and the Global: Anthropology of Globalization and Transnationalism', *Annual Review of Anthropology* 24: 547–65.

Keen, D. 1993. 'Famine, Needs-assessment and Survival Strategies in Africa', *Oxfam Research Papers*. Oxford: Oxfam.

———— 1994. *The Benefits of Famine*. Oxford: Clarendon Press.

Kibreab, G. 1993. 'The Myth of Dependency Among Camp Refugees in Somalia', *Journal of Refugee Studies* 6(4): 321–49.

———— 1999. 'Revisiting the Debate on People, Place, Identity and Displacement', *Journal of Refugee Studies* 12(4): 384–428.

Klaver, J. 1997. *From the Land of the Sun to the City of Angels: The Migration Process of Zapotec Indians from Oaxaca, Mexico, to Los Angeles, California*. Utrecht/Amsterdam: Nederlandse Geografische Studies.

Knudsen, J. 1991. 'Therapeutic Strategies and Strategies for Refugee Coping', *Journal of Refugee Studies* 4(1): 21–38.

Koser, K. 1997. 'Social Networks and the Asylum Cycle: The Case of Iranians in the Netherlands', *International Migration Review* 31(3): 591–611.

———— 2001a. 'From Refugees to Transnational Communities?'. In K. Koser and N. Al-Ali (eds), *New Approaches to Migration? Transnational Communities and the Transformation of Home*, pp. 138–52. London: Routledge.

———— 2001b. 'War and Peace in Eritrea'. Paper presented at conference, Living on the Edge: Migration, Conflict and State in the Backyards of Globalisation. Copenhagen: Centre for Development Research.

Koser, K. and N. Al-Ali 2001. *New Approaches to Migration? Transnational Communities and the Transformation of Home*. London: Routledge.

Kusow, A. 1998. 'Migration and Identity Processes Among Somali Immigrants in Canada'. Ph.D. Dissertation. Detroit: Wayne State University.

Laitin, D. and S. Samatar 1986. *Somalia: Nation in Search of a State*. Boulder, Colorado: Westview Press.

Lehman, D.v. 1993. 'Resettlement of the Mushunguli Somali Refugees of Southeast African Origins'. Dadaab: UNHCR.

Leliveld, A. 1994. *Social Security in Developing Countries: Operation and Dynamics of Social Security Mechanisms in Rural Swaziland*. Amsterdam: Thesis Publishers.

Lewis, H. 1982. 'Social Analysis: Jalalaqsi Agricultural and Relocation Project'. Mogadishu: Africare.

Lewis, I.M. 1961. *A Pastoral Democracy*. Oxford: Oxford University Press.

———— 1971. *Ecstatic Religion: An Anthropological Study of Spirit, Possession and Shamanism*. Baltimore: Penguin Books.

———— 1993. 'Making History in Somalia: Humanitarian Intervention in a Stateless Society'. Paper presented at conference, Rethinking Global Institutions, New Milton. London: London School of Economics, Centre for the Study of Global Governance.

————. 1994. *Blood and Bone: The Call of Kinship in Somali Society*. Lawrenceville: The Red Sea Press.

Loescher, G. 1993. *Beyond Charity: International Cooperation and the Global Refugee Crisis*. Oxford and New York: Oxford University Press.

Long, N. and A. Long 1992. *Battlefields of Knowledge: The Interlocking of Theory and Practice in Social Research and Development*. London: Routledge.

Makinda, S. 1993. *Seeking Peace from Chaos: Humanitarian Intervention in Somalia*. Boulder, Colorado: Lynne Rienner.

Malkki, L. 1992. 'National Geographic: The Rooting of Peoples and the Territorialization of National Identity Among Scholars and Refugees', *Cultural Anthropology* 7(1): 24–44.

———— 1995a. *Purity and Exile: Violence, Memory, and National Cosmology Among Hutu Refugees in Tanzania*. Chicago: The University of Chicago Press.

———— 1995b. 'Refugees and Exile: From "Refugee Studies" to the National Order of Things', *Annual Review of Anthropology* 24: 495–523.

———— 1996. 'Speechless Emissaries: Refugees, Humanitarianism and Dehistoricization', *Cultural Anthropology* 11(3): 377–404.

Martin, S. 2001. 'Global Migration Trends and Asylum'. Working Paper No. 41, *New Issues in Refugee Research*. Geneva: UNHCR.

Mazzucato, V., R. v. Dijk, C. Horst and P. d. Vries 2004. 'Transcending the Nation: Explorations of Transnationalism as a Concept and Phenomenon'. In D. Kalb, W. Pansters and H. Siebers (eds), *Globalization and Development: Themes and Concepts in Current Research*, pp. 131–62. Dordrecht/Boston/London: Kluwer Academic Publishers.

McMurray, D. 2001. *In and Out of Morocco: Smuggling and Migration in a Frontier Boomtown*. Minneapolis and London: University of Minnesota Press.

McNally, R. 1993. *Atlas of the World, Masterpiece Edition*. USA: Rand McNally and Company.

McSpadden, L. and H. Moussa 1993. '"I Have a Name": The Gender Dynamics in Asylum and in Resettlement of Ethiopian and Eritrean Refugee Women and Men', *Journal of Refugee Studies* 6(3): 203–25.

Menkhaus, K. 1991. *Report on an Emergency Needs Assessment of the Lower Jubba Region*, Somalia: World Concern.

Merryman, J. 1982. 'Pastoral Nomad Settlement in Response to Drought: the Case of the Kenyan Somali'. In A. Hansen and A. Oliver-Smith (eds), *Involuntary Migration and Resettlement: The Problems and Responses of Dislocated People*, pp. 105–19. Boulder, Colorado: Westview Press.

Mouffe, C. 1992. 'Feminism, Citizenship and Radical Democratic Politics'. In J. Butler and J. Scott (eds), *Feminists Theorize the Political*, pp. 369–85. New York and London: Routledge.

Nelson, N. and S. Wright 1995. *Power and Participatory Development: Theory and Practice*. London: Intermediate Technology Publications.

Nunow, A. 2000. *Pastoralists and Markets. Livestock Commercialization and Food Security in North-eastern Kenya*. Leiden: African Studies Centre.

Nyberg Sorensen, N. 2004. 'The Development Dimension of Migrant Remittances'. Working Paper No. 1, *Migration Policy Research Working Paper Series*. Geneva: IOM, Department of Migration Policy, Research and Communications.

Orwin, M.1995. *Colloquial Somali: A Complete Language Course*. London and New York: Routledge.

Perouse de Montclos, M. 2000. 'A Refugee Diaspora: When the Somali Go West'. Paper presented at New African Diasporas Colloquium. London: Migration Research Unit, University College London.

Perouse de Montclos, M. and P. Kagwanja 2000. 'Refugee Camps or Cities? The Socio-economic Dynamics of the Dadaab and Kakuma Camps in Northern Kenya', *Journal of Refugee Studies* 13(2): 205–22.

Pretty, J., I. Guijt, J. Thompson, and I. Scoones 1995. *Participatory Learning and Action: A Trainer's Guide*. London: IIED.

Quaye, E. 1994. 'Towards Sustainable Agriculture in African Drylands and Integrated Agro-ecosystems'. In M. Salih (ed.), *Inducing Food Insecurity: Perspectives on Food Policies in Eastern and Southern Africa*, pp. 180–201. Uppsala: The Scandinavian Institute of African Studies.

Reek, E.v.d. and A. Hussein 2003. *Somaliërs op Doorreis: Verhuisgedrag van Nederlandse Somaliërs naar Engeland*. Tilburg: Wetenschapswinkel Universiteit van Tilburg.

Riak Akuei, S. 2005. 'Remittances as Unforeseen Burdens: The Livelihoods and Social Obligations of Sudanese Refugees'. Working Paper No. 9, Global Migration Perspectives. Geneva: GCIM.

Richmond, A. 1988. 'Sociological Theories of International Migration: The Case of Refugees', *The Journal of the International Sociological Association* 36(2): 7–25.

———— 1993. 'Reactive Migration: Sociological Perspectives on Refugee Movements', *Journal of Refugee Studies* 6(1): 7–24.

Rogers, A., R. Cohen and S. Vertovec 2001. 'Editorial Statement', *Global Networks* 1(1): iii–vi.

Rouse, R. 1995. 'Questions of Identity: Personhood and Collectivity in Transnational Migration to the United States', *Critique of Anthropology* 15(4): 351–80.

Rousseau, C., T. Said, M. Gagne and G. Bibeau 1998. 'Between Myth and Madness: The Premigration Dream of Leaving Among Young Somali Refugees', *Culture, Medicine and Psychiatry* 22: 385–411.

Russell, S. 1986. 'Remittances From International Migration: A Review in Perspective', *World Development* 14(6): 677–96.

Ryle, J. 1992. 'Notes on the Repatriation of Somali Refugees from Ethiopia', *Disasters* 16(2): 160–68.

Safran, W. 1991. 'Diasporas in Modern Societies: Myths of Homeland and Return', *Diaspora* 1(1): 83–99.

Salih, R. 2001a. 'Moroccan Migrant Women: Transnationalism, Nation-states and Gender', *Journal of Ethnic and Migration Studies* 27(4): 655–71.

———— 2001b. 'Shifting Meanings of "Home". Consumption and Identity in Moroccan Women's Transnational Practices Between Italy and Morocco'. In K. Koser and N. Al-Ali (eds), *New Approaches to Migration? Transnational Communities and the Transformation of Home*, pp. 51–67. London: Routledge.

Salzman, P. 1980. 'Introduction: Processes of Sedentarization as Adaptation and Response'. In P. Salzman (ed.), *When Nomads Settle: Processes of Sedentarization as Adaptation and Response*, pp. 1–19. New York: Praeger.

Samatar, A. 1992. 'Destruction of State and Society in Somalia: Beyond the Tribal Convention', *Journal of Modern African Studies* 30(4): 625–41.

Samatar, A.I. 1994. *The Somali Challenge: From Catastrophe to Renewal?* Boulder, Colorado and London: Lynne Rienner.

Schrijvers, J. 1991. 'Dialectics of a Dialogical Ideal: Studying Down, Studying Sideways and Studying Up'. In L. Nencel and P. Pels (eds), *Constructing Knowledge. Authority and Critique in Social Science*, pp. 162–79. London: Sage.

———— 1993. *The Violence of 'Development': A Choice for Intellectuals*. Utrecht and New Delhi: International Books/Kali for Women.

———— 1997. 'Internal Refugees in Sri Lanka: The Interplay of Ethnicity and Gender', *The European Journal of Development Research* 9(2): 62–82.

———— 2004. 'Dilemmas of Humanitarian Aid: Supporting Internal Refugees in Sri Lanka'. In P. Essed, G. Frerks and J. Schrijvers (eds), *Refugees and the Transformation of Societies: Agency, Policies, Ethics and Politics*. Oxford and New York: Berghahn Books.

Scott, J. 1988. 'Deconstructing Equality Versus Difference', *Feminist Studies* 14: 33–50.

———— 1991. *Social Network Analysis: A Handbook.* London: Sage Publications.

Seligman, M. 1975. *Helplessness: On Depression, Development and Death.* San Francisco: W.H. Freeman and co.

Sen, A. 1981. *Poverty and Famines: An Essay on Entitlement and Deprivation*. Oxford: Clarendon Press.

Shah, N. and I. Menon 1999. 'Chain Migration Through the Social Network: Experience of Labour Migrants in Kuwait', *International Migration* 37(2): 361–73.

Shami, S. 1996. 'Transnationalism and Refugee Studies: Rethinking Forced Migration and Identity in the Middle East', *Journal of Refugee Studies* 9(1): 3–25.

Shuval, J. 2000. 'Diaspora Migration: Definitional Ambiguities and a Theoretical Paradigm', *International Migration* 38(5): 41–57.

Skran, C. 1992. 'The International Refugee Regime: The Historical and Contemporary Context of International Responses to Asylum Problems', *Journal of Political History* 4(1): 8–35.

Smith, A. 1991. *National Identity*. London: Penguin Books.

Smith, M. 2005. 'Development Aid for Refugees: Leveraging Rights or Missing the Point?'. In M. Smith (ed.), *Refugee World Survey*. Washington D.C.: U.S. Committee for Refugees and Immigrants.

Stefansson, A. 2001. 'An Impossible Homecoming? Repatriated Refugees in Bosnia-Herzegovina and the Academic Aestheticization of Displacement'. Paper presented at research seminar Beyond Home and Exile: Making Sense of Lives on the Move. Roskilde: Roskilde University.

——— 2002. '"The Monopoly of Suffering": Conflicting Moral Claims to Solidarity and Hardship Among Sarajevan Returned Refugees and Stayees'. Paper presented at AAA Annual Meeting, Homecomings panel, New Orleans.

Stoller, P. 1997. 'Globalizing Method: The Problems of Doing Ethnography in Transnational Spaces', *Anthropology and Humanism* 22(1): 81–94.

Tölölyan, K. 1996. 'Rethinking Diaspora(s): Stateless Power in the Transnational Moment', *Diaspora* 5(1): 3–36.

Turner, S. 1999. 'Angry Young Men in Camps: Gender, Age and Class Relations Among Burundian Refugees in Tanzania'. Working Paper No. 9, *New Issues in Refugee Research*. Geneva: UNHCR.

Turner, V. 1967. *The Forest of Symbols. Aspects of Ndembu Ritual*. Ithaca, NY: Cornell University Press.

UNDP 2001. *Somalia Human Development Report*. Nairobi: UNDP.

UNHCR 1996. Convention and Protocol Relating to the Status of Refugees. Geneva: UNHCR.

UNHCR 2003. *2002 Annual Statistical Report: Somalia*. Geneva: UNHCR Population Data Unit.

Unruh, J. 1990. 'Integration of Transhumant Pastoralism and Irrigated Agriculture in Semi-arid East Africa', *Human Ecology* 18(3): 223–46.

Van Hear, N. 1998a. 'Editorial Introduction', *Journal of Refugee Studies* 11(4): 341–49.

——— 1998b. *New Diasporas: The Mass Exodus, Dispersal and Regrouping of Migrant Communities*. London: UCL Press.

——— 2001. 'Sustaining Societies Under Strain. Remittances as a Form of Transnational Exchange in Sri Lanka and Ghana'. In K. Koser and N. Al-Ali (eds), *New Approaches to Migration? Transnational Communities and the Transformation of Home*, pp. 202–23. London: Routledge.

———— 2002. 'From "Durable Solutions" to "Transnational Relations": Home and Exile Among Refugee Diasporas'. In B. Folke Frederiksen and N. Nyberg Sorensen (eds), *Beyond Home and Exile: Making Sense of Lives on the Move*, pp. 232–51. Copenhagen: Roskilde University.

Verdirame, G. 1999. 'Human Rights and Refugees: The Case of Kenya', *Journal of Refugee Studies* 12(1): 54–77.

Vertovec, S. 1999. 'Conceiving and Researching Transnationalism', *Ethnic and Racial Studies* 2(2): 447–62.

Wahlbeck, Ö. 2002. 'The Concept of Diaspora as an Analytical Tool in the Study of Refugee Communities', *Journal of Ethnic and Migration Studies* 28(2): 221–38.

Werbner, P. 1999. 'Global Pathways: Working Class Cosmopolitans and the Creation of Transnational Ethnic Worlds', *Social Anthropology* 7(1): 17–35.

Wilson, K. 1992. 'Enhancing Refugees' Own Food Acquisition Strategies', *Journal of Refugee Studies* 5(3/4): 226–46.

Wimaladharma, J., D. Pearce and D. Stanton 2004. 'Remittances: The New Development Finance?', *Small Enterprise Development Journal* 15(1).

Wolf, E. 1994. 'Perilous Ideas: Race, Culture, People', *Current Anthropology* 35(1): 1–12.

Zetter, R. 1991. 'Labelling Refugees: Forming and Transforming a Bureaucratic Identity', *Journal of Refugee Studies* 4(1): 39–62.

Zitelmann, T. 1991. 'Refugee Aid, Moral Communities and Resource Sharing. A Prelude to Civil War in Somalia', *Sociologus* 41(2): 118–38.

Zolberg, A. 1983. 'International Migrations in Political Perspective'. In M. Kritz, C. Keely and S. Tomasi (eds), *Global Trends in Migration: Theory and Research on International Population Movements*, pp. 3–27. New York: Center for Migration Studies.

Zorc, R. and M. Osman 1993. *Somali – English Dictionary with English Index*. Kensington, Maryland: Dunwoody Press.

Index